T0246065

AMERICA'S FIRST PLAGUE

AMERICA'S FIRST PLAGUE

THE DEADLY 1793 EPIDEMIC THAT CRIPPLED A YOUNG NATION

ROBERT P. WATSON

Rowman & Littlefield
Lanham • Boulder • New York • London

Published by Rowman & Littlefield
An imprint of The Rowman & Littlefield Publishing Group, Inc.
4501 Forbes Boulevard, Suite 200, Lanham, Maryland 20706
www.rowman.com

86-90 Paul Street, London EC2A 4NE

Distributed by NATIONAL BOOK NETWORK

British Library Cataloguing in Publication Information Available

Library of Congress Cataloging-in-Publication Data

Names: Watson, Robert P., 1962- author.
Title: America's first plague : the deadly 1793 epidemic that crippled a
    young nation / Robert P. Watson.
Identifiers: LCCN 2022043841 (print) | LCCN 2022043842 (ebook) |
    ISBN 9781538164884 (cloth) | ISBN 9781538164891 (ebook)
Subjects: LCSH: Yellow fever—Pennsylvania—Philadelphia—History—18th
    century. | Epidemics—Pennsylvania—Philadelphia—History—18th century.
    | Epidemics—United States—History—18th century. | Yellow
    fever—Caribbean Area—History—18th century. | Hankey (Ship : 1784)
Classification: LCC RC211.P5 W38 2023 (print) | LCC RC211.P5 (ebook) |
    DDC 614.5/41097481109033—dc23/eng/20221129
LC record available at https://lccn.loc.gov/2022043841
LC ebook record available at https://lccn.loc.gov/2022043842

♾️™ The paper used in this publication meets the minimum requirements of
American National Standard for Information Sciences—Permanence of Paper
for Printed Library Materials, ANSI/NISO Z39.48-1992.

"THE SICKLY SEASON"

Those who ventured abroad, had handkerchiefs or sponges impregnated with vinegar of camphor at their noses, or smelling-bottles full of the thieves' vinegar. Others carried pieces of tarred rope in their hands or pockets, or camphor bags tied round their necks. . . . People hastily shifted their course at the sight of a hearse coming towards them. Many never walked on the footpath, but went into the middle of the streets, to avoid being infected in passing by houses wherein people had died. Acquaintances and friends avoided each other in the streets, and only signified their regard by a cold nod. The old custom of shaking hands fell in such general disuse, that many shrunk back with affright at even the offer of a hand. A person with crape [black fabric or band worn as a token of mourning], or any appearance of mourning, was shunned like a viper.

Mathew Carey
Philadelphia publisher, 1793

CONTENTS

Images. ix

Preface xi

Poem "Pestilence" xv

Prologue: Ship of Death xvii

PART I
AMERICA'S FIRST CRISIS

1 Plague!. 3

2 Revolution. 13

3 Yellow Jack 25

4 Philadelphia 35

5 The First to Die 47

PART II
THE CAPITAL UNDER SIEGE

6 "Hell Town" 63

7 Fear and Panic. 77

8 Philadelphia Responds. 91

9 Bush Hill 103

10 The Physician's War 117

CONTENTS

PART III
TURNING POINTS

11 Unlikely Heroes 135

12 A Nation without a Government 145

13 Ghost Town 157

14 The Fall Frost 167

15 Of Pestilence and Politics 177

Epilogue: One Hundred Days of Terror 193

Appendix A. Time Line of Events 207

Appendix B. Map of Philadelphia 213

Abbreviations 215

Notes 217

Bibliography 249

Index 263

About the Author 277

IMAGES

Historic charter of "Colonial Undertakings in Sierra Leona and the Island of Bulama"

Map of Bulama Island

Slave revolt in Saint-Domingue

Arch Street Ferry, Philadelphia, by W. Birch, 1800, Library Company of Philadelphia

Cartoon depicting yellow fever

Old cartoon depicting the 1793 fever in the City of Philadelphia

Bush-Hill, the seat of William Hamilton, near Philadelphia, Library of Congress

Benjamin Rush, 1812, Library of Congress

Matthew Clarkson, Library Company of Philadelphia

Mathew Carey, publisher, Philadelphia

Stephen Girard, by Albert Newsam, 1832, Library of Congress

Absalom Jones, by Raphael Peale, 1810, Library of Congress

Richard Allen, first AME Bishop, by C. M. Bell, 1873, Library of Congress

Washington's 1793 Inaugural at Philadelphia, by J. L. G. Ferris, Library of Congress

PREFACE

It is not just shipwrecks, conflict, and war that provoke our collective, morbid fascination, rather famine and disease have long terrified people and fill the pages of history, and for good reason. Plagues and pestilence have decimated entire populations and continue to threaten communities and countries today. And so, the COVID-19 pandemic that struck in the year 2020 was not the first disease to ravage the United States. Nor was the deadly Spanish flu of 1918, as one may think. Rather, in the summer and autumn of 1793, Philadelphia, Pennsylvania, then serving as the interim capital city of the new nation, was in the grip of a deadly outbreak of yellow fever. George Washington, Alexander Hamilton, Thomas Jefferson, the mayor of the city, and other leaders tried desperately to continue to govern. However, with the death toll rising, physicians soon urged residents who could do so to abandon the city. Forced to choose between fleeing or dying there, President Washington had little choice but to announce the unthinkable: he ordered the federal government to abandon the capital.

Meanwhile, the celebrated physician Benjamin Rush and the city's medical community tried in vain to address the crisis. Tragically, the primitive state of medicine at the time would have grave consequences. In the eighteenth century, there was little understanding of the causes of yellow fever and no known cure or even effective treatment. In fact, some of the efforts to treat the afflicted only contributed to their quick and painful demise. In the end, at least one-tenth of Philadelphia's population perished from the pandemic; among those who remained behind, the rate was significantly higher. Virtually no one was safe. The interim capital was soon a ghost town, leaving the United Sates in the alarming predicament of not having a functioning government or military for one hundred terrifying days.

In a parallel eerily similar to the COVID-19 outbreak, residents stopped shaking hands, kept a distance from one another, sheltered at home, and wore masks and handkerchiefs as face coverings. But not everyone. Refusing to heed the warnings from government and physicians to refrain from public gatherings, some people complained that it was an infringement on their "freedom" while others claimed the disease was not real and rejected the medical evidence. They therefore contributed to the spread of the disease—such as when churches continued to hold services, while clergy attempted to pray the fever away. Meanwhile, people continued to die.

Denial and conspiracy soon turned to anger and fear. As the death toll spiked, paranoia and panic raced through the city, then up and down the Eastern Seaboard, prompting quarantine centers to be organized throughout the country to halt the spread. The response from neighboring communities varied. Some sent aid, but others set up roadblocks outside their borders. Vigilante patrols soon appeared in an effort to prevent refugees fleeing Philadelphia from entering their towns. Ports closed, an ugly suspicion of immigrants swept the country, and fingers were pointed in many directions, including at the Black community.

At the same time, there were great displays of heroism, including by former slaves who had little choice but to remain in the city and ended up selflessly caring for the sick and burying the dead; from courageous physicians who risked their lives to try to treat their patients; and from enlightened leaders who opened a fever hospital and enacted an array of policies to stem the spread of the disease and relieve the suffering of the afflicted.

This would be America's first plague and the worst pandemic to strike the young republic. This book chronicles the events of 1793 and tells the stories of America's response to the outbreak and the nascent government's first real crisis. There are many timeless lessons that come to the fore in the face of crisis, just as there were far-reaching and unforeseen implications of the pandemic on the practice of medicine, the Atlantic slave trade, Haitian independence, and the site of the future capital. It prompted changes in sanitation and health care, governance and urban reform—including the construction of the country's first public water system in Philadelphia—and even had an impact on the patterns of growth in the country. Indeed, this pandemic would alter the course of history. The results were mixed, but the fledgling republic survived this alarming event largely thanks to the efforts of the mayor, the sacrifices of "free Blacks," President Washington's order to vacate the capital . . . and the winds of good fortune.

A word to the reader: You may occasionally find unusual spelling and language in some of the quotes. However, wherever and whenever possible, I chose to use the original words spoken by the characters in the book, even if eighteenth-century grammar was a bit informal.

This book benefited from several helpful individuals. I wish to thank my colleagues at Lynn University: Katrina Carter-Tellison, Vice President of Academic Affairs; Gary Villa, Dean of the College of Arts and Sciences; Jared Wellman, reference and research librarian; and Lea Iadarola, archivist, for their continued support and assistance. I would also like to acknowledge my friends Bob Seidemann, George Goldstein, MD, and Samuel Stockhamer who read early drafts of this book and provided valuable feedback.

A special thanks to Peter Bernstein, my literary agent, for his assistance and ongoing interest in my work, to Ada Rosa for her support, and to Jon Sisk, Benjamin Knepp, Sarah Sichina, Katie Berlatsky, Della Vache, Christine Florie, and the team at Rowman & Littlefield Publishers for publishing another one of my books. And, as always, I acknowledge my son and daughter—Alexander and Isabella—for inspiring me.

Like everyone, I found the ordeal posed by COVID-19 and its variants to be taxing and trying. The devastating results of the outbreak, the inspired courage of health-care workers, and the appalling reaction to the crisis by too many of our elected leaders and neighbors all prompted me to think about the history of disease and epidemics. The result was this book. I hope you, the reader, find some useful lessons from this long-forgotten early chapter in our history.

Robert P. Watson
Boca Raton, Florida

"PESTILENCE"

Hot, dry winds forever blowing,
Dead men to the grave-yards going:
Constant hearses,
Funeral verses;
Oh! what plagues—there is no knowing!

Priests retreating from their pulpits!
Some in hot, and some in cold fits
In bad temper,
Off they scamper,
Leaving us—unhappy culprits!

Doctors raving and disputing,
Death's pale army still recruiting—
What a pother
One with t'other
Some a-writing, some a-shooting.

Nature's poisons here collected,
Water, earth, and air infected—
O, what a pity,
Such a City,
Was in such a place erected!

Philip Freneau
Philadelphia, 1793

PROLOGUE
SHIP OF DEATH

Beware and take care
Of the Bight of Benin
For the one that comes out
There are forty go in

—Early sailors' warning about West Africa[1]

Human Chattel

The wooden ship creaked and groaned as oceangoing vessels of the day did, slowly making her way from the African coast westward across the vast Atlantic. To those aboard, the voyage must have seemed cursed or haunted. The skeletal crew and few surviving passengers looked the part—gaunt, starving, sick, and in various stages of a ghastly death. This was in stark contrast to their ship, the *Hankey*, described as a "remarkably fine and stout" ship. Built only eight years earlier, she was a "relatively large oceangoing vessel for the time," measuring 110 feet in length and 30 feet at the beam. Snapping in the trade winds were several large square sails on her three masts—the fore, main, and mizzen—along with a few smaller, sleek and triangular sails above the bowsprit jutting out from the bow of the ship. The vessel was "designed to sail across the Atlantic" and so it was. This was not the *Hankey's* first sailing to the West Indies. However, this fateful passage in November of 1792 would be different than other voyages and would ultimately have dire and far-reaching consequences.[2]

The expedition that took the *Hankey* from England to the west coast of Africa, then to the West Indies and ultimately Philadelphia, Pennsylvania, was part of a bold and controversial expedition. Indeed, the mission held the promise of ending slavery and promoting an array of social reforms. Though well intentioned, it would do neither. The "Bolama experiment," as it came to be known, would end in complete failure. After losing most members in Africa, the few survivors of the expedition continued to face death during the desperate transatlantic crossing. Unbeknownst to those aboard, the *Hankey* carried a deadly secret that would soon spark a pandemic that would claim thousands of lives throughout the West Indies and America.[3]

The pages that follow tell the tragic story that began exactly one year earlier, on November 2, 1791, when six abolitionists organized a meeting at Old Slaughter's Coffee House in central London. It was a fitting location for such an enlightened gathering, as Old Slaughter's was a favored haunt of fellow progressive thinkers Benjamin Franklin, Thomas Paine, and Mary Wollenstonecraft, an early proponent of the women's rights movement. There, six men—Philip Beaver, Henry Hew Dalrymple, Robert Dobbin, Sir William Halton, John King, and John Young, all veterans of the wars against the Dutch and Spanish—agreed to plan an audacious experiment, toasting what they hoped would be "the most effectual means for abolishing the slave trade."[4]

Those who gathered that day at the famous coffee house were inspired by William Wilberforce,[5] the British politician and philanthropist, who, four years earlier in 1787, began a campaign to abolish the slave trade. This native of Yorkshire, England was a social reformer, member of Parliament, and close friend of Prime Minister William Pitt "the Younger." Influenced by a former slave trader turned pastor named John Newton, Wilberforce embraced evangelical Christianity and had his own spiritual transformation, which led him to help found the Society for Effecting the Abolition of the Slave Trade. Under his leadership, it grew in both popularity and controversy, and later adopted the much simpler moniker, the Anti-Slavery Society.[6]

Of course, that wretched practice—and opposition to it—long predated Wilberforce. By the end of the fifteenth century, Portuguese ships filled with enslaved Africans were regularly sailing for the islands of Cape Verde off Africa's west coast and the Madeira Islands, an archipelago off Africa's northwest coast, where sugar plantations benefited from the exploitation of free labor. In the opening years of the next century, Spanish conquistadors began enslaving Africans for work in Spain's Caribbean colonies. Prior to the year 1600, it is estimated that a few hundred thousand Africans had been transported to the Americas. However, the next century saw European powers scramble to add colonies throughout the Caribbean as the demand for sugar increased dramatically. As a result, plantations were established throughout the islands and in the Chesapeake region of North America. Soon, millions of Africans would be taken to the New World in bondage.[7]

Through the seventeenth century, Dutch and Portuguese traders dominated the slave trade and acquired additional, lucrative colonies in the western hemisphere, which only increased demand for the "peculiar institution." The practice expanded at an alarming rate. It is believed that nearly three-fifths of all enslaved Africans taken to the western hemisphere arrived in the eighteenth century alone—the time of the sailing of the *Hankey*. Not to be outdone, the British and French expanded both their colonies and reliance on slavery, resulting in their eventual control of roughly half of the entire transatlantic slave trade.

The impact of the burgeoning slave trade had global consequences. A "triangular trade" route emerged, in which ships sailed from Europe to Africa, then along the five-thousand-mile Middle Passage[8] to the Americas with enslaved Africans packed below decks in unsanitary and inhumane conditions, then back to Europe with their holds full of tobacco, sugar, rum, molasses, and other lucrative by-products of the slave economy. Records reveal that as many as 15 to 25 percent of those suffering below decks did not survive these voyages. In one particularly shocking incident in November of 1781 aboard the infamous slaver *Zong*, an infectious disease tore through the ship, killing many of the Africans below deck and the European crew above deck. The captain, Luke Collingwood, desperate to halt the spreading scourge, ordered that more than 130 of the enslaved Africans be thrown into the ocean in what would become known as the *Zong* massacre.[9] After surviving the ill-fated voyage, Collingwood filed an insurance claim on behalf of the Liverpool-based slave-trading company to be reimbursed for his lost "cargo."[10]

PROLOGUE

The slave trade tore African families apart and devastated the economies of entire villages. With so many healthy young men captured, the challenges of maintaining viable agricultural and hunting practices proved too much for many villages. Likewise, many of those enslaved were young women of childbearing age, which further exacerbated the depopulating of the region. The fear of captivity among the locals, utter disregard for humanity among the invaders, and the resulting social, economic, and psychological upheaval in western Africa caused by the slave trade was profound and lasting.

Cruelly, the monetary incentives were such that some local chiefs were complicit in aiding and abetting the slavers. Warlords even began hunting their fellow Africans in order to sell them to the Portuguese slavers, creating a climate of lawlessness and violence. As the slave trade grew, the Portuguese were no longer content with purchasing slaves from chiefs after tribal wars. They began establishing bases deep in the interior of Africa to hunt and capture ever larger numbers of people. Soon, long lines of human chattel bound by ropes, chains, and shackles snaked for hundreds of miles, from trading and enslavement centers in the Congo-Angola region and along the Senegal and Niger Rivers to the coast.

With slavery growing and spreading rapidly, in 1789, Wilberforce introduced through a series of speeches, considered to have been among the most eloquent and impassioned ever heard in the House of Commons, one dozen resolutions that attempted to abolish the slave trade. Although the measures had the support of Prime Minister Pitt and such noted leaders as Edmund Burke, they failed. In 1791, Wilberforce reintroduced legislation to end the slave trade, but these efforts also met resistance from conservative politicians and those with an economic interest in the enterprise. However, the antislavery movement was growing in Britain and a compromise was achieved in 1792, calling for a gradual curtailment of both the slave trade and the institution itself. Although not to the satisfaction of Wilberforce and his supporters, the seeds of abolition had finally been planted. In 1807,[11] a bill to end the slave trade in Britain's West Indies colonies finally passed and did so by a wide margin.[12]

Ultimately however, the transatlantic slave trade is estimated to have carried at least ten million—and possibly as high as twelve million—enslaved Africans to the New World from the sixteenth to the nineteenth centuries. It would mark one of humanity's largest and most despicable migrations in history, and one in which the British were complicit.[13]

The Bolama "Experiment"

Against the contentious backdrop of the antislavery debate and imbued by both the horrors of the *Zong* massacre and heroic example of Wilberforce, the organizers of the Bolama experiment hoped to inspire Africans and build support among White Europeans for abolition. To do so, the group of well-intentioned reformers would attempt to prove their theory—though shockingly colonial and condescending by modern standards—that it was possible to employ and "civilize" Africans, enabling them to live free. As Philip Beaver,[14] a former naval officer and one of the original six members of the undertaking, stated, their goal was "to purchase land in their country, to cultivate it by free natives hired for that purpose and thereby to induce in them habits of labour and of industry [that] might eventually lead to the introduction of letters, Religion and civilization, into the very heart of Africa."[15]

Not only would this help the cause of abolition, but the organizers intended for their experiment to make amends for English involvement in slavery by "improving" the lives of Africans. Despite their colonial mindsets, the planners of the expedition were motivated by a sense of duty, religiosity, responsibility, and hope. As Captain Beaver stated, they set about to "increase of the general happiness of mankind."[16]

It was also hoped that the Bolama experiment's advocacy for "cultivation and commerce" among Africans would lead Europe to "civilize" the continent rather than view it as a source of slave labor.[17] According to the founding members of the experiment, the colony would constitute a "reparation to Africa, as far as we can, by establishing a trade upon true commercial principles."[18] They thus proposed the then-radical idea of hiring and paying—rather than enslaving—Africans. If they were successful in their grand experiment, it would constitute "the most effectual means for abolishing the slave trade." At least that was the idea.[19]

The plan was not entirely new, nor was the theory of hiring and civilizing Africans. A similar colony and commercial enterprise was under way in Sierra Leone, which also inspired the leaders of the Bolama experiment.[20] Indeed, during the 1780s, numerous social reformers in Britain hoped that the idea of pursuing a combination of "commerce, civilization, and Christianity" would replace slavery as a "new Africa policy." The idea had also gained support in Denmark, France, and Sweden.[21] The organizers, however, still needed members, financing, ships, and supplies for their voyage—and a location in Africa for their experiment. They intended to purchase land and settle it, yet never visited the continent or bothered to consider the perspectives of those already living there.

Over the ensuing weeks, additional meetings were held, and public announcements appeared in newspapers in London and eventually in Manchester. As support built for the Bolama experiment, the group began meeting regularly and the original six organizers formed the Bulama Association,[22] so named for the island of Bolama just offshore from present-day Guinea-Bissau on Africa's western coast. The selection of the small island of just twenty-five square miles in the Bissagos archipelago[23] was symbolic in that it sat right in the middle of where the transatlantic slave trade began. As early as 1446, two Portuguese ships had identified the islands and over the ensuing century, Portugal established a trading base on nearby Cape Verde.[24]

Of roughly eighty-eight tiny islets that extend nearly eighty miles from the mainland, the easternmost island of Bolama was surrounded by mangrove swamps, had a densely forested interior teeming with monkeys, and was otherwise largely uninhabited at the time. Over the subsequent two decades, the British would try repeatedly to colonize the island, but failed miserably. Bolama was later claimed by Portugal and, in 1941, finally transferred to Bissau, a country that had been ruled by the Portuguese since 1687. Today, Bolama has a population of just six thousand and is known for its cashew nuts and the ruins of the old colonial settlement that is now a World Heritage Site.[25]

So many people signed up for the Bulama Association's expedition that the organizers quickly ran out of space on the ships and accepted no further applications. Interestingly, the lion's share of those enlisting in the expedition were from London's and Manchester's working class. They had never heard of Bolama, much less had any notion of the island's whereabouts or conditions.[26] Yet, in the words of Captain Beaver, they were all willing "to lay the foundation of a permanent settlement."[27]

Despite their fear of Africa, ignorance of what awaited them, the threat of tropical diseases, and utter lack of preparedness, the settlers seem to have been motivated by the naive promise of a better life—not ending slavery. To be sure, the working class and poor of London and Manchester toiled long hours in miserable work conditions and many were unable to feed their families. Life spans were short, infant mortality rates were high, housing was wholly insufficient, and poor laborers were jailed for an array of offenses such as stealing food in order to eat. A few passengers even saw their futures as a choice as between jail and poverty or Bolama.[28]

Accordingly, many signed up for the expedition as indentured servants who would have to work for their passage to the west coast of Africa, one of several cruel ironies surrounding an experiment allegedly about equality and rights. Others were wealthy idealists and social reformers with a moral commitment to opposing slavery. Of course, the expedition also included the usual land-grabbers and opportunistic businessmen.

Not only did volunteers rush to join the expedition, but donors provided ample funding for the bold plan. The Bulama Association sold "subscriptions" in London and Manchester, with each donor being recorded as either a "subscriber" who would join the expedition or those who simply supported it financially. In addition to the efforts of Wilberforce and his supporters, the fight for abolition was being led by several women's groups in Britain. Recognizing this, one of the expedition's organizers, C. B. Wadstrom, a Swede, appealed to women's groups who responded with additional funds, prompting him to write, "This is one instance among many to show how warmly the Ladies interest themselves in liberal and humane enterprises. To what sublime degrees of humane feeling and heroic virtue might not mankind arrive if, in union with the sex, they would always set before them the amiable pattern of female goodness?" In fact, the Bulama Association ended up being funded in good measure by at least a half dozen women.[29]

The organizers of the expedition enlisted forty families plus single male passengers and servants who agreed to work with the later promise of owning land. They then hired two large ships and purchased a small cutter. The initial plan to settle Bolama was calculated to take six months, but that was where any reasonable planning ended. As it would happen, their enthusiasm did not extend to preparedness, just as their noble intentions would not make up for their colonial naivete. They knew nothing about the climate, agriculture, or customs and language of those living in Bolama or its neighboring islands. Their supplies lacked adequate stocks of carpentry tools and medicine, and they did not include enough farmers, builders, or soldiers in the expedition, and one of the ship captains was inexperienced. All that could be said in a positive vein was they at least hired a physician and a surveyor.[30]

There was even a Black colonist named James Watson, who had gained his freedom by fighting in the Revolutionary War but was on the voyage serving as Captain Beaver's servant. He would later prove to be about the only useful member of the expedition.[31] There were also a few Jewish colonists, including John King, one of the original six members and later part of the governing Bulama Council. King's father, Jacob Rey, had moved his family from Gibraltar to London, where King was born in 1763. As a young man he anglicized his last name, preferring King to Rey, and became a successful financier and broker to a descendent of Lord Byron. Yet, because of the prevailing anti-Semitism, he was often derided as "Jew King."[32]

A charter was drawn up for the proposed colony prohibiting slavery and guaranteeing the right to vote for all male settlers, even those not owning land. In this respect, the Bulama Association was not only inspired by the American Revolution and Constitutional Convention, but it went beyond what the Framers had proposed in extending voting rights. The organizers of the expedition cited Pennsylvania as an example of providing voting rights to all adult males, while also, through the state's Gradual Abolition Act of 1780, being among the first places in America to end slavery.[33]

Much like the Pilgrims over a century and a half earlier who had drawn up the Mayflower Compact constituting rules for self-government, the document drafted by the leaders of the expedition established a republican form of government for their settlement, one rooted in the belief that "sovereignty resides in the people."[34] The charter even advocated an "equitable" distribution of land and redistribution of wealth in an effort to avoid the type of "plantocracy" dominated by a few plantation owners, as was the case in the West Indies and the American South. No single person could own a sizeable area of land; instead, both English and Africans would work together to grow tropical fruit, sugar, cotton, and indigo. While sounding quite noble, few of these principles would come to pass.[35]

In simple terms, Captain Beaver maintained that their primary ambition was for the colony to be "humane."[36] Yet, Beaver also claimed to express the sentiment of the group when he wrote, "It was resolved that no female should be admitted as a settler on her own account," meaning they could only travel as wives, daughters, or servants.[37] Fully fifty-eight women sailed on the initial voyage to Bolama, seventeen of which signed up as "personal servants."[38] Yet, despite the leaders' rhetoric and beliefs, there was a distinct pecking order on the ship, and servants were treated as such and forced to fulfill menial work on board. Most of the female travelers were treated in the same fashion, reflecting Captain Beaver's view that any member of the expedition not from the upper echelons of society was mere "rabble." Accordingly, the wealthy travelers enjoyed private cabins, while everyone else crowded into cramped quarters below deck. Sure enough, while the ships were still at sea, the leaders and wealthier members of the expedition began divvying up the land, allocating vast parcels to themselves despite their promise of an egalitarian colony.[39]

Beaver also summed up the difficult expedition, saying simply, "If we fail, they will be just where they were. . . . If we succeed, it promises happiness to myriads of living and millions of unborn people."[40]

An Ill-Fated Voyage

The organizers of the Bolama experiment would have been wise to heed the warnings from English and Portuguese sailors who long cautioned that few, if any, travelers to Bissau and Benin ever returned.[41] In the eighteenth century, explorers were still mapping the largely unknown coasts of Africa and most of the interior and islands such as the Bissagos archipelago, to which Bolama belonged. While thousands of sailors had made transatlantic crossings and visited Africa, the continent remained dangerous and shrouded in superstition, tall tales, fear, and inaccuracies. Likewise, there was little information on the people who lived in Bissau or the Bissagos Islands, other than secondhand accounts from slavers—and these were ominous.

None of this stopped the colonists from setting sail in March 1792 from England—275 men, women, and children, including a few infants—on three vessels, the *Beggar's Benison*, a small 34-ton cutter, the *Calypso*, a 290-ton ship, and the ill-fated 260-ton *Hankey*.

The small convoy embarked from Greenwich, England, near where the River Thames flows into the sea, and set their clocks to the exact time of the prime meridian, which would help with navigation. As they were about to sail for the open ocean, however, they received a communication that the British Foreign Ministry had not yet approved their expedition. It turned out that the home secretary was Henry Dundas, who was in the pocket of pro-slave interests. He advocated a slow, gradual end to the slave trade, perhaps in an effort to derail any progress. There was also simply too much money to be made from slavery. Moreover, Britain was still gaining colonies and eyeing trade in present-day Gambia, Senegal, and Sierra Leone, while, simultaneously, the prime minister had little patience for political agitators and radical proposals. It appeared as though the expedition would be over before even getting under sail.[42]

While the leaders of the expedition petitioned the government for permission to sail, the three ships docked at Motherbank on the Isle of Wight along the southern coast of England. While waiting, a smallpox contagion struck the ships. Debate arose as to whether those afflicted, including an infant child and her parents, should be allowed to remain on board. As the days passed, fear gripped the ships and divisions among the passengers and between the leaders and colonists heightened tensions. For instance, the day after the diagnosis of smallpox, five people abandoned the ships. Captain Beaver and the leaders of the expedition would later have to expel four others for "unruly" behavior. As the days passed, morale plummeted. Then the news arrived that the petition to establish the colony was rejected. This was an omen of things to come, but with the entire expedition now in jeopardy, the leaders chose to proceed without permission from the government. They quickly and secretly set sail the next morning, April 11.[43]

There was no wind that first day and progress was frustratingly slow. It became worse when a newborn child, a young girl, and an adult man died that same day, most probably from smallpox, and were buried at sea, another ominous start to the grand experiment. The winds improved in the coming days, allowing the ships to finally leave English waters and make their way south. Yet, the ships soon became separated. The *Calypso*, as the fastest of the three ships, far outpaced the other two, while the *Beggar's Benson* fell far behind. The plan was to rendezvous in the Canary Islands off the coast of northwestern Africa.

In the open ocean, rough seas battered the ships. The passengers, unaccustomed to sailing, struggled mightily. Both the leaders of the expedition and colonists, most of whom had never been to sea, underestimated the rigors of sailing. Ocean travel in the eighteenth century was harrowing even for the most seasoned of sailors—much less the clerks, bookbinders, tailors, cooks, laborers, preachers, and housewives from London and Manchester aboard the *Hankey* who were completely unprepared for the long trip. Soon, people's skin, hair, and clothing dried and hardened in the salty air. The more literate of those on board must have found the famous quip by the noted English writer and intellectual Samuel Johnson to be painfully accurate: that sailing ships were like "being in a jail with the chance of being drowned . . . [only] a man in jail has more room, better food, and commonly better company."[44]

The ship's carpenter, boatswain, cooks, and other crew members toiled during the difficult voyage, and it was all-hands on deck for the passengers. The men were expected to wash the decks, adjust the sails, and stand watch at all hours; the women were expected to cook, clean, and mend clothing. The constant rocking, creaking, and groaning of the wooden planks of the ship reminded everyone that they were on a relatively small craft in the middle of the open ocean. Everyone on board became violently seasick. The smell of vomit and human sweat mixed with the odors of the live farm animals held in the deep holds to create a pungent aroma that infiltrated every nose and every nook and cranny of the *Hankey*. Fresh water was to be had only when it rained and food was hard to preserve on the open ocean, forcing them to subsist on hardtack, a simple type of biscuit or cracker made from flour and water, which lacked taste, and had the consistency of a leather shoe. Beef, pork, and fish were dried and placed in barrels of salt so that they would last through the voyage. Of course, the presence of vermin of all varieties not only contaminated the food stores but harassed the passengers.

The ship itself, like most vessels of the age, was not designed for comfort or for passengers. It was built to carry goods back and forth across the Atlantic: sugar, molasses, rum, tobacco, rice, and other agricultural commodities as well as gold, silver, and slaves. The *Hankey* had a few decks, with supplies stored in the lower decks alongside the goats, sheep, and chickens that were brought in order to raise populations in Bolama. The stores also included extra wood, sails, thick rope, tar, turpentine, and tools required to sail the ship and make any necessary repairs while at sea. All this served as a form of ballast to stabilize the ship in rough winds, waves, and currents. Consequently, the living spaces below decks were anything but; rather, they were cramped, dank, and dark, without privacy or personal space. Pans were used for human excrement, then dumped overboard. No one bathed, unless a bucket of cool saltwater was pulled up from the side of the ship, but for puritanical Englanders and especially the women, this would not have even been considered.

The crew's quarters were in the front of the ship and were nothing more than wooden bunks and hammocks, while the captain's cabin sat on the top deck in the stern of the ship. The *Hankey* had but a skeletal crew and too few soldiers and artillery aboard to defend itself, all of which meant the ship was at risk of being lost at sea and vulnerable to attack. Piracy was common and warships and privateers from rival countries prowled the seas ready to attack, sink, capture, or loot all vessels. The threat of piracy was ever present, especially as they sailed along the entrance to the Mediterranean where Barbary pirates routinely harassed Western shipping and seized prisoners.

There was another threat: Amid the poor drainage onboard, lack of ventilation below deck, crowded conditions, and the hot sun, the ship was ripe for an array of maladies. As expected, the three ships in the convoy suffered additional outbreaks of smallpox, while lice tormented the colonists. The threat of scurvy was ever present for long, oceangoing voyages, while other diseases waited at the ports to visit their wrath upon all ships. Not only were they harbingers of disease, but the few ports and forts established along the route to western Africa were often lawless. With tensions among the various European powers heightened, stopping for trade, repairs, or resupplies was dicey at best.

Each craft in the small three-ship convoy faced challenges, the worst of which were aboard the *Calypso*, as it was not designed for the open sea. Rather, the small cutter was built to move goods and people around the docks and ports along the Thames. Her passengers were therefore battered mercilessly in the rough seas and the small cutter was nearly lost a number of times. Partway into the trip, smallpox tore through the ship, killing many aboard and foreshadowing the fate of the entire expedition. Meanwhile, the main problem aboard the *Hankey* was the inexperienced captain who was commanding his first voyage. As if on cue, Captain John Cox became lost, sailing the ship in the wrong direction and putting all 120 passengers on board at risk.[45]

Confrontation

The ships sailed for Tenerife in the Canaries, a collection of thirteen islands whose moderate climate, natural ports, and location along the northwest coast of Africa not far from the shores of Morocco made them a popular way station for ships headed to the continent. The likes of Christopher Columbus, Charles Darwin, Alexander von Humboldt, and other notable explorers had resupplied in the volcanic isles. Similar to other isolated islands, the prevailing trade winds and currents guided more than ships to the archipelago—diseases such as smallpox and measles brought to the Canaries by European seafarers had decimated the local populations.

The islands were Spanish territory and prevailing tensions between Spain and Britain were such that the three ships could have been fired upon, confiscated, or looted. Despite the risks, the small convoy was desperate for respite from the rough seas and needed to be resupplied. They would dock. Because the *Hankey* was far off course, she arrived late and anchored off Gran Canaria. The *Calypso* had arrived earlier and, when it was discovered that she carried smallpox onboard, was quarantined. Nevertheless, Captain Beaver ignored warnings not to come ashore and led the landing party. They had no papers from the British government, so they were detained by authorities in the Canaries, who were also panicked by the obvious signs that the newcomers were carrying diseases.

While they waited for the *Beggar's Benson* to arrive, Beaver attempted to negotiate for their release and tried to procure supplies, which were belatedly sold to them but at an inflated price, depleting much of the expedition's finances. Making matters worse, some members of the expedition went ashore and ended up getting into a drunken brawl at a pub; they were arrested and detained. Once the *Beggar's Benson* arrived and the *Hankey* procured supplies, they quickly set sail in the middle of the night, joined by the *Calypso*, which fled its quarantine. However, all three ships again became separated at sea.

After another two weeks of sailing farther south, the *Hankey* arrived at the Cape Verde islands, sitting off the coast of Senegal and not far from their destination. The *Calypso* followed, but there was no sign of the *Beggar's Benson*, and it was feared that the cutter had been lost at sea or sunk by the Spanish or pirates. While waiting on Cape Verde, the crew of the *Hankey* acquired donkeys, livestock, and further supplies. After a few days, the two ships set sail for Bolama.

The first to arrive was the *Calypso*, but as she sailed by Bissau the ship encountered other ships, most likely from the Portuguese slave base and fort there, whose sailors warned them about the islanders they were about to encounter at Bolama. There were tales of bloodshed and cannibalism. Dismissing the threat, the crew traded for barrels of water and made for Bolama. In late May, after several weeks at sea, an outbreak of smallpox, and multiple leaks, the *Calypso* finally anchored off the island. They met a few locals who, through a Portuguese-Creole dialect, echoed the warnings of the Portuguese slavers: a nearby island was home to the Canabacs, a tribe of the Bijago people who were "very hostile to Europeans" and known to practice cannibalism.[46]

The *Hankey* was the next to arrive, after having docked in Bissau because Captain Cox could not find Bolama. Furthermore, when Captains Cox and Beaver went ashore in Bissau to ask Portuguese authorities to help them sail to the island, they were arrested as possible pirates. Though they lacked official papers, nothing about the ship or crew would have suggested piracy. The most likely explanation for the detention was that the arrival of abolitionists was seen as a threat to the slave traders who controlled the port. The captain and leader of the expedition were eventually freed, although they too heard horror stories about Bolama. Undeterred, they sailed for the island and arrived in early June of 1792. Days later, on the eighth, the *Beggar's Benson* finally reached the colony. All three ships were lucky to have made it; it appeared to them to be divine providence. But things were about to get far worse.[47]

In many ways, the English colonists could not have selected a worse place for their experiment. While it was symbolically near the heart of the African slave trade, Bolama was only four hundred square miles. The low-lying island was surrounded by mangroves and coastal savannas, with interior semiarid palm forests. It was too small for agriculture or animal husbandry on the scale known in Europe or the Americas, and too far from Europe to be a viable trading post for anything other than slavery. Moreover, much of the region remained uncharted and the customs, native languages,[48] and land was totally alien to untraveled, fair-skinned Englishmen used to living in urban areas.

In typical colonial fashion, the new arrivals began cutting down trees and burning grasslands in order to make way for planting and their livestock, all without consulting the islanders they allegedly came to "save." Without adequate provisions of food, they hunted monkeys that lived in the interior forests and which, unknown to the colonists, carried a strain of a deadly disease—yellow fever.

It did not take long for word of the settlers to spread around the islands. "Armed Indians" arrived in canoes near the site where the colonists had dropped anchor. One member of the expedition, Joshua Montefiore, was dispatched with a flag of truce, which had no cultural meaning to the locals. Montefiore met the arriving party on the beach. His description of the Canabacs reflects prevailing views and hints at the coming confrontation, noting they possessed "very disagreeable features, their lips being exceedingly thick, and their noses remarkably broad and flat. Their complexion was of a coal black, and they had no clothing, except a small leather apron."[49]

The next morning, the colonists discovered that all their supplies, tools, and livestock that had been rowed ashore had been taken by the Canabacs. A few days later, the Canabacs returned. This time it was a war party. They caught several of the colonists in the fields planting and building housing. A tailor was immediately killed. Then one of the council members of the colony, Henry Gardiner, was seized and his hand cut off. The fleeing colonists and those aboard the ships watched in horror as Gardiner was then killed. The panicked colonists ran for the rowboats at the water's edge and frantically paddled to the *Calypso*, anchored nearest the shoreline. Most made it into the boats and water, but several more colonists were captured. From the ships, terrified members of the expedition could do little but watch the ensuing massacre on the sandy beaches. Six settlers were summarily hacked to death, prompting Montefiore to write that it was "a scene to shocking to dwell upon." The Canabacs took a few remaining women and children prisoner and departed in their canoes as quickly as they had arrived.[50]

I

AMERICA'S FIRST CRISIS

CHAPTER ONE
PLAGUE!

For now I will stretch out my hand,
that I may smite thee and thy people with pestilence;
and thou shalt be cut off from the earth.

—Exodus 9:15

A History of Pestilence

Thousands of epidemics have taken place worldwide throughout human history. No culture, country, or century has been immune from these scourges. Some of the more well-known include the bubonic plague, cholera, influenza, polio, smallpox, typhus, and yellow fever. In the twentieth and twenty-first centuries, the world has grappled with AIDS, SARS, avian and swine flu, and COVID-19. These silent, invisible, and deadly agents have shaped history.

These diseases seem inevitable. Microbes, far too numerous to count, populate the human body, inside and out. Invisible to the naked eye, they are measured in millionths of a meter. Most are single-celled bacteria and are found in the water we drink, foods we eat, and even in the air we breathe. They, therefore, colonize the human body to the extent that, in an ironic twist, because our intestinal tract needs the bacterium that resides in it, our lives become dependent on this symbiont relationship.[1] However, microbial parasites can be dangerous. Infectious microbes called pathogens can spread and make the hosts ill or even cause death.

When this occurs on a widespread level it creates an epidemic. When the outbreak extends beyond a localized area, it becomes a pandemic.[2]

According to the World Health Organization, one of the first recorded instances in human history of what we call a "plague" was the plague of Justinian. Likely introduced to the Mediterranean by centurions returning from Ethiopia, it struck the Roman Empire in 541 CE. Lasting for several years, this scourge killed thousands, including an estimated one-fifth of the imperial capital of Constantinople and nearly claimed the life of the Byzantine emperor Justinian,[3] for whom the pandemic was named. It would eventually return for nearly three centuries and claim the lives of millions.[4]

Yet, a millennium before the plague of Justinian, another disease threatened Western civilization. During the famous Peloponnesian War between Athens and Sparta that started in 431 BCE, people across the Grecian world died not just from warfare but from disease. Thucydides, who wrote the masterpiece *History of the Peloponnesian War*, devoted considerable time to describing a pandemic that he estimated killed almost one-third of the Athenian people in the summer of 430. In fact, it is believed that the outbreak claimed more lives than the fighting. Thucydides described those afflicted as suffering with fevers, delirium, vomiting, and red pustules on their bodies. Interestingly, he does not attribute the disease to the gods or human sins; he merely describes what some scholars have suggested was typhoid fever, while others suspect a corresponding outbreak of smallpox, and maybe even the bubonic plague. Either way, bodies piled up, fear ran rampant across the islands, and civil society broke down. One of the casualties of the Plague of Athens was none other than the "father of democracy," the great Pericles, who may have succumbed to the scourge. The disease contributed to the collapse of the Athenian empire as well.[5]

However, the worst pandemic in history struck Europe in the fourteenth century. It began around 1346 when an unknown disease decimated towns and later entire countries. Its symptoms were gruesome: high fever, severe abdominal pain, vomiting, diarrhea, difficulty breathing, and painful welts and sores on the body that oozed pus and blood and gave off a particularly foul odor. It had no known cure. The so-called Black Death derived its haunting nickname from the dark blotches that formed on the human skin. Roughly half of the unfortunate souls who contracted the disease succumbed to it. The primitive state of science and medicine at the time also precluded an understanding of the origins and means of transmission of the disease. Today, it is known that the malady lodges in the lymph nodes by the groin and armpits, causing swelling known as buboes (thus, the origin of the term "bubonic"). Likewise, science has determined that the disease is carried in droplets in the air and is highly contagious. The culprit has also been identified. In 1894, Alexander Yersin,[6] a student of Louis Pasteur, located and described the problematic bacterium. Today, it is known as *Yersinia pestis* in honor of its discoverer.[7]

The exact origin of the Black Plague remains uncertain, but medical and historical communities point to fleas and rats from South Asia as its source. It is possible that the conquering Mongol army may have carried the infected pests with them during the wars in Central Asia in the 1330s. Likewise, traders from Venice and elsewhere were both traversing the Silk Road and sailing to and from China, which would have provided a handy means for introducing the malady to Europe.[8]

In the 1340s, the disease was already on the continent's doorstep. It was then that the Tartars, an army of Turks, Mongols, and Muslims under the leadership of Genghis Khan, began their siege of communities along the Black Sea. The fighting not only forced European merchants to flee from the Crimean Peninsula, but in a macabre scene, the corpses of the dead were used as weapons. Bodies were catapulted over fortress and city walls, both terrorizing populations and introducing the disease to large populations. By 1346, millions were dying in Europe and along the trade routes and battlefields in Asia. In trading centers such as Venice, Rome, and Paris, hundreds of people were dying each day, a rate faster than bodies could be buried, resulting in corpses being placed in great piles at the docks, stacked outside city walls, and dumped into nearby rivers.[9]

Europe was ripe for the affliction. In the previous century, the planet started to cool. Global climate change of only a few degrees resulted in diminished summer harvests and harsher winters, both of which contributed to widespread starvation. Meanwhile, wars continued to rage, and monarchs governed with incompetence and impunity. It must also be remembered that people rarely bathed; nor did they wash their clothing regularly, brush their teeth, clean their hair, or visit physicians. There was no indoor plumbing, and hospitals were a thing of the future.

Raw sewage was poured onto the unpaved streets or dumped into nearby rivers and streams. Hygiene, as we know it today, was virtually nonexistent. If a person living today were to travel back in time to the fourteenth century, the smell would likely be the first thing to greet them. And it would be overpowering.

It did not help that the population remained largely ignorant and illiterate, and a feudal economic system relegated most Europeans to relatively short, miserable lives. For most of human history, life was precarious—our hunter-gatherer ancestors could expect to live but twenty-five years. For thousands of years afterward, there were few advances in health care. Combined with bad diets and a scarcity of food, life expectancy rates remained low. English citizens living in the eighteenth century, including the passengers on board the *Hankey*, could expect, on average, to live perhaps thirty-seven years. This did not mean, however, that half the population lived to that ripe old age. Rather, infant mortality rates and death during childbirth were ills that plagued humanity throughout history. Perhaps fully one-quarter of people living in Europe died prior to the age of five. Therefore, if one survived childbirth and made it to adulthood, there was a chance of living to fifty or even sixty, although the quality of life would have been abysmal.[10]

The disease with many names—the Great Mortality, Black Death, the Great Dying, the Pestilence, or the bubonic plague as it is known today—was so deadly that it is believed to have claimed in excess of one-third of the continent's population in under five years, earning it the generic name the plague. It also decimated populations in Asia and Africa. More than just claim lives, it caused widespread societal upheaval. Trade ceased, governments were unable to rule, and entire villages became ghost towns, all marking major transitional periods in the Middle Ages. Indeed, it took Europe decades to recover.[11] DNA samples from skeletons from the time of the plague reveal the *Yersinia pestis* bacterium to be the culprit.[12]

Etiology

In a case of truly bad timing, a few years before the Black Death struck Europe, Pope Boniface VIII banned the practice of dissecting the human body, which further limited science and the understanding of health and disease.[13] Most physicians had little education beyond reading the works of Hippocrates, the Greek father of medicine from the fifth century BCE. Consequently, a visit to a physician, which was a privilege for only the most affluent, often ended up doing more harm than good.[14]

Perhaps realizing the folly of his predecessor's decision, Clement VI later reversed the papal bull prohibiting dissections. After all, the plague claimed the lives of many church leaders. Others saw the plague as God's punishment for human sinfulness. Some stopped drinking, gambling, and committing what they believed to be sins. Others behaved less humanely. Some devout Christians adopted the practice of flagellation to atone for their sins. They punished themselves by striking their backs, legs, and genitals with sticks and knotted ropes containing iron spikes that flayed the skin. These radicalized Christians began attacking both non-Christians other Christians believed to be less devout. They even destroyed churches and threatened clergy suspected of being too lenient or secular, such that Pope Clement VI was forced to ban these flagellant brotherhoods in 1349.[15]

The finger of blame was pointed in many directions. Once again, the Jewish community was scapegoated in tragic ways. Amid fear and death, rumors circulated that Jews were the cause. One malicious source of gossip from the South of France held that Jews had poisoned the wells in order to kill Christians. Others thought that the death toll in Jewish villages was far lower.[16] Christians responded by slaughtering Jews. In Mainz, Germany, it is estimated that twelve thousand Jews were murdered during the years of the plague, mostly by being burned alive. Near Basel, Switzerland, a small island in the Rhine River was used as a detention center for Jews, until they were later burned. Tragically, attacks against the Jewish community were nothing new in Europe, but the killings in the fourteenth century were so extensive that Pope Clement VI issued another decree banning the attacks. It did not work.[17]

Likewise, during such catastrophic outbreaks, many Christian leaders and their flock believed the second coming of Christ was at hand, as described in scripture. Other faiths saw it as the "end of times" or the result of sin in the eyes of a vengeful deity. It is undeniable that superstition and religiosity contributed to many human ills of the period. Indeed, the state of science, medicine, and education had regressed during the Dark Ages, owing to centuries of superstition and oppressive church dogma that suppressed learning and progress. The arts, science, human-ism, rights, and medicine were all repressed.[18]

Medical thinking at the time did not understand bacteria or microbes; instead, it embraced the idea of imbalances in blood, phlegm, and bodily fluids, which called for bleeding and purging. Another early effort to explain the origins of diseases from the plague to yellow fever was known as miasma, or the idea that foul air or poisonous gases carried disease or entered the human body and caused afflictions. This theory would later guide many physicians trying to treat the pandemic that would strike the American capital in 1793. Their misunderstanding of the nature and causes of disease would result in a great loss of life. Many other superstitions and inhumane actions from earlier pandemics would again rear their ugly heads during the outbreak of 1793.

Etiology, a branch of medical science, is the study of diseases and their causes. There are numerous transmittal types, from airborne and waterborne to human contact and insects. Perhaps the first person to undertake the systematic study of the causes of diseases, or at least record it, was the Greek physician Hippocrates.[19] Known as the father of medi-cal ethics and arguably the most influential healer of the ancient world, Hippocrates sought to understand and explain health and disease independent of actions of the gods; rather, he considered natural causes and consequences of lifestyles and actions. This caused a paradigm shift not only in medicine but in science, as superstition and religious zealousness gave way to environmental factors as the primary causes of illness, including cold winter winds, summer heat, and unhealthy marshes. While Hippocrates may be forgiven his many mistakes, he at least set medicine on the path of observation, investigation, and rationality—in short, science.[20]

Among the few positive developments in combating diseases was the advent in seventeenth-century Europe of birdlike masks that had a protrusion that housed a cloth drenched in vinegar, which was thought to minimize transmission, and physicians wearing gloves and black robes. Later, in Venice, the advent of *quaranta giorni*—or the quarantine—was a necessary step forward in combating the spread of infection. As the word *giorni* implies (i.e., "days") ships were required to remain at anchor for forty days before entering the city.[21]

Fortunately for all of us today, the late eighteenth century was a period of transition, as the former American colonies gained independence and introduced new ideas about rights and self-governance. Ideas about monarchy and absolute power were beginning to change along with other social reforms. By the twentieth century, the way had been paved for science and medicine to make great progress toward both understanding and combating contagious diseases. An array of antibiotics, vaccinations, and treatments are now a part of standard medical practices and have successfully defeated, mitigated, or minimized scourges that ran unchecked throughout human history. One of the most important of those moments occurred in 1928 during an incident in a lab when Alexander Fleming noticed that the mold *penicillium notatum* came in contact with a sample of a bacteria and proceeded to kill the harmful bacteria. Thus, penicillin was discovered and has since become a wonder weapon in the fight against disease, while extending human life expectancies to previously unimaginable ages.[22]

The New World

After remaining in relative isolation for thousands of years, the inhabitants of the Americas and West Indies were vulnerable to the myriad diseases brought by European explorers and, later, enslaved Africans. The indigenous peoples had no immunity to the ticking biological bombs—hepatitis, influenza, measles, mumps, smallpox, typhus, and other contagions—that arrived in the New World during the Age of Exploration. As early as 1492–1493, Christopher Columbus described seeing the native peoples of the West Indies beginning to die in unusual ways and in alarming numbers. On the island of Hispaniola alone, where his expedition set foot, some estimates were that the indigenous population was as high as one million; yet it is thought that just a decade later the population was as low as a few tens of thousands.

In subsequent years, entire armies attempting to defend against European encroachment were felled by disease. At the same time, communities throughout the western hemisphere were ravaged by sexually transmitted outbreaks of syphilis. The depopulating of Central America and the West Indies as well as modern-day Mexico and the United States was unstoppable. The result was some of the highest death rates in world history. It was not just enslavement and massacre, advanced weapons and technology, ruthlessness, religious dogma, or a penchant for raping, robbing, and exploitation that contributed to the conquest of the Americas—rather, disease was a primary culprit.[23]

For example, in just three months in 1521, Hernán Cortés successfully took the Aztec capital of Tenochtitlán[24] in present-day Mexico and the entirety of Montezuma's grand empire with only three hundred men. The Spaniards benefited by the Aztecs believing Cortés was their god Quetzalcoatl incarnate; however, once again, it was disease in the form of smallpox that defeated Montezuma's warriors. It certainly was not Cortés's strategy; after all, he was busy fighting with his rival invader Pánfilo de Narváez, whose soldiers appear to have been the source of the smallpox outbreak. In fact, Cortés was initially defeated by the Aztecs but after the outbreak he regrouped and defeated what remained of Montezuma's army. It has been suggested that one-quarter of the population of the capital city, including Montezuma, died within weeks, while perhaps half the population throughout the empire perished in the years after the Spanish invasion.[25]

A friar by the name of Toribio Motolinia kept a journal of the conquest, which described the devastation. In it, he wrote that the Aztecs perished "in heaps, like bedbugs" and offered a chilling account of the atrocities, noting "in many places it happened that everyone in a house died, and, as it was impossible to bury the great number of dead, they pulled down the houses over them in order to check the stench that rose from the dead bodies, so that their homes became their tombs." They endured a grisly death with severe fever and headaches, the possibility of blindness, weakening of internal organs, irritated throat, and visible rashes and bumps known as pustules that oozed a foul pus. It is not hard to understand why, confronted with the outbreak, the Aztecs abandoned their gods, culture, and, ultimately, any resistance. Across the Americas, it soon mattered not whether frightened populations converted to Christianity; they died either way.[26]

A decade later, in 1532, Francisco Pizarro arrived from Europe with a few hundred men, but his ships also carried smallpox and soon there was another outbreak. Populations already teetering on anarchy, famine, and fear could not endure another pandemic, and entire civilizations collapsed. Another explorer-invader—Hernando de Soto—arrived in 1539 to chart and loot North America, telling the people he encountered that he was a god from the sun; he then went about burning locals alive. As de Soto traveled through the Americas, he found entire populations dead and once-thriving villages reduced to ghost towns. Through the 1500s, European diseases tore across the continents, helping the Spanish conquer the Americas and islands in the West Indies, and the Portuguese to do the same in Brazil.[27]

By the time British and French colonists arrived to claim North America, smallpox and other diseases had been decimating native populations for a century. The story would repeat itself along both the New England and Virginia coasts, where settlers, soldiers, and explorers brought diseases to the first Americans. So would the pillaging and inhumanity, such as when Cotton Mather,[28] the noted New England puritan and religious leader who, despite advocating inoculations, suggested the epidemics were sent by God to destroy "the pernicious creatures to make room for better growth"[29] or when, a century later, political leader Jeffrey Amherst went so far as to recommend during the French and Indian War that blankets and clothing contaminated with the pox be given to Native leaders to kill off the "Execrable Race"—a Trojan horse with the gift of death.[30]

Smallpox had likely originated in Africa and through warfare, trade, and slavery, spread across the globe to Persia, India, China, and, of course, the New World, where it ended up killing more Native people than war, enslavement, forced relocation, or other diseases. The result was one of history's worst travesties. Entire cultures and civilizations were eradicated in a matter of years, while perhaps 90 percent of all Native populations disappeared over the ensuing four centuries from disease.

Some cities in America had also dealt with yellow fever, and accounts suggest it was deadly. Records dating to William Penn and the founding of Philadelphia describe an unknown disease that some referred to as "Barbados distemper." Yet, the city had managed to go decades without a major outbreak of the scourge. Those who remembered it "feared no disease more," even noting that the city was overdue for an outbreak.[31]

Like smallpox and other disorders, the yellow fever pandemic in the 1790s that first hit the West Indies and came to the US capital, originated with those fleeing both disease and violence. Indeed, the ravages of yellow fever long predated the years 1792 and 1793 when the *Hankey* sailed to the West Indies and America, laden with the scourge.

CHAPTER TWO
REVOLUTION

Toussaint—the most unhappy of men!
Whether the rural milkmaid by her cow
Sing in the hearing, or though liest now
Alone in some deep dungeon's earless den,
Oh miserable Chieftain, where and when
Wilt thou find patience? Yet die no!
Do thou wear rather in thy bonds a cheerful brow;
Though fallen thyself, never to rise again,
Live, and take comfort! Thou hast left behind
Powers that will work for thee—air, earth, and skies
There's not a breathing of the common wind
That will forget thee! Thou has great allies:
Thy friends are exultations, agonies,
And love, and man's unconquerable mind.

—William Wordsworth's "To Toussaint L 'Overture," 1803

Devils

Back in Bolama, few slept the night after the attack by the Canabacs. For their safety, the colonists stayed on board the *Hankey* and the other two ships, while sentries remained on alert. They waited until daylight before sending an armed party ashore to search for survivors. What they found were bones along a nearby beach, which seemed to lend credence to the rumors of cannibalism. Unnerved and not finding any survivors, the small search party hurried back to the safety of the ships. They did not have long to wait, as the Canabacs returned to the beach that day wearing the clothing of the murdered and kidnapped colonists. According to Montefiore, one of the expedition's leaders who had earlier attempted a meeting under a white flag of truce, the assumption was that those taken prisoner must have been killed. Montefiore added that the Canabacs began "hallooing, hooting, and treating us with contempt and derision."[1]

From the safety of the ships, the leaders of the expedition attempted to communicate with the natives, hoping to "buy" Bolama and pay a ransom for the return of any women and children that might still be alive. Money and valuable items were eventually exchanged, but the English would later discover that the Canabacs did not "own" the island—it was controlled by the Biafada tribe who lived on an adjacent island. The settlers had been fooled. At least the Canabacs later returned all but two of the prisoners, keeping a pregnant woman and her young daughter. The prisoners who were released had been stripped naked, which appalled the sensibilities of the puritanical English and prompted Captain Beaver to declare of the Canabacs, "Their devil is white."[2]

In desperate need of livestock, supplies, and hoping to regroup to determine the future of the expedition, the ships sailed to the mainland, arriving at a Portuguese slave fortress in Bissau. After a heated debate about the fate of the settlement, nine colonists abandoned the expedition and waited at the port for a ship headed to Europe or, hopefully, England. The remainder of the members of the expedition purchased armaments and supplies and decided to return to Bolama. They could not have known, but a worse enemy awaited them.

With the ships again at anchor along the coast of Bolama, the colonists picked up where they had left off, going ashore to plant, build, and hunt. Sentries were posted, but they made another costly mistake. After building corrals for their livestock, they took the cows, goats, and donkeys they had just purchased ashore. However, when the colonists awoke the next day, they found that the Canabacs had killed and eaten all the animals. It was then that it began.

A mysterious, deadly fever fell upon the ship's colonists. Many fell ill and six died within days. Every aspect of the expedition was unraveling. On July 19, panicked, 150 of the colonists boarded the *Calypso* and sailed away, traveling to Sierra Leone, where they were turned away because of the obvious signs of fever. Desperate and with the disease ravaging the passengers, the crew of the *Calypso* decided to forego additional precautions and the procurement of supplies and sailed for England. At least sixty of the passengers succumbed to the malady before making it home.[3]

The fate of those remaining at Bolama was the same. By the end of July, only about ninety colonists remained alive. The idealistic mission to employ Africans in order to make a case for abolishing the slave trade had changed to one of survival. The blame game started, resulting in a vote to replace Henry Hew Dalrymple as the governor of the settlement with Captain Beaver, who was given the title of "president."[4] Beaver saw himself as the absolute ruler, immediately imposing strict naval discipline on the colony.[5] The twenty-six-year-old leader posted guards at all hours and organized crews to go ashore and build housing, cultivate the fields, and hunt. He even made them work on Sundays, which angered the devoutly religious settlers. However, Beaver's efforts were undermined by the rainy season on the coast. Torrential downpours battered the ships and freshly planted fields, preventing the colonists from doing much of anything except hunkering down in the two remaining ships.

The rain provided them with much needed fresh water, but the containers in which they collected it likely served as their undoing; they doubled as breeding grounds for disease-carrying mosquitoes. Other members of the expedition soon fell ill. It was yellow fever. Between the relentless fever and ongoing attacks from the Canabacs, by the end of August, only sixty-nine people remained alive at the Bolama settlement.[6]

The situation remained precarious. The Canabacs continued to assault the settlers who ventured off the ships to build houses or tend to the fields. Soon, a fatalism overtook many of the colonists, who began referring to themselves as "Canabac chickens" to be "harvested" at will. Unable to tend to their fields and with the livestock gone, the colonists began to starve, so they began hunting more of the monkeys that populated the island. However, they observed that entire troops of monkeys were dying. It turned out the monkeys "harboured a vicious strain of yellow fever, circulated among them by mosquitoes that infested the mangrove swamps of Bolama." Soon, the disease plagued the entire island.[7] Even though some colonists starved to death and others were killed by the Canabacs, yellow fever was, in the words of one historian, "the most disastrous factor for the colony."[8]

Most every member of the settlement had either suffered from the malady or succumbed to it. There were now so few of them remaining that homes were not completed, fields became unproductive, supplies were not replenished, and the settlement was undefended. September and October of 1792 had been particularly difficult months. The fever claimed several more lives, and torrential downpours and the threat of attack prevented them from leaving the ship. The colonists were now living—and dying—on the *Hankey*.

Ghost Ship

On November 23, 1792, roughly two dozen of the colonists abandoned the experiment. They set sail on the *Hankey* with water caskets filled with the larva of mosquitoes, leaving behind only twenty-eight fellow colonists. Most of those on the ship were weak, ill, or in the grips of the fever. They intended to set a course for England but would first need to repair the ship and procure supplies for the long voyage home. Therefore, they sailed to the port at Bissau on December 3, but, because so few of those on board were able to work or go ashore, they had trouble obtaining the items they needed for the voyage. Once it was discovered that a fever was aboard the ill-fated ship, they were ordered out of the port. After the delays, the *Hankey* sailed to the Cape Verde islands, arriving on January 4, 1793. There, the inept Captain Cox ran the ship aground, damaging its hull, causing the vessel to leak and list to one side.[9]

It is doubtful either the captain or the unseaworthy ship would have made it to England. However, the British warship HMS *Charon*,[10] a forty-four-gun frigate that, by the end of the year, would be converted to a hospital ship, encountered the *Hankey* on the open seas. The *Charon's* captain, whose name was Dodd, had his crew repair and provision the *Hankey* and informed Captain Cox that it would be too dangerous to sail for England. The existing tensions between the British and French had resulted in numerous French warships prowling the waters along the entrance of the Mediterranean and European coast.[11]

The *Hankey* carried only six cannons, no sailors or marines, and, even if they knew how to man the naval artillery, there were not enough healthy passengers to operate them. They were told to sail for the British possessions in the West Indies. Captain Dodd, likely realizing that his counterpart on the *Hankey* was incapable of making it to the West Indies, sent two of his crew to join the settlers in order to help sail the cursed ship to the islands. Not long thereafter, the ship encountered the HMS *Scorpion*,[12] whose captain offered two more sailors to assist the disease-laden vessel in crossing the Atlantic. Why neither captain recognized the fever onboard or, if they did, why they allowed crew members on board, is unknown.

One can only imagine the devastating blow to the passengers aboard the *Hankey* eager to get home. After all they had endured, they found out they would have to set sail across the Atlantic Ocean. The West Indies might provide sanctuary from Bolama and any prowling French warships in European waters, but the ship was still carrying the disease that seemed to be bled into its planks. With each day, the *Hankey* sailed farther westward away from England while, unbeknownst to them, within days the fever tore through the *Charon* and *Scorpion*, killing several crew members. The captains and more seasoned sailors aboard the British warships belatedly recognized the symptoms—it was yellow fever. Stories had long circulated among sailors about "ghost ships" adrift in the Atlantic or off the coast of Africa, their crews dead from the dreaded "yellow jack," as sailors called the disease, a reference to the small yellow flags flown off the bow to indicate the presence of the scourge on board.[13]

It would not be the *Hankey's* first voyage to the New World; she had earlier transported people and sugar to and from the region. But this time she was carrying passengers living on borrowed time and a terrible disease that would soon decimate ports in the Americas. The doomed ship was about to sail on a six-month voyage to the West Indies and America, bringing yellow fever to every port she visited.[14]

The West Indies

The *Hankey* arrived in the British island of Barbados on February 14. She set sail soon after docking and was in St. Vincent on February 16. The island's recent turbulent history included the British conquest of the indigenous Caribs to take control in 1763, but losing the colony to the French in 1779, then having it restored in 1783 at a treaty signed at

Versailles. None of that mattered, because yellow fever was about to despoil Barbados and add to the turbulence on St. Vincent. Three days later, the ship made port in Grenada.

It was in St. George, the capital of Grenada, that Dr. Colin Chisholm, a Scottish surgeon who moved to the island after the Revolutionary War, recognized the connection between the "death ship" and the outbreaks and nicknamed the disease "Bolama Fever." Within days of the *Hankey's* arrival, locals took ill and began to die, prompting Dr. Chisholm to note of the disease that it was, "I believe, unknown in this country, and certainly unequalled in its destructive nature."[15] Other physicians and government officials soon recognized that the ship was carrying a deadly disease. The Grenadian physician, Dr. Joseph Gilpin, added in disbelief, "Of the infected state of the *Hankey*, I never did nor ever shall entertain the least doubt, nor do I recollect that any medical man in Grenada held an opposite opinion."[16]

The colonial governor of Grenada therefore summoned Captain Cox for a meeting, where the inept sailor was ordered to throw all of the *Hankey's* cargo overboard. The cursed ship was then ordered out of port; it anchored some distance offshore. The governor also had a message dispatched on a ship bound for London informing His Majesty's government of the yellow jack. Ironically, one of the officials receiving the communiqué was Sir Henry Dundas, the home secretary who had originally denied the colonists aboard the *Hankey* a permit to establish a colony at Bolama on account of his support of slavery.[17]

Within just weeks of the *Hankey* reaching Grenada, the authorities reported that hundreds of sailors at the port died. Death followed the British soldiers who were stationed at the port back to Fort George, the English stronghold on the island. Within just one week, so many soldiers at the fort died of Bolama Fever that the entire garrison was in the grip of fear. Ultimately, the death toll among the troops stationed on the island was such that the British were unable to defend the fort or Grenada. The British military was forced to rush additional troop transports to their colonies in the West Indies. However, many of these replacements suffered the same fate.

One of the British officers sent to Grenada aboard the troop ships was Lt. Thomas Howard, who recorded the state of crisis in the islands, writing, "In the West Indies the Months of June, July, August, September and the beginning of October are what are called the sickly months." During the "sickly" season of 1793 after the *Hankey* visited its wrath upon the islands, Lt. Howard estimated that twenty British soldiers died each day on Grenada and claimed that, of the seven hundred York Hussars who sailed from Portsmouth to the island, only two hundred survived the fever. The young lieutenant concluded, "It is impossible for words to express the horror that presented itself at this time."[18]

The British ordered that flags warning of the disease be flown for months. So many corpses piled up that enslaved locals were made to bury the dead. "From sunrise to sunset" they toiled, remembered Lt. Howard, yet could not keep up with the demand. The scenes harkened back to the bubonic plague, as carts filled with corpses were pushed around St. George and mass graves were dug on the island. The British soon ran out of lime to cover the burial sites.[19] By summer, it is estimated that fully half of the European population in Grenada was dead. Soon, horror stories about "yellow jack" were racing through the West Indies. The *Hankey* was forced out of Grenadian waters.[20]

In each port, those members of the *Hankey* still able to walk and work dropped off dying passengers and replenished the dwindling stock of water and supplies. The fact that she sailed to three islands in just five days suggests the unwillingness of local authorities to allow a diseased ship to stay in port. Each of the ports visited—Barbados, St. Vincent, and Grenada—recorded an outbreak of yellow fever within days of the *Hankey's* ill-fated arrival. Moreover, epidemics later arose on other islands visited by ships that were docked next to the *Hankey*.[21] These included Antigua, Dominica, Jamaica, St. Kitts, Trinidad, and Tobago. The evidence for the ship being "patient zero" includes the fact that yellow fever had not struck those islands in decades. As expected, the outbreaks in 1793 were deadly. Ultimately, in the words of historian Billy G. Smith, the "*Hankey* created the first yellow fever pandemic in the Western Hemisphere."[22] And the cursed ship's travels were not over.

Saint-Domingue

The French colony now known as Haiti comprised the western third of the island of Hispaniola, which had been transferred from Spain, which controlled the eastern two-thirds of the island by the Treaty of Rijswijk in 1697. The island, known by the Spanish as Santo Domingo, was rechristened with the French variation of the name. It grew quickly to become France's most prosperous colony and constituted the lion's share of the motherland's foreign investments, which included developing the large port at Cap Français[23] and sprawling plantations in the island's lush interior to make the colony an international agricultural power. As the jewel of France's colonial empire, Saint-Domingue produced roughly half the world's sugar and coffee. Europe was addicted to the island's exports, which also included a lucrative trade in cocoa, cotton, indigo, and tobacco. As a result, the need for slaves became a priority.

The horrors of slavery were many, yet the institution was likely more brutal on Saint-Domingue than anywhere else. Day and night, slaves cleared fields, planted and harvested crops, toiled in the sugar mills, worked on steep slopes in sweltering heat and torrential rains, and suffered dehydration, malnutrition, and injuries. When a slave died, a replacement was simply brought to the plantation. Awash in profits, plantation owners worked their slaves even harder. The rapid increase in wealth and exports resulted in the French colony importing even more enslaved Africans—and the cruel cycle continued. Appallingly, when the *Hankey* sailed into port, over a half-million enslaved Africans worked the island for roughly 56,000 White slaveholders. Yet, with so many slaves, the White ruling class had become fearful of slave uprisings, resulting in the relentless, violent crackdown on any infraction, perceived or real.

It is hard for people living in the West today to comprehend how widespread and accepted the abysmal institution had become. Voices of dissent were a minority. Views of racial superiority and inferiority were accepted as doctrine by politicians, the church, and educational institutions. When combined with colonial and imperialistic mindsets, cultural and linguistic barriers, and the lucrative nature of a slave-economy, a dangerous concoction resulted. Fellow humans were shackled, beaten, and raped on the long Atlantic voyage and then suffered the same fate upon arrival before being auctioned, branded, and either worked to death or murdered. Families were separated. The process repeated itself year after year until millions of Africans filled the fields of the Americas and of Saint-Domingue.

The social conditions and institution of slavery on Saint-Domingue spiraled into madness, sowing the seeds for an inevitable uprising. Even White settlers were organized into a strict caste system comprised of a small number of *grands blancs*, the ruling White plantation owners; a few thousand *petits blancs*, the craftsmen, tradesmen, and plantation overseers; and a few thousand *blancs menants*, the White peasants. The rest were *affranchis*, literally "freed" or "mulattoes."

One account from a servant who spent many years in Saint-Domingue, complained of the inhumane treatment of slaves as follows: "Have they not hung up men with heads downward, drowned them in sacks, crucified them on planks, buried them alive, crushed them in mortars?" He went on, adding, "Having flayed them with the lash, have they not cast them alive to be devoured by worms, or onto anthills, or lashed them to stakes in the swamp to be devoured by mosquitoes?" The treatment was nothing shy of torture and evil, as described by the servant: "Have they not thrown them into boiling cauldrons of cane syrup? Have they not put men and women inside barrels studded with spikes and rolled them down mountainsides into the abyss? Have they not consigned these miserable blacks to man-eating dogs until the latter, sated by human flesh, left the mangled victims to be finished off with bayonet and poniard?"[24]

Another account comes from a resident of the island named Francis Stanislaus, who documented slaves being branded and forced to wear irons around their wrists and ankles nearly all day and even while sleeping. He offered an insight into the morning routine on a plantation, remembering "the cracking of whips, the smothered cries, and the indistinct groans of the Negroes, who never see the day break but to curse it, who are never recalled to a feeling of their existence but by suffering." Stanislaus escaped the horror when he became one of the first White people to flee the island when the uprising started.[25]

"Die Like Flies"

Not only was the *Hankey* driven out of port after port, but the few experienced sailors on board jumped ship. With a growing reputation as a diseased ship, Captain Cox could not find new crew members for the cursed vessel. To make matters worse, those aboard the *Hankey* were out of money. They were also out of time. They needed to find a safe harbor and medical care. With few options, Cox sailed for Cap Français on the northern coast of the island of Saint-Domingue to obtain supplies and sailors.[26] The port where they docked happened to have been the exact site where Christopher Columbus established the first European settlement in the New World. Thanks to the large, natural port that the *Hankey* entered, Cap Français was the wealthiest community on the island, perhaps the most lucrative colony in the world, and a major trading center, exporting sugar, molasses, rum, and other crops, while importing the major enterprise on the island: slavery.[27]

Yet, as the ship approached the port in late June of 1793, Cox and his few remaining passengers could see smoke across the entire horizon. The port and many homes and large buildings in the city were burning. Cap Français had boasted a large theater, a hilltop fortress, a cathedral inspired by Notre Dame, and other impressive structures, as well as a population of over 170,000 people. It was the pride of French colonialism in the West Indies, which explained the once-vibrant city's nickname back in Europe, "Paris of our Islands." This also explains why the port city was a prime target during the slave uprising occurring on the island.[28]

The ideals of the French Revolution had made their way across the Atlantic Ocean, just not in the way envisioned by the residents of the Republic. They inspired enslaved workers to escape. Beginning in August of 1791, slaves began running away in large numbers. Within weeks, over ten thousand "Maroons," as they were known, were hiding in the thickly forested hills and mountains on the island. Away from the cities and the former coffee plantations they formed communities and militias. A year later, the French military sent troops across the Atlantic to quash the uprising. The number of former slaves in open rebellion soon reached a staggering 100,000.

The rebels conducted an ever-increasing number of guerrilla attacks against their former masters along with lightning assaults to free other slaves. Hundreds of plantations were attacked and liberated. In response, the grands blancs organized militias to both hunt the Maroons and defend the plantations. At the same time, Britain and Spain sent support to the rebellion, hoping to hurt their historic rival France and eventually gain control over the island's plentiful resources. By the end of 1791, the uprising turned to a full-fledged war, with former slaves revisiting brutality on the severely outnumbered White plantation class by burning cities, massacring White people, and destroying plantations.[29]

The island's economy ground to a standstill and with it the lucrative trade and finances France relied upon. A furious Napoleon

Bonaparte dispatched an additional 65,000 soldiers and sailors to Saint-Domingue with orders to put down the revolt and show no mercy. Signifying the importance of the island's productivity, Napoleon appointed his brother-in-law, General Charles LeClerc, to command of the mission. The ensuing campaign was barbarous. It is believed that roughly 150,000 slaves and former slaves were slaughtered. In the process, the French momentarily reasserted control over the island, but their reprisal was so bloody that it sparked a second and more determined rebellion.[30]

The former slaves were led by Toussaint L'ouverture, a gifted military and political leader known as the "Black Napoleon," who was inspired by Simón Bolívar's campaign to promote independence from the European powers for the people of the Americas. L'ouverture realized "we have only destruction and fire as our weapons." As such, he wisely instructed his followers to simply hide in the forested mountains, conduct surprise guerilla strikes on the main city and port of Cap Français, then retreat into the bush. He had a secret weapon. L'ouverture decided to let the island kill the massive French army by simply "waiting for the rainy season, which will rid us of our enemies." To be sure, the second wave of rebellion was given a boost when a yellow fever outbreak tore through the island. Writing to his top commander Jean-Jacques Dessalines, L'ouverture noted, "The whites from France cannot hold out against us here in St. Domingue," predicting, "they will fight well at first, but soon they will fall sick and die like flies." And that is precisely what happened: some fifty thousand French soldiers died, most from the yellow fever pandemic brought, in part, by the *Hankey*.[31]

CHAPTER THREE
YELLOW JACK

Then it came to pass that a pestilence fell on the city,
Presaged by wondrous signs, and mostly flocks of wild pigeons,
Darkening the sun with their flight, with the naught in their craws but an acorn
As the tides of the sea arise in the month of September
Flooding some silver stream, till it spreads to a lake in the meadow,
So death flooded life, and, o'erflowing its natural margin,
Spread to a brackish lake the silver stream of existence.
Wealth had no power to bribe, nor beauty to charm, the oppressor;
But all perished alike beneath the scourge of his anger

—Henry Wadsworth Longfellow "Evangeline: A Tale of Acadie," 1847

Fleeing the Bloodshed

The *Hankey* docked at the chaotic port in Saint-Domingue without hindrance from the authorities—they were otherwise either overwhelmed with the bloody revolution . . . or dead. Cap Français was in complete ruin. It had become a refuge for White settlers fleeing attacks throughout the island. Captain Cox and the few surviving members of the Bolama expedition were met at the port by terrified colonists who shared horrific stories of entire families being hacked to death while their homes burned. Rather than pick up agricultural goods for trade, Cox decided to line his own pockets by selling seats aboard the *Hankey* to the throngs of desperate French colonists willing to pay handsomely to flee the island. The savagery—on both sides of the fighting—was such that anyone able to get to the port would pay any price to leave . . . and live. At the same time, the ship of death brought yet another yellow fever outbreak to yet another island.

The population on both sides of the revolution suffered from the starvation that gripped the island brought on by the fallow fields, disruption of trade, and many bloody attacks. Ultimately, the impact of both yellow fever and the revolution were far-reaching. Desperate for cash to make up for the losses in Saint-Domingue and to fund his war in Europe, in 1803 Napoleon sold the lucrative Louisiana Territory to President Thomas Jefferson, thus instantly doubling the size of the young United States and promoting the westward expansion of the fledgling republic. The French were also forced to abandon Saint-Domingue, and on January 1, 1804, General Dessalines and his Maroon fighters declared independence. Saint-Domingue became the first successful slave uprising resulting in an independent Black nation in the New World. The response from the European powers, colonists in the West Indies, and slave owners in the American South was to panic, then crack down in even harsher ways on their large, enslaved populations.[1]

Sadly, General L'ouverture did not live to see independence for the people of Saint-Domingue. Accepting an invitation to parley from a French general, the leader of the rebellion was tricked and arrested. The freedom fighter was sent to France where he was jailed and succumbed to his mistreatment in 1803. However, the die had already been cast for the defeat of the French army and the colonial masters they were sent to defend.

Meanwhile, colonists were fleeing Saint-Domingue in droves, rushing to the port and clamoring to board the *Hankey*, not knowing that death awaited them on the ship. Leery of other possible slave uprisings throughout the West Indies, their preferred destination was the United States, which, at the time, was barely into its fourth year as a new nation. A few ships carrying French refugees managed to set sail, heading for the large ports of Baltimore, Charleston, New York, and Savannah, but others like the *Hankey* sailed for the capital city of Philadelphia, followed by a small flotilla of vessels.

Within days of their arrival at the port in Philadelphia, a rash of illnesses and fever appeared along the dock and waterfront. The public and physicians initially assumed they were the usual maladies that plagued the city each July and August. Philadelphia's weather that time of year could be stifling and various ailments—some carried by mosquitoes—were quite common. Unbeknownst to them, the French colonial refugees, their slaves, and the handful of surviving passengers aboard the *Hankey* brought with them mosquitoes infected with a deadly strain of yellow fever.

AÉDES AEGYPTI

Anthropologists are in wide agreement about an African genesis for humanity. The continent appears to have been the wellspring of human development. From Africa, early humans spread outward beginning around 1.8 million years ago. Yellow fever is also believed to have originated in Africa around 3000 BCE. But it was the age of sail and discovery from the fifteenth to the eighteenth centuries that accounted for the spread of deadly microbes and diseases from tropical Africa to the far reaches of the world. Yellow fever, in particular, is endemic to West Africa—the region from which the transatlantic slave trade originated—and was most certainly brought to the Americas and West Indies by slave ships carrying infected mosquitoes. The sudden contact among populations that had never had contact with one another and were thus lacking immunity from foreign diseases, followed by the onslaught of ships, colonists, slaves, and trade, had devastating consequences.

Dr. John Blake, a scholar who studies the disease, stated flatly that the "history of yellow fever, like that of most diseases, is difficult to unravel." At times, it has been blamed for an epidemic when the culprit was another disease, or vice versa. After all, it shares symptoms with a few other contagions. Such was the case for smaller, isolated outbreaks in American history, which scientists and historians now doubt were instances of yellow fever. One such example was an epidemic in 1688 in New York, which may not have been yellow fever. Yet, Blake also notes that medicine has "assurances" that the 1793 episode was indeed the dreaded yellow jack.[2]

Most scholars and medical researchers now believe, in the words of Dr. Blake, that "yellow fever probably came to the New World from

Africa." Of course, there is a "paucity of records," so the evidence is not conclusive. However, the disease's origins are tropical, and outbreaks corresponded to incidents of trade and slavery between Africa and the Americas.[3] As early as the closing years of the 1640s, Dutch slavers began transporting enslaved Africans to the islands in the West Indies. Yellow fever followed.[4] These outbreaks would later kill countless slaves, White people, and Native Americans throughout the hemisphere, however, some physicians and White colonists noted that some Africans were immune, which later led to the discovery of the fever's origins.[5]

Yellow fever thrives in tropical and subtropical areas and, ever since the age of discovery, this included the hospitable climates in Central and South America as well as the Caribbean. It was therefore known by sailors of the time who docked in warmwater ports—and often saw the "yellow jack" flags flown by ships infested by the disease. Yellow fever is an acute and infectious disease that, like malaria and typhus, is not spread from person to person; rather, it is transmitted by the bite of an infected mosquito. It is the females of the *Aedes*—which includes *Aedes africanus* and *Aedes aegypti*, in the *Haemogogus* genus of mosquitoes—that carry the disease, typically after contracting it from an infected primate. In the case of the *Hankey* and the outbreaks in Bolama and elsewhere in the West Indies, the culprit was *Aedes aegypti*, meaning "unwelcome Egyptian," a reference to it killing thousands in that region.[6]

According to the National Institutes of Health, yellow fever is one of over two hundred known human viruses that includes HIV/AIDs, Ebola, measles, mumps, polio, smallpox, and the coronavirus. An RNA virus that is part of the family *Flaviviridae*, yellow fever is also related to the West Nile virus and encephalitis, and is a hemorrhagic disease, meaning it is defined by bleeding. It is a particularly painful affliction. The African strain of the disease attacks the red blood cells, disrupting the flow of blood in the body. Internal bleeding occurs in the stomach and intestinal mucous membrane, producing the disease's signature "black vomit." Bleeding can also occur through the nose and anus.[7] Other symptoms include severe fever followed by chills, heightened pulse, headache, muscle pain or soreness, numbness in the limbs, dryness and discoloring of the tongue, decreased bowel movements, urinary problems, and kidney and liver failure, which taints the skin and eyes a yellowish color, thus giving the disease its name.[8] The influential preacher

Cotton Mather, who encountered it in colonial New England, wrote that people were "turning yellow then vomiting and bleeding every way."[9]

Quite simply, yellow fever is a wretched disease. Dr. William Currie, a Philadelphia physician who would end up treating countless residents who suffered and died from the disease that struck his city in 1793, made a careful study of its symptoms, recording details of each of his patients. Currie described the onset of the fever this way:

> The patient first complains of weariness and weakness, which, in a few hours, is succeeded by a sense of chilliness, and an oppressive dull pain and giddiness in the head, an oppressive weight and stricture about the breast, particularly at the region of the heart, as if the space was too narrow for its pulsation. The breathing is performed with quickness and uneasiness.[10]

Currie's observations included the next stage of the illness, which, he recorded, gets progressively worse. "In most cases," he chronicled, "the initial symptoms are soon succeeded by . . . a frequent propensity to puke, and this by a quick, full, but soft and irregular pulse." The patient also suffers from a "great heat about the head, neck, and breast," while the skin becomes "generally hot." At this point, the patient either stabilizes or gets worse, which occurs "about the third and fourth day" when the symptoms "become more distressing and alarming, with the pulse low and sunk." From there, "frequent vomiting of matter resembling coffee grounds in colour and consistence, generally occurs before the disease terminates, when it proves mortal, together with a cadaverous appearance of the countenance, succeeded by a deep yellow or leaden colour of the skin and nails." Even "the eyes become suffused with blood, and the countenance appears like that of one strangled" and "in some cases, a profuse discharge of blood from the nose, concludes the catastrophe," wrote Currie.[11]

In the end, the delirious patient is often described as "walking dead." There was no known cure, however, yellow fever is not fatal in all cases. It is estimated that for every one life-threatening case, there are up to seventy that are asymptomatic or mild. Of those infected, many die about a week after infection, but it could be as quick as a day or two after infection, and those who survive often take weeks to recover, but have a lifelong immunity to the scourge.[12]

The American Plague

Yellow fever likely first arrived in the western hemisphere in the mid-1600s, as described by the ancient Mayans. According to scholars, "The earliest epidemic generally accepted as yellow fever [in the Americas] occurred in Yucatan in 1648." Perhaps the first cases documented by Europeans occurred in Barbados when thousands died during outbreaks in 1647–1650. Over the ensuing years, there were believed to have been yellow fever episodes in Cuba, Guadeloupe, and St. Kitts, as well as Brazil in 1685. Periodic epidemics followed every few decades, such as when a French warship traversing the globe arrived in Martinique in the 1690s and likely caused a deadly outbreak there.[13]

The devastating nature of the disease and its impact on larger events was seen around the same time when Sir Francis Wheeler's British fleet sailed from Antigua and Barbados to sack French-controlled islands such as Martinique in 1693, but his crew fell ill with yellow fever. History records that Wheeler lost roughly half his crew to the disease. He later sailed for Boston, which appeared to trigger the deadly outbreak in that city when he arrived that July. The few surviving members of the deadly expedition sailed back to England, and the disease abated only after the late fall when frost killed the mosquitoes carrying it. This pattern repeated itself time and again as it would soon do so in Philadelphia.[14]

The disease is believed to have been responsible for deaths in Charleston, South Carolina, in 1699, New York City in 1702, and elsewhere in the 1700s. Charleston, in particular, had several outbreaks of the fever or similar afflictions throughout the century because it was home to a large slave trade and boasted long, hot summers. In 1741 and 1742, there was thought to be a yellow fever outbreak in Virginia. Those afflicted were diagnosed, treated, and then written about by Dr. John Mitchell, who would give his notes to Benjamin Franklin. Franklin then donated them to Dr. Benjamin Rush, the foremost physician of the revolutionary and postrevolutionary eras, whose treatments during the 1793 outbreak were informed by Mitchell's notes. Science now questions whether the Virginia episode was even yellow fever, just as medicine would later show Rush to be wrong in his theories about and treatments of the disease, all of which would have deadly consequences.[15]

The 1793 pandemic was not the first time yellow jack is thought to have menaced Philadelphia. There are recorded episodes in 1699, 1741, 1747, and 1762.[16] So, why the thirty-year absence of yellow jack in the latter half of the 1700s? Dr. Currie, who treated patients in the 1793 outbreak in Philadelphia, wrote that, to his knowledge, the fever had not been in America since, at least, the Revolutionary War.[17] Dr. Blake offers a possible answer, suggesting that Philadelphia was "probably saved by a combination of luck, trade regulations, and the fortunes of war." While the slave trade continued largely unabated through the century in both the West Indies and America, most colonial powers did not trade with one another; rather their trade was restricted to the motherland and their colonial possessions. Yet, trade, shipping, colonial conquest, wars, and slavery spread throughout the century, thus, as Blake admits, "providing an ideal setting for yellow fever." There was also the matter of the revolution in Saint-Domingue, the war between England and France, and the naive ambitions of English abolitionists trying to colonize the island of Bolama on the African coast that brought the scourge to Philadelphia.[18]

In the late eighteenth century, the months of August and September were referred to as the "sickly season" in Philadelphia and other communities around the United States. The condition was also known as the "summer complaint," the "autumn fever," or simply the "ague." This was true in the blisteringly hot and stagnant Deep South and in boggy and marshy regions in the Southeast's low country. Sitting at sea level, the low-lying city of Philadelphia in southeastern Pennsylvania is often hotter and damper than communities farther south such as Charleston, South Carolina; Savannah, Georgia; and Williamsburg, Virginia; and, despite its proximity, tends to be more inclement than Baltimore, Maryland. Therefore, anyone with the means to do so abandoned the city each August. The same was true for visitors. Shipping and trading typically slowed during the "sickly season," and Congress used to wait until cooler weather arrived in November before returning to the people's business.[19]

Despite being the largest city in the young republic and the home to many of the revolutionary events that led to independence, Philadelphia was very much a city surrounded by, and carved out of, bogs and marshlands, which invited pestilence. High tide impacted the Delaware, Schuylkill, and other rivers, often washing over their banks and depositing not only dead fish but trash and debris in the city. Afterward, pools of stagnant water remained, which invited mosquitoes. Likewise, residents both stored and captured rainwater in large open barrels. Few streets were paved at the time, and the city had yet to build its water or sewage systems. At the waterfront, the area around Dock Street contained a large, foul sewer. Nearby, large holes, known as "sinks," collected human waste and even dead animals, emitting what was described as a "noxious effluvia." Even though Philadelphia was considered "clean, safe, and prosperous by the standards of the day," it was a city ripe for the pandemic that was coming.[20]

Not surprisingly, the mere mention of "yellow jack" at the time the *Hankey* sailed for the Americas was enough to send entire ports into a panic. As historian Bob Arnebeck concluded, "Fever was to the 18th century what cancer is to today. Fever is what people feared would cause their death."[21]

Yet, ports throughout the world were spared the scourge because most slave and trade ships did not have any or many infected mosquitoes onboard. Fortunately for humanity, mosquitoes have a short life span, far too brief to survive the long voyage across the Atlantic Ocean on slow, wooden sailing ships. Adults mate, the female lays her eggs, and dies. But mosquitoes lay their eggs in moist or wet areas and any infected stowaway could lay eggs in the many barrels of water stored on sailing ships. Alarmingly, a female mosquito lays anywhere from 350 to 700 eggs at one time. With the infected adult mosquitoes no longer living, the hatchlings would need to bite an infected human on the ship, contract the disease, and pass it along to the next person they bit. Making matters worse, mosquitoes are nearly invisible, they hunt and feed on blood at dawn and dusk, and are very adaptable to warm, wet climates.

Descriptions onboard the *Hankey* reveal that a thick cloud of mosquitoes swarmed throughout the ship. Because the ship made port in the tropics or during the wet, summer months, the infected mosquitoes found stagnant pools of water, rain forests, and swamps—in short, welcoming environments for surviving and plenty of hosts to bite. The *Hankey* unknowingly "unloaded" its deadly cargo in port after port, leading historian Billy G. Smith to describe its sailing as "detonating the yellow fever bomb."[22]

Consequently, outbreaks of yellow fever struck during the rainy, warm seasons, and so it was that the *Hankey* arrived in warm, wet islands throughout the West Indies, then in Philadelphia during a particularly hot summer. The origin of the deadly contagion that plagued Philadelphia was therefore most certainly the "Fever of Bolama" brought by the *Hankey* and refugee ships from Saint-Domingue.[23] It was about to decimate the interim capital city, earning yet another nickname and for good reason: "The American Plague."[24]

Back in Bolama

By November 1792, "every colonist suffered not just one but a series of illnesses," leaving only a few dozen English settlers alive. Captain Beaver stubbornly insisted on remaining along with just twenty-some settlers, all but four of which were inflicted with the fever. They continued to die. Even Beaver appeared to have lost his faith, noting dispassionately in his journal the deaths of his fellow colonists. On December 9, for instance, he recorded matter-of-factly, "Died of a fever, and was buried, Mrs. Harwin . . . Myself a little feverish." The next day, his journal contained the entry: "Died of fevers, and were buried, Peter Box, Henrietta Fowler, and Hannah Riches. . . . Myself ill of a fever."[25]

After only a half-year at the Bolama settlement, the few remaining colonists had had enough. They had endured starvation, attacks from the Canabacs, the gruesome sight of watching their fellow settlers be hacked to death, and waiting for what seemed to be their own inevitable fate. The stubborn Beaver finally admitted defeat. He and just five other dying colonists boarded the *Beggar's Benison* and, with torn sails and broken masts, limped to Sierra Leone. Beaver's Black servant, James Watson, remained behind in Bolama, then found his way to the West African coast. Beaver alone somehow made it back to London to tell the tragic tale of the Bolama expedition. He arrived in May of 1794 weak and near death, and facing bankruptcy from his failed investment.

CHAPTER FOUR
PHILADELPHIA

Columbia's genius, veil thy brow,
Guardian of freedom, hither bend:
The prayer of mercy meets thee now,
With healing energy descend

—A Citizen's "Philadelphia, An Elegy," 1797

America's City

Philadelphia, Pennsylvania, has rightly been called the "Cradle of Liberty" and the birthplace of America." Its official name came courtesy of William Penn, who was granted a charter from England's King Charles II in 1681 to establish Penn's namesake colony—Pennsylvania. For the colony's foremost city, Penn looked to the Greek word meaning "brotherly love," a nickname that has stuck with Philadelphia ever since and was inspired by the Quaker commitment to religious freedom and tolerance. A Quaker himself, Penn, his city, and colony were known for their openness, opposition to slavery, and social progressivism.[1]

It was the site where the First Continental Congress met in 1774 to discuss independence from British rule.[2] It remained—off and on—the temporary seat of government during the Revolutionary War when the Second Continental Congress met there several times from 1775 to 1781, then again when the Congress, under the Articles of Confederation, gathered at the Pennsylvania State House from 1781 to 1783. Of course, Philadelphia was famously the site where Thomas Jefferson put quill to parchment and produced the Declaration of Independence in 1776 and the meeting place for the Convention of 1787 that created the US Constitution. The culmination of these momentous events, and the fact that the city was the cultural and intellectual center of the new nation, even gave rise to another nickname for the city in the early 1780s: the "Athens of America."

Consequently, it was the city that hosted George Washington, John Adams, Alexander Hamilton, Thomas Jefferson, and its own favorite son, Benjamin Franklin.[3] Thanks in part to Franklin, Philadelphia was not only the political capital of the young republic, but the civic, social, educational, intellectual, medical, and scientific hub of the country. It was there in 1751 that Franklin established the Academy and College of Philadelphia—later named the University of Pennsylvania—and would go on to found the American Philosophical Society, a publishing company, newspaper, the first public library (that allowed patrons to take books home), and a fire department, as well as advancements in street lighting, public safety, health, and other civic improvements. From his office in the city, Franklin also made numerous discoveries, advanced important theories, and produced his famous inventions. He was also an abolitionist and helped to not only identify Philadelphia with the cause but contribute to the larger social movement.

In short, Philadelphia was the foremost community in the nation. Even the noted historian and chronicler of the birth of America, Henry Adams, gushed, "If Bostonians for a moment forgot their town meetings, or if Virginians overcame their dislike for cities and pavements, they visited and admired, not New York, but Philadelphia."[4]

In 1793, the city's residents would have been well aware of the special place where they lived. Indeed, all but children would have had firsthand experiences with, and vivid memories of, the momentous events that defined the Revolution and independence. Many would have seen or met the Founding Founders and Framers as well as such influential revolutionary residents as Betsy Ross, Samuel and Elizabeth Powel, Chaim Salomon, Charles Thomson, Thaddeus Kosciuszko, and others. They would have followed closely the fighting of such bloody and important battles as Brandywine in September 1777, the largest battle of the entire war, and Germantown the next month, both fought on the outskirts of the city.

They would have shared in the emotions of General Washington's bold and brilliant crossing of the Delaware River on Christmas night of 1776, a feat that likely saved the Continental Army, and his difficult encampment during the winter of 1777/1778 at Valley Forge, events occurring just miles from the city. They would have endured the crushing blow when the British army marched into the city on September 26 to begin their occupation of America's political capital, just as they would have rejoiced the following June when the redcoats abandoned the city and returned to their headquarters in New York City.[5]

In the late eighteenth century, Philadelphia was the largest city in the young nation. The first federal census completed in 1790 put the population of the city at just over 44,000, but it continued to grow rapidly, especially after it became the interim site for the nation's capital. By 1793, Philadelphia likely had a population of roughly 50,000 people. By 1800, it had swelled to nearly 68,000 residents. It was a bustling city with over four hundred shops and stores, including one of the most popular markets in the country on High Street. There, vendors lined up to sell their wares. Residents and visitors alike who gathered at the busy marketplace were treated to the smell of freshly baked bread and roasting meats, the sounds of caged pigs and poultry, and the bright colors of cut flowers and fresh vegetables.[6]

Philadelphia was also a city of professions, with attorneys, blacksmiths, bookbinders and booksellers, builders, candy makers, carpenters, coopers, druggists, grocers, hatters, ministers, printers and publishers, tailors, teachers, and wool combers. In addition to the markets and shops, the city boasted numerous houses of worship for the widest array of faiths and congregations found anywhere in the country.

So, too, was the character of the city forged by this surprising diversity. Philadelphia contained a large Quaker population, whose abolitionist views, religious devotion, and commitment to education affected the whole city. It was, consequently, the center of Quakerism in the country. The semiannual meetings of the Society of Friends were among the largest events hosted by the city. There was a large German-speaking population, some French and Irish immigrants, and roughly 2,500 Black people, including many former slaves who were now living freely in the city. By the year 1800, the Black community is estimated to have grown to nearly 6,500 residents, lured by Philadelphia's abolitionism and tolerant reputation. The city also attracted both farmers and merchants from the sur-rounding rural communities in Delaware, New Jersey, and Pennsylvania who came to sell their wares and marvel at all the city had to offer.[7]

Philadelphia was also known for its almshouses. These "poorhouses" were charitable endeavors licensed and supported by the city as well as by donations, that provided clothing, food, shelter, and even basic medical care to its poorest citizens. Groups such as the Quakers established almshouses and a number of related organizations such as the Overseers of the Poor likewise offered an array of care and support for the city's needy and shelters for orphaned and homeless children. They would end up figuring prominently into Philadelphia's response to the coming yellow fever crisis.

Located in southeast Pennsylvania, the city stretched about two miles in length north to south but less than a mile in width, hugging the shore of the Delaware River. Its somewhat compact size came courtesy of an enlightened and orderly grid design. The square blocks began near the expansive wharf, whose docks ran from Southwark in the southern part of the city to Kensington on the north side. Philadelphia's waterfront was not only the lifeblood of the city but one of the most important ports in the country, contributing to its status as a major center of trade. It also brought both immigrants and new residents to the city, with a whopping 23,000 people estimated to have arrived at its docks in the decade of the 1790s alone.[8]

Like every community at the time, the defining characteristics also included the odors and health problems created by a lack of a clean public water supply, indoor plumbing, or closed sewage system, and the presence of an abundance of horse manure from the many carriages and wagons that clattered across the cobblestone streets. On the unpaved roads and Philadelphia's signature narrow alleyways, it gathered and mixed with mud and trash on rainy days. Along the wharfs, intersecting streets, and narrow alleys, the city boasted a large and planned series of oil-burning streetlamps. Though pungent, they kept the life of the city going long after smaller villages and towns were asleep. The waterfront was also marked by rows of cheap wooden shacks and boardinghouses where a strange mix of the poor, sailors, recent immigrants, and young men came and went. This part of the city lacked adequate schooling, fire and policing services, and, though bustling from the busy port, had a lawless and frontier character to it.

The lack of a reliable water supply was a matter of life and death, not only for Philadelphia but for other cities at the time. Obviously, the challenges of safe and abundant water for drinking, "basic hygiene," and fighting fires in a time of crowded wooden structures was paramount. Yet, as was the case with other cities in the eighteenth century, the interim capital was reliant on "an inadequate hodgepodge of wells, cisterns, and springs for most of its water." The quality of public water at the time was such that people actually drank little of it, preferring teas, beer, wine, and rum.[9]

That fateful summer, the first cluster of cases of yellow fever would be found by the Arch Street wharf, which would be a victim of its location on the water.

Interim Capital

In 1793, Philadelphia was once again front and center in the young nation's politics. It was serving as the interim capital while a permanent seat of government was being built along the shores of the Potomac River on land ceded by Maryland and Virginia. That site would soon be named for the first president, whose vision and leadership would make the capital a reality. It must be remembered that the American colonists had since 1775 fought a war, gained their independence, and formed a government, all without the benefits of a permanent capital city. Accordingly, a proposal had been negotiated at great political expense for General George Washington to be inaugurated as the nation's first president in the spring of 1789 in New York City. That northern city would serve as the temporary seat of government, with Washington residing at the Osgood Cherry Street home and taking the oath of office at the majestic Federal Hall by Wall Street.[10]

There were, however, numerous unsolved and contentious issues that threatened the very existence of the fledgling experiment in popular government and which contributed to the birth of political factions—the Federalists and Anti-Federalists—that would soon become political parties. Foremost among them were the location of a permanent seat of government and the large debt stemming from the war. These two issues undermined the continuity of the nation which, predicted by Thomas Jefferson, would "burst and vanish, and the states separate to take care of everyone of itself."[11] Washington concurred, believing the debates over the capital were the most "heated" of all the issues discussed at the Constitutional Convention, prompting the general to write that the prospect of selecting the site of the capital "is pregnant with difficulty and danger."[12]

The debate over the location of the capital and massive debt lasted for years. All the while, Philadelphia remained in the minds of many political leaders and the public as the natural, if not obvious, site. However, Southerners generally remained opposed to any site not in the South, while over thirty cities were, at one time or another and with varying degrees of seriousness, proposed to host the capital. It seemed that everyone wanted their city to be selected, believing that their community was best or realizing the obvious economic advantages and enhanced value of land and property from having the federal government move in.

Alliances formed to support or oppose Philadelphia and other sites, such as when representatives from Pennsylvania and New Jersey worked together to support the city. There were several votes and most of them were both close and contentious. One proposal forwarded by Robert Morris on May 24, 1790, to make Philadelphia the capital was postponed by a narrow two-vote margin in the Senate.[13] Little progress was made and the twin debates over how to cover the massive debt from the war and where to locate the capital became so intense that, in the words of the Pulitzer Prize winner Ron Chernow, "It seemed the union might dissolve in acrimony."[14]

Both matters were resolved during what has been called "the dinner table bargain" or "the bargain of 1790," a deal struck between Thomas Jefferson and Alexander Hamilton while dining at Jefferson's rented home on 57 Maiden Lane in New York City.[15] Of course, over the years the difference between fact and legend has blurred, but what is known is that few political leaders wanted the capital to remain in the temporary location of New York City. Therefore, the two met on June 20 and Jefferson invited his friend and political ally, James Madison, another Virginian and advocate for the Jeffersonian perspectives on the two great debates, to join them. Jefferson thus attempted to stack the deck two to one against Hamilton. It was an unlikely—and most likely frosty—gathering. Hamilton was the leader of the Federalist faction and Jefferson was the leader of the Anti-Federalist faction. So, too, as Hamilton was the secretary of the treasury and Jefferson served as secretary of state, they were rivals for power in the Washington administration.[16]

The Virginians wanted a small, rural capital comprised of simple, one-story brick buildings located in the South and preferably in their home state, while also opposing taxes, any mandate to pay the debt incurred by the war, or internal public improvements.[17] This position was echoed throughout most of the South and by nearly all members of Congress from the region. Hamilton preferred the capital remain in New York City and contain imposing structures, while also expressing concern about the inability of government or the states to pay the debt, veterans, its allies from the war, or desperately needed roads, bridges, and ports. Northern states such as Massachusetts, New York, and Pennsylvania, after all, had shouldered much of the burden of the war and were not in an economic position to pay the debt. Although the details of this important dinner party remain unknown, it appears Hamilton agreed to his rivals' positions.

Yet, unbeknownst to Jefferson, the treasury secretary had walked them into something of a trap. Given his close relationship with Washington, Hamilton would have known all along that the president favored a location by the Potomac, near his home. As such, Hamilton "gave away" that which the great general would support and used it as leverage for other deals. Likewise, by agreeing that Virginia and the South did not have to contribute to the debt, the only way to cover the massive amount owed and therefore put the nation on firm financial footing was for the federal government to assume the states' debts. This would require a national bank, debt plan, the advent of public credit, a strong treasury, and an active role for the fledgling federal government in economic matters, all actions that Hamilton had longed for and which went against everything Jefferson stood for. When the secretary of state later realized he had been duped, he admitted, "Of all the errors of my political life, this has occasioned me the deepest regret." That was an understatement, as the deal set the course for the new government and nation.[18]

The gridlocked issues had been resolved. Madison and Hamilton agreed to get their respective factions to endorse the deal, and Washington provided symbolic support—and cover—for the plan and even helped to flip votes needed to pass the 1790 Residence Act, which codified the deal.[19] Supporters of the Philadelphia location took comfort in their belief that the proposal to build from scratch a grand capital city along the Potomac on land comprised largely of bogs, fields, and forests was doomed to fail. In fact, it sounded like madness. There were few trained architects, and the federal government was broke, but the deal included a provision that the interim capital would move from New York City to Philadelphia on December 6, 1790, when Congress reconvened from its recess. Philadelphia would then host the government until 1800, when it was scheduled to move into the newly built city on the banks of the Potomac.[20]

Second Term

The year 1793 also marked the start of Washington's second term in office, which he had to be coaxed into. He had been experiencing some health issues, including a fading memory, and he longed for retirement at his beloved Mount Vernon. He had tired of the emerging political divisions and bickering and believed in the principle of a citizen-statesman serving a limited tenure in elected office. But trusted advisers such as Hamilton, close friends such as Eliza Willing Powel, a prominent socialite and both the wife and daughter of mayors of Philadelphia, and others implored him to remain in office. The nation was not yet on firm footing politically. It took some convincing, but Washington ran for a second term in 1792.[21]

In a joint session of Congress on February 13, 1793, the Electoral College's votes were tabulated, and Washington was unanimously elected for a second time. John Adams would again serve as his vice president. However, as Washington wished, his second inaugural address and ceremony, held on March 4, 1793, in Philadelphia, were far less public than the first; in fact, that address would end up being only 135 words in length, a record as the shortest in history. Because the former general was first sworn in as president in New York City in April 1789, Washington has the distinction of being the only occupant of the office to have inaugurals in two different cities. The president resided in downtown Philadelphia on High Street near Independence Hall in a mansion he rented from the wealthy founding father Robert Morris.

As the Constitution was purposely rather vague about the details of the duties of the president, the second term saw Washington continue to establish precedents both for the office and nation. He had, for example, created customs that would become sacrosanct, such as how he selected his cabinet, the manner in which treaties were signed, the process for following the constitutionally mandated "Advise and Consent" clause for the Senate, and even how he entertained guests. But the second term would bring him great challenges, including the arrival of a deadly pandemic in the interim capital city.[22]

Among the issues Washington wrestled with was the building of the new capital city, a shortfall in funding for the massive project, a shortage of trained architects and builders, and continued opposition from across the country from those who wanted their own cities to host the government. Moreover, the brilliant architect, Pierre Charles L'Enfant,[23] hired by the president to build his "grand city for the ages" had to be dismissed because of his difficult personality and inability to work with the federal commissioners Washington appointed to oversee the capital. The enormous undertaking was not only Washington's great passion but was consuming his time and energy.[24]

The president was also dealing with treaties with Native Americans and military preparedness. The frontier and Northwest Territory were anything but secure, and the new nation's military was not yet in a position to defend these outposts from either the Indigenous people who were in conflict with White settlers or the British, who still maintained a presence along the border in Canada and were believed to have been inciting native attacks against Americans. So, too, were southern "war hawks" agitating for reprisals and military expeditions against the Cherokee, Creek, and other Indian nations. Ultimately, after consulting with his secretary of war, Henry Knox, his appointed governor of the Northwest Territory, William Blount, and his federal Indian agent, James Seagrove, Washington humanely decided against war with the native peoples. But the issues of military preparedness, British fortifications along the border, and what to do about the many Indian nations remained far from resolved.[25]

The problems were, however, about to become far worse.

Omens

The year 1793 started off in crisis. In January, the city suffered a minor outbreak of mumps. The very next month, several cases of scarlet fever were documented. The winter of that year had been very mild and without the usual snows. In fact, some waterways had not frozen, and parts of the city had not even experienced frost. Water shortages followed. Elizabeth Drinker, a Quaker housewife in the city who was an avid diarist, recorded, "This has been an uncommon moderate winter," which she noted was "remarked by every one" to the extent that it was a frequent topic of conversation.[26]

That troubling winter was followed by an early spring. Philadelphians welcomed the songbirds back to their city along with the first blossoms. However, the balmy weather was accompanied by drought. Water levels dropped dangerously low, and wells were compromised. This included marshes, ponds, and both the Delaware and Schuylkill Rivers—the lifeblood of the city—which by summer had a few feet of exposed muck and mud where there had once been water. Dead fish along the banks of the waterways attracted insects, especially in April, which was abnormally hot. One account noted that "moschetoes hung over the city like a cloud." Residents soon complained of the constant high whirring and buzzing from the swarms that harassed them. Philadelphia was desperately in need of cooler and wetter weather to alleviate the situation.[27]

May, which was chilly and very wet, brought that relief. Rainfall was recorded nearly every day that month, but the parched land could not absorb the rain and flooding ensued. The rivers and creeks around the city overran their banks and Philadelphia's streets and alleys filled with water, mud, and debris. The storms and relief lasted only one month, as June was one of the hottest and driest months that any local could remember. It ended up being an unbearably hot and humid summer up and down the Eastern Seaboard, the worst in memory for many. With the absence of any breeze, the air was eerily still and quiet.[28]

Indeed, the year was already one of the worst in memory. Mathew Carey, a publisher in Philadelphia, recalled that "from November 1792, to the end of late June, the difficulties of Philadelphia were extreme." It was not only a series of health and ecological crises, but a financial one as well. The economy of much of the country had been impacted by "numerous failures in England" as well as "distress" among American banks and businesses. However, the threat appeared to be waning, thanks in part to "the opening, in July, of the bank of Pennsylvania," which Carey claimed put the city "on favourable footing" and rescued "many" of Philadelphia's merchants from "ruin."[29]

Then, in July, just as the *Hankey* and other ships carrying the deadly yellow fever were about to dock, influenza and other unidentified ailments appeared in Philadelphia. The adjacent state of Delaware was suffering through a bout of the "bilious" fever. Suddenly and strangely, people began to notice cats dying in large numbers and unusually large flocks of migrating birds streaming out of the city. Oyster beds throughout the region began dying and the small harvests were inedible. There were reports of cows and horses dying and unusual illnesses in nearby Maryland and New Jersey, as well as in Harrisburg, Pennsylvania.

Coming on the heels of drought and floods crops started to fail, and livestock fell ill or died. The city's water sources were again brackish or dry. Open river and streambeds cracked in the blistering sun and the stench of rotting fish permeated the city. With food stocks affected from prolonged drought, farmers' markets resorted to selling large numbers of pigeons, which harkened to the old wise tale that pigeons were a portent of bad things to come. Elizabeth Drinker, a keen observer of events in the city, made mention in July that something ominous was afoot. She could not have known how true her prediction would be.[30]

Interestingly, on the morning of September 12, 1793, a chunk of a meteorite crashed into Third Street in downtown Philadelphia. The more superstitious of the city's residents, along with many religious leaders, saw it as foretelling a pending calamity such as the yellow fever outbreak that was menacing the capital that month. Some said it was the judgment of God. Even among the more learned and rational, it appeared something was seriously awry that year. What's more, Dr. David Rittenhouse, a noted scientist and inventor who was a member of the city's esteemed American Philosophical Society and served as the first director of the U.S. Mint, recorded that a comet was visible in the city's night sky and that it became a topic of conversation to Philadelphians. Soon, speculation ran rampant about whether it, too, was a foreboding sign or manifestation of the outbreak in the city.[31]

The year 1793 was turning out to be a challenging one. Residents were looking forward to the fall, but an invisible enemy aboard the "ship of death" docked at the city's wharf was causing one of the deadliest outbreaks ever to strike an American city. It would soon claim thousands of lives, grow into a nationwide pandemic, necessitate the evacuation of the capital city, and spark a governing crisis. And it was born of tragedy and irony.

45

CHAPTER FIVE
THE FIRST TO DIE

The sky is pure, the clouds are light,
The moonbeams glitter cold and bright;
O'er the wide landscape breathes no sigh;
The sea reflects the star-gemm'd sky,
And every beam of Heav'n's broad brow
Glows brightly on the world below
But ah! the wing of death is spread;
I hear the midnight murd'rers tread;
I hear the Plague that walks at night,
I mark its pestilential blight;
I feel its hot and with'ring breath,
It is the messenger of death!

—Lucretia Maria Davidson
"The Yellow Fever," 1824

Death Comes to the Docks

It was not the first time the *Hankey* had sailed to Philadelphia. In 1784, she had transported a few hundred indentured servants from Ireland who came to Philadelphia in search of a better life—once, of course, their servitude had been paid. In late July 1793, the *Hankey* made her way from the bloody revolution in Saint-Domingue to Philadelphia.

The cursed vessel dropped anchor by the city's main wharf for only one week in order to unload her passengers and resupply before sailing for England, but it was time enough for the disease-carrying mosquitoes and infected travelers to bring yellow jack ashore.[1]

The *Hankey* anchored next to the *Sans-Culottes*, a small French merchant craft-turned privateer that arrived in Philadelphia on July 22 along with the *Flora*, a ship she had recently captured in the West Indies.[2] Around the same time, the ship *Amelia* also docked and began unloading rotted coffee and other agricultural products at the dock. All these ships had been to Saint-Domingue and their crews were sick, most probably with the fever.

Aboard the *Hankey* were Captain Cox, a handful of survivors from the original Bolama expedition, and refugees fleeing the violence in Saint-Domingue, most of whom were wealthy White colonists and their families. In a shocking act of irony and inhumanity, some brought their slaves with them from the island, intending to perpetuate the bondage in America. Other ships followed, likewise escaping the revolution. Almost every day another ship arrived filled with refugees packed into their holds. Ultimately, it is estimated that perhaps one thousand refugees arrived at the port in July and another thousand in August. It is hard to know for sure, but perhaps fifteen thousand colonists fled Saint-Domingue for ports in the West Indies and the Americas. Of course, death was hidden away on many of these ships.[3]

So, too, did they bring horrific tales of death and destruction. The colonists shared shocking stories of plantation owners and their families being murdered, blood-soaked sugarcane fields, cities aflame, and disease tearing through the port. Cried one refugee, "Would to God I had the courage to take my own life and escape from the horror of such a cruel recollection."[4]

The war had raged for a few years, wreaking havoc on trade and the island's economy. Consequently, many of the refugees, though once prominent members of Saint-Domingue's plantation society, were now destitute, barely clothed, starving, and sick. Some had to be carried ashore, and several showed obvious signs of being in the grips of a serious disease. Some hoped to be reunited with friends and family members who had also fled among the chaos. As such, announcements were placed in Philadelphia's newspapers and posted on pub doors. Word of the plight of the refugees and of the turmoil in Saint-Domingue was soon on the lips of Philadelphians.[5]

Accommodating roughly two thousand refugees was a tall order, even for the largest city in the country. The number, after all, amounted to roughly 4 percent of the city's total population. Given the limited infrastructure, public services, and housing at the time, it would have been difficult for cities to take in a few hundred refugees, yet alone the number of sick and destitute arriving at the wharf. Moreover, Philadelphia was geographically somewhat compact and already overcrowded from the recent and rapid rise in its population on account of the federal government moving to the city. The refugees seriously strained the city.

Mathew Carey, a prominent publisher in the city, put it this way: Philadelphia was "a victim of its own liberality." It was a welcoming city, which Carey boasted was its "most respectable point of light." Carey also proudly reported that "nearly 12,000 dollars were in a few days collected for their relief." However, within a "few weeks" the "unfortunate refugees from Cape Francois" were utterly dependent on the "public charity" of residents.[6]

Additional charities were quickly established to collect and distribute clothing and food for the refugees. Horse shows, theater performances, and other events in the city were organized to raise money, while politicians spoke about the plight of the former colonists from Saint-Domingue. It helped that Philadelphia had a large Quaker population, known for its benevolence. They led the effort to help raise funds and organize "camps" by the waterfront. So, too, was there a French population in Philadelphia that proved eager to help their countrymen. This included prominent leaders such as Stephen Girard and Peter LeMaigre, who organized the Société Française de Bienfaisance de Philadelphie to aid in the relief effort.

Waterfront

The docks at any large city are always busy, and so it was in Philadelphia. Ships from Baltimore, Boston, Charleston, New York, and elsewhere, including Europe and the West Indies, regularly brought cargo and passengers to the city. Nearby, large warehouses were filled with merchandise from the ships and crates and boxes to be loaded onto outgoing ships. As was the case at any major port, taverns were but a few steps away from the waterfront, as were cheap boardinghouses filled with sailors, prostitutes, and recent immigrants. The crews and refugees from the *Hankey* and other ships found accommodations by the docks, many between 2nd and 4th Streets, which ran parallel to the waterfront. They also boarded at Front Street, which sat next to the river and dock, and Walnut, which intersected Front by the main wharf.[7]

Ports were also wretched places at the time. Ships brought rats, spoiled agricultural produce, and rowdy sailors itching to drink and brawl. The horrors of the Philadelphia docks near Water Street where the fever would soon manifest itself were described by a British traveler named Isaac Weld: "Behind these wharfs, and parallel to the river, runs Water-Street. This is the first street which you usually enter after landing, and it does not serve to give a stranger a very favourable opinion either of the neatness or commodiousness of the public ways of Philadelphia."[8]

In the summer, the conditions and odors were worse. Of Water Street, Weld went on to say, "It is no more than thirty feet wide, and immediately behind the houses, which stand on the side farthest from the water, a high bank, supposed to be the old bank of the river, rises, which renders the air very confined." The picture he painted was anything but pleasant, noting, "Added to this, such stenches at times prevail in it, owing in part to the quantity of filth and dirt that is suffered to remain on the pavement, and in part to what is deposited in waste houses, of which there are several in the street, that it is really dreadful to pass through."[9]

Given the poor sanitation and hygiene that defined dockyards, the unregulated housing, and unwillingness of authorities to enforce the law on the waterfront, it was a prime area for the spread of the disease. This was especially true of the pools of stagnant water and muck along the docks. Indeed, they would soon prove to be fertile breeding grounds for the mosquitoes brought by the *Hankey*, *Sans-Culottes*, *Amelia*, and other ships.

Many passengers on board these ships were likely already carrying yellow fever. We will never know who was the "index case" or "patient zero" in Philadelphia. This person may have been at the rundown establishment on an alley off North Water Street known as Denny's Boardinghouse, run by Richard Denny.[10] The boardinghouse was popular with sailors, poor immigrants, and the refugees who arrived from Saint-Domingue. Within a day of the arrival of the *Hankey* and refugees, two boarders at Denny's who arrived from Saint-Domingue fell ill. By the end of July, several others at the boardinghouse and elsewhere by the port were feverish. One was a French sailor whose name is not remembered by history, who died on Saturday, August 3, of a "severe fever." Diarist Elizabeth Drinker recorded another death that day, noting that on August 4 that "Samuel Lewis departed this life yesterday morning, after two hours sickness." It continued when an Englishman by the name of Moore, who was lodging at Denny's, contracted the fever on August 2, and died just two days later. Within days, a number of its boarders showed signs of the disease. The neighborhood near the port was living up to the unceremonious nickname used by sailors: "Hell Town."[11]

On August 6 or 7, a Mrs. Parkinson, a recent arrival from Ireland, died just three days after falling ill. On August 7, the man rooming with the deceased French sailor also succumbed to the fever. They were followed by the owner, Mr. Denny, and his wife, both of whom died within days. That same week, two people lodging next door to Denny's passed. The situation was about to get even worse when, on the seventh, the ship *Mary* arrived at the port, her hulls filled with sick and dying refugees from Saint-Domingue.[12]

Despite the sudden deaths and obvious presence of a new and terrible disease, Philadelphia's residents had yet to panic, and its leaders had yet to react. The city's newspapers rarely reported on what happened at the port and in Hell Town. The docks were, after all, home to the poor, illiterate sailors, and newly arrived immigrants. Every port suffered from maladies and recurring outbreaks, especially in late July and August. Plus, those who passed included the refugees who had arrived starving and ill, so their deaths were somewhat expected. What city officials did do was to see that corpses from the waterfront were removed at night, although they were buried within city limits. According to Rev. Justus Helmuth, a popular preacher in the city, "Several dead bodies had been brought ashore" from early ships, but "this was done in the night time and persons who had seen it, were taken sick immediately, and died."[13]

But soon the cluster of cases moved beyond the port and Denny's, then beyond Water Street and spread to Arch Street and elsewhere. Soon, the people of Philadelphia began expressing alarm that their neighbors appeared to be in good health one day, but deathly ill the next, and dead within a week. Within weeks of the first cases, a shocking percentage of the residents had either evacuated, were violently sick, or had died. The young resident and diarist Elizabeth Drinker observed, "There has been an unusual number of funerals lately here." She worried that it was "really an alarming and serious time," and concluded, "tis a sickly time now in Philadelphia."[14]

Something is "Ravaging" the City

What was killing the people of the capital city? This question consumed the medical community as they tried desperately to find a cure or even a way to treat the sick and comfort the dying. However, the primitive state of medicine was such that they did not know that the mosquito, *Aedes aegypti*,[15] that bred in small pools of stagnant water, was the cause of the scourge. Even though Philadelphia was the center of medicine for the entire country at that time, neither the city nor its many physicians were prepared for the coming epidemic. Nonetheless, several brave physicians persisted in the face of the growing body count, attempting to identify the source of the disease and experimenting with an array of desperate treatments, and all the while putting their own lives at risk. In fact, several of the physicians contracted the disease. Some died.

At the time, the medical community did not understand viruses and bacteria. Rather, a popular explanation for infections was that they were caused by foul environmental factors—a "mephitic" or what we today would call a noxious gas or vapor. The most prominent physician in the nation at the time, Dr. Benjamin Rush, was an adherent to this theory, advocating the idea of "miasmas" as a cause for many of the maladies that plagued his native Philadelphia. In Rush's mind, a variety of diseases including cholera and the Black Death were believed to come from "bad air." Relatedly, others pointed to the general unhealthiness of the city and thought the preponderance of the bogs and marshes surrounding the city were to blame. There were, it seemed, constant sicknesses plaguing the city. In particular, fingers began to be pointed at the filth at the docks and garbage that piled up around the city. One possible culprit was the open sewer that festered on Dock Street, described as a "large and offensive canal."[16]

Another possible mephitic was the rotted coffee that had been unloaded in late July when the first cases of fever at the port appeared. It had come from the sloop *Amelia*, which had sailed from Saint-Domingue laden with coffee that had gone bad during the voyage. This was causing a strong and foul odor. It was also known that the ship's captain and five crew members were in the grips of some disorder when they arrived. Since July 24, the large mound of foul coffee sat festering less than a block from the wharf, prompting one of the city's physicians—a Dr. Foulke—to suggest it as the cause, noting it was "a great annoyance of the whole neighborhood" and could be detected throughout Hell Town and over a one-quarter mile away.[17]

Publisher Mathew Carey agreed, noting of the Englishman named Moore who was one of the first to die, that he "had been walking along the wharves, where the coffee lay" and near where "the *Sans Culouttes* was moored."[18] Carey reported on Moore that "in the morning; and on his return home, was so extremely ill, as to be obliged to go to bed, from which he never rose again." Likewise, the crew of the *Sans Culouttes* fell ill.[19]

Such explanations fit Dr. Rush's belief in miasma. He, too, would embrace the idea that the rotted coffee and other putrid vegetable matter at the docks were the cause of the "bilious remitting Yellow Fever," as he would later call it, beginning to plague the city. Of course, Rush and others were dead wrong, but such beliefs and the loss of so much life would prompt the city, in the months and years after the 1793 pandemic, to at least clean up such unhealthy places and improve the disposal of garbage.

A few alternative theories quickly emerged about the origins of the disease. When the outbreak was discovered, many residents knew about the various maladies that struck the city that time of year, but because this one was different, they assumed it did not come from their city. As such, some people and physicians began to question the idea of a foreign or new mephitic as the culprit. The current disease, it was reasoned, must therefore have come from abroad, and most probably from where the recent arrivals and refugees had come. It was known that troops from Pennsylvania (when it was a colony) that had fought with His Majesty's army in the West Indies often returned with various afflictions. Likewise, the refugees from Saint-Domingue talked openly about the fever that struck their island, an illness that had many names including the Barbados distemper, Siamese fever, spotted yellow fever, and others, while sailors recognized it as yellow jack. Many therefore pointed to the refugees and Saint-Domingue as the cause of their new problem.[20]

The struggle to explain the disease would last through the duration of the affliction that year, and even through the next century. The debate over both the causes and best treatment also raged among the medical community, becoming so heated that it divided the city and even poured over into newspaper coverage of the fever and factored prominently in the growing, deep political divisions in Philadelphia and the country. A few of the city's physicians, however, did not hesitate to head straight to the blighted docks to attend to the sick along Water Street.

The First Doctors to Respond

Two of the first physicians to respond were young men who worked at the Dispensary, which was part of a larger organization known as the Overseers of the Poor,[21] a charity that, since 1705, was funded by a city tax and also accepted donations. As the name implies, it existed to provide services to the poor.[22] Dr. Phillip Syng Physick, who was born in Philadelphia in 1768,[23] and Dr. Isaac Cathrall were accustomed to treating sailors and immigrants, and to having patients from the docks. Physick had studied medicine in Edinburgh, Scotland, under Dr. John Hunter, perhaps the most famous physician in England and Scotland at the time. Physick himself would go on to be a famous surgeon, even earning the honor of being one of the "Fathers of American Surgery." In that capacity, he served on the staff of the Pennsylvania Hospital for many years and became the first professor of surgery at the University of Pennsylvania's medical school in 1805, even operating on Chief Justice John Marshall in 1831.[24] Cathrall, born in 1764, had also attended medical school in Edinburgh and continued his studies in London and Paris.[25] He was also a highly capable and selfless physician.

On August 3, Richard Parkinson, a new immigrant from Ireland had asked the Overseers of the Poor to send a doctor to see his wife, who would end up being one of the first to die from the fever on the sixth or seventh of that month. Mrs. Parkinson had been lodging at Denny's with her husband and two daughters since early summer after arriving from Ireland. It was there that Dr. Cathrall, just twenty-five years old at the time and sent by the Overseers of the Poor, met his patient. The young physician was shocked by what he encountered. Mrs. Parkinson was in severe pain, vomiting a foul black mucus, dehydrated, had an inflamed throat, and had suddenly gone nearly blind. Cathrall was told an Englishman named Moore, also staying at Denny's, had similar symptoms. The young physician notified the Overseers of the Poor, who sent Dr. Physick to assist with the mysterious new scourge at the docks.[26]

Cathrall attempted to treat Mrs. Parkinson and also visited Mr. Moore, who, as was noted earlier, died the next day. The two physicians discussed their patients and the strange malady—they were perplexed. Both patients died, but Mrs. Parkinson's family seemed fine and shared the same cramped room. Therefore, they reasoned, she had not been contagious. Likewise, neither physician became ill despite repeated visits to Hell Town.

Physick's autopsy of the two patients concluded "some derangement in the colon" and the vessels of the brain were "uncommonly distended and turgid with blood." Moore had died right away, so Physick initially suspected poisoning, but an autopsy suggested otherwise. On the other hand, Mrs. Parkinson lasted a few days. The physicians pondered whether the two cases were related and concluded that such illnesses usually happened at the wharf and were often "seasonal" maladies that seemed to occur at the filthy docks and among the poor. Beyond that, they had no answers.[27]

But then the young physicians observed other cases in early August, all among sailors, immigrants, and refugees who stayed or had eaten at Denny's or were living nearby on Water Street. Their patients included French sailors, both Mr. and Mrs. Denny, and others. All had fevers, chills, black vomit, severe stomach and throat pain, and other similar conditions, but also had a curious case of jaundiced skin. Yellow fever was not fully understood by American physicians at the time, nor was it even identified; however, Cathrall and Physick understood that the scourge they were facing was tied to Saint-Domingue and the West Indies, and not caused by the rotting coffee or filth at the docks.[28]

Another bit of evidence came a few weeks later and also seemed to confirm their theory. It involved Samuel Powel, the beloved mayor of Philadelphia who had served during the revolutionary years of 1775 and 1776 and again from 1789 to 1790 and was close friends with George Washington. Powel had recently dispatched an aide to Barbados. The man died of yellow fever while there. His clothing and belongings were then returned to Philadelphia. Powel and others who opened the chest were all said to have become violently ill. Was there a connection?[29]

Yet, despite the reports by Cathrall and Physick, the alarm had yet to be sounded in the city. The physicians were young, had only recently returned from Scotland, were working for a charity, and treating the poor at the docks. At that point in their careers, they lacked the high profile and political connections necessary to issue such an alarm. Moreover, unlike some of the more prominent physicians in the city like Rush, they did not opine on medical issues in the newspapers. Tragically, their progress in studying the disease went largely unrecognized and their warnings disregarded . . . for the time being.[30]

Rush Arrives at the Waterfront

Benjamin Rush was without question the most famous physician in the country at the time, even earning the nickname "The American Syden-ham," a reference to the acclaimed doctor and teacher Thomas Sydenham, a founder of clinical medicine and epidemiology in seventeenth-century England.[31] Known as the "English Hippocrates," Sydenham was famous for his detailed study of epidemics, using careful observations rather than the prevailing religious doctrine, mysticism, and hocus-pocus that defined much of medicine through the ages. Consequently, even though the Oxford educated physician wrote important medical books[32] and was among the first to systematically analyze scarlet fever and other well-known but little understood disorders, he was often seen as controversial by his contemporaries. In many ways, Rush both sought to be like Sydenham and a worthy heir to the great physician.[33] Indeed, one historian noted that Rush "remains to this day the most imponderable single figure in the history of medicine in the new world."[34]

Rush had impeccable credentials and was well connected politically. He had served as General Washington's surgeon general during the Revolution, was one of the signers of the Declaration of Independence, had traveled and studied across Europe, and had been taken under the wing of none other than Benjamin Franklin. Rush was also one of the fathers of American psychiatry, having developed new and scientific approaches to treating mental illness. Not surprisingly, Rush was a leader among the medical community in Philadelphia. Yearning to be placed alongside other medical luminaries in history and imbued with ample ego, Rush viewed the outbreak of a terrible disease in his native city not only as a way to serve but as his "moment"; he would be the rescuer of the capital city. In fact, many residents took solace in knowing their famous protector was on the case.

The forty-seven-year-old doctor looked and acted the part: lean, impeccably dressed, and known for his attention to detail and insistence upon good hygiene, he was widely recognized wherever he went and his writings were just as widely read. Rush was also careful about his diet (something that was rather unusual for the time), even refraining from alcohol and tobacco. A moralist, the noted surgeon espoused a number of social reforms including abolition and access to education. Rush was also a workaholic, spending long days and nights at his office on Walnut Street and Third. This tendency, along with his practice of frequent bloodletting and purges, likely contributed to the chronic nagging cough and other lung ailments from which he suffered . . .

There were other, less admirable, sides to the surgeon, however. As author J. H. Powell noted bluntly, "He had no common sense." Moreover, Rush could be thin-skinned to the point of being vindictive, judgmental to the point of being puritanical, and opinionated to the point of being overly confident in his abilities. Such traits at times interfered with his impartiality as a scientist and, when combined with his dogged partisan political views, would end up stoking deep divisions among the medical establishment about how to treat the pandemic. He would also be at the center of bitter political disagreements about how the city should respond to the outbreak. As others have aptly stated, "Boring, Rush never was!"[35]

Regardless of his complicated personality, Rush was fearless and dedicated to his patients. And so it was that he headed to Philadelphia's waterfront on August 3 after hearing about the mysterious ailment. One of his first patients was a fellow physician's daughter. Hugh Hodge, a surgeon during the Revolutionary War, had asked his colleague to examine the Hodge family's two-year old, who was in the grips of a bad fever. Rush arrived at the home, which was just a half-block from Denny's lodging house, and found the girl with a high fever, vomiting a foul black bile, and "yellow skin." Both surgeons were stumped by the unusual symptoms. Sadly, the toddler died within days, prompting Rush to later conclude that Hodge's daughter was the pandemic's first victim. Such a statement reflects Rush's ego—the first patient he saw had to be, in his mind, the first to pass from the mysterious disease, even though a number of refugees and sailors arriving at the docks in late July had already succumbed to the fever.[36]

Infant mortality rates were high during the eighteenth century, and a shocking number of children did not live to see the age of two, which may have been the reason the famed physician did not immediately sound the alarm about the new ailment. Rush and his wife, Julia, for instance, lost four of their eleven children in infancy. Over the next two weeks, Rush continued to see and treat those by the waterfront suffering from the fever. and a pattern soon emerged.[37]

On August 7, Rush treated a young man by Water Street, then a week later the patient's brother fell ill of apparently the same affliction. On August 15, Rush saw another woman with yellowed skin. She died quickly; the famous surgeon learned that five people who lived next to her also passed. On August 18, Rush visited a man who was, alternatively, suffering from high temperatures and cold, clammy skin. He, too, had a jaundiced appearance.[38]

Another one of Rush's early patients was Polly Bradford, wife of Thomas Bradford, a prominent publisher and close friend. As was the case with Dr. Hodge, Bradford had summoned Rush. Interestingly, Polly, the daughter of a hatter, happened to be the famous surgeon's first love. However, their budding relationship ended when Rush sailed for Europe to study medicine and met the beautiful sixteen-year-old daughter of the wealthy Earl of Leven. Polly was forgotten.

Polly—now Mrs. Bradford—was suffering from severe headaches, a very inflamed throat, nausea, and yellow eyes and skin, symptoms resembling the other patients. Rush treated her with bleeding and purging, his preferred and trusted approach to a number of ailments. Such treatments, as we shall soon see, often killed more patients than saved them and would soon embroil the city in controversy. Happily, Polly recovered. Rush took it as proof-positive that he had found a way to cure the mysterious malady, although he did recognize that something new and terrible was plaguing the waterfront.[39]

"'Tis a Sickly Time"

Drs. Cathrall and Physick were also overrun with patients. One resident who observed the alarming trend was Rev. Helmuth, the popular, fire-and-brimstone preacher. "As early as in the middle of the month of August," he noted, "we had a funeral" for one of the congregants. The reverend added that, while in hindsight it "seemed rather suspicious . . . nobody at that time had the least idea, that the deceased had been affected with a contagious disorder." But the situation soon worsened. Helmuth was summoned to see a member of his church on August 19, whose "breathing was very short, but who did not shew in his countenance the least symptoms of approaching death." The preacher recorded that "to my very great surprise he was a corpse on the 20th." The congregant, it was declared, had died of a "contagious fever." Then, on August 21, another member "of the same family was buried. That same day, several of Helmuth's parishioners shared "terrifying accounts" of the disease now ravaging Water Street.[40]

Another Philadelphian would end up rendering history a great service as a reliable chronicler of the disease and corresponding events that deadly year. Her name was Elizabeth Drinker. Born on Second Street in Philadelphia in her family home, she was the daughter of William Sandwith, a recent immigrant from Ireland but with family roots near Whitehaven in England. Accounts of Elizabeth noted her "sweetness of disposition and singular propriety of conduct." In a Quaker ceremony, she married Henry Drinker, who ran a shipping and importing business. The family, which included three daughters and two sons, lived on Water Street by the docks for ten years before moving to nearby Front Street adjacent from the site where the *Hankey* would drop anchor.[41]

The avid diarist recorded on August 10 that "Wm Shipley died this week" and again six days later, "John Gillenham was buried on second day last." She expressed the opinion of many when she wrote, "'Tis a sickly time now in Philad. and there has been an unusual number of funerals lately here."[42] Indeed, by the end of the month, thousands would take ill, and hundreds were dying.

Rev. Helmuth described it as "a merry, sinful summer." The reverend believed God was visiting his wrath on the people of Philadelphia in the form of a plague, just as he had allowed the British to seize and occupy the city during the Revolutionary War. Of his beloved city and his sinful neighbors, Helmuth observed, "There are few cities upon which the Lord had poured forth richer blessings, than on this; and there are but few indeed, that have been plunged by his just judgment into a deeper abyss of distress, than our now weeping Philadelphia."[43]

II

THE CAPITAL UNDER SIEGE

CHAPTER SIX
"HELL TOWN"

In the sad chambers of unkind disease,
Where Rush prescribed, he never failed to please;
His gentle manners, sympathetic fire,
Constrained to love, respect him and admire!
Where anguish palled, whenever Rush appear'd,
Fear fled the bosom and the heart was cheered

—Elegiac poem dedicated on the death of Dr. Benjamin Rush, 1813

August 19

Dr. Benjamin Rush had seen several patients in August, a few of whom died. But August 18 was a particularly difficult day. Rush lost two more patients that morning—a twenty-five-year-old woman named Mary Shewell, wife of a wealthy Baptist merchant, and John Weyman, a longtime resident of Philadelphia. That same day he was asked by a fellow physician, Dr. Benjamin Say, to consult with one of his patients. Say had tried everything and was out of ideas. No treatment seemed to work. The patient in question, Peter Aston, happened to be a friend of both physicians and a prominent resident of the city. Rush arrived, as requested, and found Aston "sitting upon the side of his bed, perfectly sensible." Aston seemed to be recovering so Rush and Say conferred about the unusual case before them. Before long, however, Rush recorded that Aston was "without a pulse, with cold clammy hands, and his face a yellowish color." The man died that very day.[1]

The loss of three patients in one day, including one that was a friend, seemed to affect Rush. Moreover, all three were residents of the city, not recent refugees, although they all lived near the docks. And they were not the only deaths that day. The diarist Elizabeth Drinker recorded on the evening of August 18 that others succumbed to the disease that day.[2]

The following morning, on the fateful day of Monday, August 19, Rush set out from his office determined to tackle the mysteries of the disease now threatening his city. He headed back to the waterfront and to the home of a young boy named McNair who was in the throes of the contagion. Rush noted that the boy was feverish, suffered from nausea, and was vomiting a foul black vile. He treated the young patient as he had others—with bleeding and purging. McNair died. Rush saw two other young boys that day and encountered the same "vicious, violent symptoms" and peculiar yellowish skin and eyes. They, too, became casualties of the disease.[3]

Still undeterred, Rush headed to the home of Peter LeMaigre, a French trader who had moved to Philadelphia several years earlier and ran a boardinghouse on Water Street. The Frenchman was spearheading a project to collect clothing, food, and supplies for the recent refugees from Saint-Domingue now sheltering in the squalor of Hell Town. LeMaigre's wife, Catherine, had recently taken ill and was showing signs of the disease. Dr. Hugh Hodge, the Revolutionary War surgeon whose two-year-old daughter had died earlier in the month, and Dr. John Foulke, Rush's former student who had gone on to become a Fellow with the city's College of Medicine, had been treating Mrs. LeMaigre at the request of her husband. The thirty-three-year-old was extremely ill and vomiting a black vile. Like the other patients, her skin had turned a strange yellow hue. Hodge and Foulke tried a number of treatments, including a laudanum compound comprised of barley water and apple water with opium.[4] The prognosis did not look good, so the two physicians went to meet with Rush.

In typical fashion, Rush agreed to see the patient right away and recorded that she "vomited constantly, and complained of a great heat and burning in her stomach." She had the other symptoms Rush had seen throughout the month of August. Catherine LeMaigre was, Rush concluded, "in the last stage of a highly bilious fever."[5]

Rush shared the news with Hodge and Foulke and also informed them that several of his patients had not recovered. Hodge responded that he knew of "an unusual number" of people who died of the fever, and they, too, lived along Water Street "within sight of Mr. LeMaigre's door." Hodge described the alley as "the narrowest, yet one of the most populous in the city." Foulke concurred, adding that another patient who lived there had died within hours of contracting the fever. The three physicians were convinced that the answer that eluded them might be found in Hell Town, an area Rush described as "much confined, ill aired, and, in every respect . . . a disagreeable street."[6]

Mrs. LeMaigre died the next day. Records show that twelve more residents were lost on August 20 and thirteen passed on August 21. Mathew Carey, the publisher, pointed to the loss of Peter Aston and Catherine LeMaigre as "the first deaths that attracted public notice." They were leading citizens in the city, after all. There was a custom of ringing church bells when a person died or when there was a crisis, and the bell towers across Philadelphia were soon ringing throughout the day, which only furthered the growing fear and panic in the city. From that point on "for some weeks," he wrote, "almost every hour in the day, carts, wagons, coaches, and chairs, were to be seen transporting families and furniture to the country in every direction."[7]

Although he would flee the city during the height of the plague, as a publisher, Carey had numerous sources still in the city and would later write an account of the fever that would prove to be invaluable to our understanding of this history. Born in Dublin, Ireland, in 1760, Carey had worked in printing and the book industry as a young man then began publishing essays on controversial topics in politics such as his opposition to dueling and Ireland's harsh criminal justice system. After the British House of Commons threatened to have him arrested, he fled to Paris in 1781 where he met Benjamin Franklin. The great founding father invited Carey to work for him and encouraged him to return to Ireland and continue to publish.

Carey did, but again found himself running afoul of the authorities and was forced to escape in 1784 disguised as a woman, sneaking aboard a ship headed for the new United States. In America, Carey used his connections with Franklin and the Marquis de Lafayette to open a bookstore and publishing business. Soon, a few of his newspapers and magazines such as *The Pennsylvania Herald, Columbian Magazine,* and *American Museum* were making money. Carey become an important publisher of Bibles, including the first Roman Catholic version and the now-famous King James Bible, as well as atlases, maps, and political essays. Carey soon emerged as an important publisher and political leader in the city.[8]

The diarist, Ms. Drinker, put a face on the scourge when she wrote on the twentieth that she "called" on a few friends including "at ye widow Rigers, a poor woman with three children, who lost her Husband a week or 10 days ago." Despite the danger, Drinker continued to visit neighbors and console the grieving. She added the concern that people were dying "rather suddenly."[9]

Through the remainder of August, people began dying in ever-increasing numbers. A newly arrived citizen, Samuel Breck, who lived through the epidemic and went on to become a teacher for the blind, commented that his neighbors were "in health one day were buried the next." As Carey described it, "The streets wore the appearance of gloom and melancholy."[10] Drinker added an ominous diary entry on August 21 that "8 or 10 persons buried out of Water St. between Race and Arch Sts.; many sick in our neighborhood, and in ye City generally." Indeed, another frightening development struck: the fever was beginning to spread beyond Hell Town. Cases appeared throughout the city.[11]

Rush Identifies the Disease

Rush had served as a young physician's apprentice during the 1762 outbreak and subsequently read accounts of yellow fever, recalling the symptoms from his studies. The characteristics of the malady had been recorded. Moreover, it was believed that the 1762 outbreak was started by a ship from Havana that brought sugar to Philadelphia's Sugar House Wharf near South Street in the Hell Town neighborhood. It was written that one of the sailors who came ashore was already quite sick with a mysterious malady. The man died soon afterward and those who tended to him fell ill and died. Regrettably, even though Rush knew that incident likely came from a ship from the West Indies, that information did not point him to correctly identifying the source of the 1793 outbreak. But he did realize that his patients around the Arch Street wharf and Water Street all shared the same array of troubling symptoms—delirium; cold, clammy skin; high pulse; severe stomach pains; vomiting black blood; yellow tinge to eyes and skin; and so on. All were characteristic of the descriptions of yellow fever found in his medical books.[12]

Rush noted another characteristic of those stricken with the disorder, one that should have helped him to identify the true cause. He wrote that the patients had "*petechiae*," or reddish pinpoint spots on the skin, usually the result of bleeding within the mucous membrane. He even said they "resembled moscheto bites" and "appeared chiefly on the arms, but they sometimes extended to the breast." He also observed that they often "disappeared . . . in the course of the disease." Rush had inadvertently named the precise source of yellow fever, but never put one and one together to identify the cause of the disease.[13]

Rather, he was blinded by three factors. The first was that all the cases at that time had clustered around Water Street and in Hell Town, which led him to conclude that the malady originated there. He wrote that those who died had either lived by, worked at, or visited Water Street, the wharf, or the Hell Town neighborhood. The only person Rush knew of who succumbed to the disease but did not fit such a profile was Elizabeth Hill, yet he recalled that her husband was a fisherman who worked at the docks.[14]

The second problem was that Rush was an adherent to the miasma theory that held that diseases were caused by "bad air." The famous surgeon commented, "There was something in the heat and drought which was uncommon, in their influence upon the human body." While we know this to be true today in the form of dehydration, fatigue, or sunstroke, Rush was referring to something entirely different. He had read about the outbreak a few decades earlier and concluded it was the result of "pestilent air." He thus felt the culprit was "some damaged coffee which putrefied on the wharf near Arch Street."[15]

In Rush's defense, such conclusions were medical truisms at the time. The medical books he consulted blamed "miasmata," including the foul air of the marshes and the rancid smell of decomposing animals and vegetation for a whole host of physical afflictions. Physicians had, after all, been trained in such ideas for centuries.[16] Moreover, Rush was supremely confident in his abilities. He was, after all, methodical and scientific in documenting every detail of what he encountered, taking careful notes. Writing that he had seen "an unusual number of bilious fevers, accompanied with symptoms of uncommon malignity," Rush consulted his library before arriving at a diagnosis of the contagion.

Yet it was his zealous nature and dogmatic faith in his own ideas that posed the third and perhaps main obstacle to an accurate diagnosis. Unlike the younger physicians in the city, Rush was even slow to realize that the disease did not spread through human contact and that similar afflictions ended during the cold months, even though such conclusions were obvious.

The Announcement

It appears that Rush was the first to publicly announce that the city was in the throes of a terrible disease and was also the first physician to correctly identify it. Thus began a debate about what disease was tearing through the city and how to treat it. Both Drs. Hodge and Foulke respected Rush but felt they needed to consider additional cases before rendering a diagnosis. Other physicians soon weighed in on the issues. However, as shall soon be seen, this was about all that Rush got right about yellow fever.

Rush initially offered his theory in the parlor of LeMaigre's home on August 19, then sounded the alarm, going public with news that Philadelphia was facing a "highly contagious, as well as mortal . . . bilious remitting yellow fever." Rush used the term "bilious," which meant it pertained to stomach maladies and was often a descriptor for discolored stool or vomit. The term "remittent" implied sweating and chills as part of the fever. As to labeling the disease itself, this came as a surprise to many, as the city had not experienced a yellow fever outbreak since 1762 and nothing quite as lethal as the current affliction.[17]

Rush began notifying fellow physicians, political leaders, and the press that Philadelphia had an epidemic on its hands. He also began reading vigorously on the disease, poring over old manuscripts on the history of the fever. Rush also developed treatments, some of which were beneficial to public health such as cleaning the docks and streets, but others, as we shall soon see, did more harm than good.

On the August 20, diagnosis in hand, Rush also went to see Mayor Matthew Clarkson and Governor Thomas Mifflin to inform them of his conclusion and warn that "all was not right in our city." He claimed to be confident that the plague ravaging their city was yellow fever but was equally as sure that it originated with the rotted coffee at the port. The only good news, Rush claimed in an August 21 letter to his wife, Julia, who was then summering with the family in Princeton, New Jersey, was that the affliction would remain localized by the wharf and mound of coffee. His diagnosis was dealt a blow when, within days, the disease spread throughout the city.[18]

Mayor Clarkson had been elected to his first term on April 13, 1792. Though born in New Jersey, he had quickly established himself as a leader and social reformer in Philadelphia. Mifflin assumed office as the new state's first governor in 1790, after having served in the Revolutionary War as an aide to General Washington and as a delegate to the Constitutional Convention. Both men knew Rush, as was the case with most of the state's leaders, and trusted him. After all, the city, claimed Rush, was his responsibility—he would lead the effort to combat the outbreak.

Just two days later, on August 22, Mayor Clarkson issued his first public "notice" about the disease, sharing Rush's assessment. Two days after that, Rush notified Dr. James Hutchinson, former surgeon general of Pennsylvania, Fellow of the College of Physicians, and, at the time the doctor overseeing the port. Initially, most of Philadelphia's physicians disagreed with Rush's diagnosis and assumed the malady was the usual fever that struck the city most years during the "sickly season" of August. As he would repeatedly do, Rush bristled at dissent. Not one to tolerate opposition or disagreement, he began complaining that he was "treated with ridicule and contempt." Not one to confer, Rush tended to dictate to other physicians. In short time, a "controversy" erupted over the causes of and treatments for the disease, as "everyone had opinions on it," and over Rush's autocratic approach.[19]

Treatment

In addition to the idea of miasma, Rush accepted the conventional wisdom that the body contained blood, phlegm, and bile. Illness was the result of an imbalance of such fluids. Known as humoral theory, this idea dated to the teachings of Hippocrates, the Greek physician and paragon of medicine in the ancient world.[20] From the classical Greeks through the Roman Empire and up to the eighteenth century, bloodletting was believed to restore balance.

Rush vigorously examined as many books and sources as possible on the history of such diseases, hoping to find a treatment. This included the letters of Dr. John Michell, a physician who tended to the afflicted during an outbreak of yellow fever in Virginia in 1741. These letters were given to Rush by a trusted source, none other than Benjamin Franklin. Mitchell observed that the stomach and intestines filled with blood and advocated emptying those organs through bleeding and purging. Wrote Mitchell, "I can affirm that I have given a purge in this case, when the pulse has been so low that it can hardly be felt, and the debility extreme, yet both one and the other have been restored by it." Rush found his treatment.[21]

With an inclination for the medieval practice of drawing blood and purging, Rush sought to treat those suffering from yellow fever with regular bleedings and forced vomiting. When a patient recovered, Rush credited his treatment; yet, when a patient passed away, Rush failed to question his methods. Rather, if the treatment was not working the noted surgeon often pursued increasingly aggressive bloodletting and purging. He also tried sweating the disease out of his patients and used a "mercurial sweating powder" that only made matters worse, which some of his critics pointed out. To be sure, even though he was a meticulous chronicler of the fever, he ignored any connection between his treatment and those who died. A man of strong faith and unshakable confidence, Rush boasted, "To every natural evil, Heaven has provided an antidote."[22]

It is quite probable that Rush's treatments were, in some cases, what killed the patients and not the yellow fever. Nevertheless, he remained wedded to his aggressive bloodletting and purging, but added two new approaches. One was a powder formulated of ten grains of a mercury-based calomel and ten grains of the cathartic drug jalap, which was derived from the poisonous root of the Mexican plant *Ipomoea purga*, a type of morning glory. This concoction, which he ground into a powder then made into pills, was given to patients to prompt even more violent vomiting and diarrhea. The other involved tree roots and bark to "blister" his patients, then coat their bodies with a heavy salve of herbs. Nothing worked. "Finding them all ineffectual, I attempted to rouse the system by wrapping the whole body . . . in blankets dipped in warm vinegar," wrote Rush. For the myopic and overly confident Rush to experiment with alternative treatments suggests his frustration with the disease and awareness that his efforts were not working.[23]

The surgeon at least deserves credit for not blaming immigrants and refugees, which soon became the politically expedient path for some. So too, his ideas to clean the streets, alleyways, and docks, while emptying toilets regularly, though obvious today, were innovative and positive urban reforms at the time. Perhaps most impressively, while patients and physicians started dying in frightening numbers and with residents streaming out of the city by late August and through September, Rush stoically remained and was relentless in meeting his patients. He commented bravely, "I have resolved to stick to my principles, my practice, and my patients to the last extremity," which at the least gave people some hope and the promise of a cure. To be sure, the public sent him letters of thanks, which only further buoyed his confidence.[24]

Rush's use of bleeding, purging, and mercury would, with much consequence, become standard medical practices for decades. At the time, however, his announcements and methods did cause controversy. Ms. Drinker, the diarist, wrote in late August of the debate over Rush's announcement, "Some say it was occasioned by damaged Coffee and Fish, which were stored at Wm Smiths'; others say it was imported in a Vessel from Cape Francois, which lay at our wharf, or at ye wharf back of our store." Concerns were raised on all sides of the debate. Drinker added, "Doctor Hutchinson is ordered by ye Governor to enquire into ye report. He found, as 'tis said, upwards of 70 persons sick in that square of different disorders; several of this putrid or bilious fever. . . .'Tis really an alarming and serious time."[25]

Of course, the port was vital to the economy of the city, state, and young fledgling nation. What impacted the city impacted the country as well. The mere mention of the fever sparked fear throughout the city and nation, as it seemed there was little that could be done to stem the spread of the fever. Though trying to appeal to calm, Rush recalled that "about this time began the removals from the city." Lines of wagons, horses, and people soon appeared on the roads leading out of the interim capital.[26]

At the end of August, Rush wrote to his wife describing his frustration, "The fever's symptoms are very different in different people."

He underscored the severity of the horrid and deadly disease that gripped the city, noting that "few survive the 5th day, but more die on the 2 and 3rd days," and admitted in a rare moment of candor about his work that "the common remedies for malignant fevers all have failed." Rush closed the emotional letter, "O! that the hand of the Lord may be with me."[27]

Rush Falls Ill

In late August, Dr. Rush wrote to his wife predicting "our neighborhood will be desolate in a day or two." He was losing close friends, patients, and colleagues. Yet, despite the threat of the disease and mass evacuations, he did not hesitate to remain on the job. It must be remembered that the nature of the disease was still largely unknown, and Rush and others believed it to be highly contagious. Likewise, a few physicians had abandoned the city, others fell ill, some stopped seeing patients, and fully ten had succumbed to the disease. Yet, more than simply remain in the city, Rush was tireless in treating his patients, including the poor, those in Hell Town, and others in the last fitful throes of the disorder—typically seeing "dozens of patients" per day.[28]

Rush wrote again to Julia, "Parents desert their children as soon as they are infected, and in every room you enter you see no person but a solitary black man or woman near the sick." Likewise, Rush added, "Many people thrust their parents into the street as soon as they complain of a headache"[29] The physician added, "My dear Julia, The fever has assumed a most alarming appearance. . . . It not only mocks in most instances the power of medicine, but it has spread thro' several parts of the city remote from the spot where it originated. . . . In one house I lost two patients last night, a respectable young merchant and his only child. His wife is frantic this evening with grief. . . . Five other persons died . . . yesterday . . . and four more last night." The disturbing accounts continued. A few days later he wrote, "I hope I shall do well. I endeavor to have no will of my own. I enjoy good health and uncommon tranquility of mind. While I depend upon divine protection, and feel that at present I live, move, and have my being in a more especial manner in God alone, I do not neglect to use every precaution that experience has discovered, to prevent taking the infection."[30]

Rush's treatments put him at risk. For instance, Rush and a nurse would turn down the sheets and open the windows in order to allow the "infected air" to "disperse" the contagion. This would have allowed mosquitoes to enter the room. He also sprinkled vinegar around the room, including beside the open windows. Despite his belief of it being contagious, Rush touched his patients and checked their temperature and pulse, although he often dipped his fingers into a "mild acid" before doing so.[31]

On September 12, after a day of seeing patients, Rush broke out in a sweat, felt dizzy and nauseous, and suffered pains in his stomach and joints. Initially, the physician thought he might have simply overworked himself and had become overheated. He was, after all, a workaholic and was used to being exhausted from long hours of seeing patients. However, he later diagnosed himself, recording, "My body became highly impregnated with the contagion." Having seen more patients than any other physician, he recognized the symptoms, including a racing pulse, adding, "My eyes were yellow, and sometimes a yellowness was perceptible in my face." Yet, he continued to see patients, despite barely being able to walk and his concern about spreading it to others.[32]

In mid-September, few physicians were still seeing patients, so news of Rush's affliction spread through the city and worried the population and Philadelphia's leaders. He had given residents hope that he would rescue them and was receiving piles of mail from across the country, pleas from 50 to 150 prospective patients a day, and requests for advice from other physicians. Rush somehow managed to answer some of the mail each evening and agree to a good number of the requests.[33]

Rush's close friends and fellow physicians, Doctors Griffitts, Mease, and Say, all contracted the disease, yet survived. This seems to have emboldened him to continue. Plus, he felt that having contracted it himself, he might now be immune, dismissing caution and writing, "Streams of contagion were constantly pouring into my house, and conveyed into my body by the air." Ever the narcissist, Rush even pronounced that his home was the most infected spot in city! Either way, he continued tending to the dying, noting, "I laid aside all this, and all other precautions."[34]

Rush's dedication is all the more admirable because he was dealing with the difficult losses of his apprentices. On September 11, the day before his own illness, one of Rush's students named Washington contracted the fever. The young man downplayed the extent of the illness, hoping to not distract Rush and even attempted to treat himself. However, he died not long after. Rush commented that the student was particularly "effective" in "curing others." Exactly one week later, one of his assistants named Stahl fell ill while in Rush's home. Stahl "refused" to take medicine and "resisted" his mentor's efforts to treat him. The student passed on September 23. The next day a third student named Alston fell ill and died just one day later. Rush seemed unable to face the reality of the losses, attributing, for instance, Alston's death to being "worn down because of his sickness," and to "uncommon exertions in visiting, bleeding, and even sitting up with sick people." He did admit that he struggled to recover "from the shock" of his students and assistants dying. Then, Rush's main apprentice, a young man named Fisher, came down with the disease; the day after that, his only other apprentice, a student named Coxe, fell ill.[35]

That same difficult September, Rush's sister Rebecca, in his words, "yielded to the disorder." He added, "My heart has flown into the coffin with her." Soon thereafter, his mother fell ill, followed by his Black servant. The only member of his remaining household and office not stricken with the disease was an eleven-year-old "mulatto boy" of whom Rush said became the only person "able to afford me the least assistance." The strain was becoming almost too unbearable, even for Rush, who admitted to his bout with "melancholy" that month. Fortunately, a former student of his named James Woodhouse returned to take some of the load off his mentor.[36]

Among the few accommodations Rush made for his own illness were carrying a "rag wetted with vinegar," as it was thought to mitigate diseases and foul air. He also both stopped eating meat during his ordeal and gave up drinking "wine and malt liquors." After making these changes, he noticed that his "troublesome headache . . . now suddenly left me." During his six-week ordeal he wrote that he "did not taste animal food, nor fermented liquors of any kind"; rather, he lived "intirely upon milk and vegetables." He noted that he lost weight but felt better and entertained the idea that he had possibly found another cure for the disease.[37]

Mostly, Rush continued to work, exhausting himself from the tireless schedule. He recorded in his notes that he was "frequently" too tired even to eat and often had "anxiety of the mind" such that he "was forced to lie down a few minutes" before continuing. No wonder. In a single day during his ordeal, he saw an astonishing forty to fifty patients! "When it was evening," he recorded, "I wished for morning; and when it was morning, the prospect of the labours of the day, caused me to wish for the return of evening." It did not help that he also continued his infamous catch-all treatment on himself: bloodletting and purging, typically pulling ten ounces of blood before going to sleep and sedating himself with his elixir of mercury. He would draw another ten ounces in the morning capped with tea and "purging powder" to force himself to vomit and empty his bowels before heading off to see patients.[38]

Rush's personality can be seen in all its complexity—his stoicism, dedication to his craft, and fearlessness, but also his arrogant belief that only he could address the outbreak, his overconfidence in his own conclusions and treatments, and his vanity insofar as he was also determined that other physicians would not get credit for any progress against the disease. He expressed anger, for example, that people, in his view, "were dying under the care of a French physician" that dared to disagree with him.[39]

Rush remained weak through the fall and winter, suffering all the while from, in his words, "a cough and a fever somewhat of the hectic kind." Finally, in the spring of 1794, the combination, he claimed, of warm weather and "divine goodness" allowed for a complete recovery. Philadelphia exhaled.[40] However, by the end of that terrifying month, one hundred people a day were dying in the capital city.[41]

CHAPTER SEVEN
FEAR AND PANIC

O! may thine arm, Lord, now stretch out
Upon a guilty land
Make them consider and not doubt
It's thy almighty hand

—Popular poem in Philadelphia, 1793

Exodus

Despite the alarming signs in late July and the number of people dying in August, it was the passing of Dr. Hugh Hodge's young daughter while in the care of Dr. Rush that ultimately caught the attention of the city. After all, she did not fit the profile of those who died at Denny's and the waterfront. It was no longer a malady impacting only refugees and the poor. The child's passing spurred the prominent newspaper publisher, Mathew Carey, who, unaware of those who had fallen ill at Denny's and at the port in late July, wrote, "Dr. Hodge's child, probably the first victim, was taken ill on the 26th or 27th of July, and died on the 6th or 7th of August." He concluded, a "malignant fever" had struck and "made its appearance here, about the end of July" and was now "ravaging" the city.[1]

After appearing by the wharf in August, then spreading to adjacent neighborhoods, by the end of August yellow fever was ravaging the entirety of the nation's largest and most important city. A mere six years after it played host to the Constitutional Convention, just four years removed from the optimism surrounding George Washington's inauguration, and only three years since the temporary seat of government relocated from New York, Philadelphia found itself in the grip of a full-fledged crisis. In a scene reminiscent of the bubonic plague in Europe, crews walked the streets and alleys yelling, "Bring out your dead!" Wagons filled with bodies became a common sight. Teams of neighbors and city workers were forced to go door-to-door to collect the dead, as family members were either dead themselves or too ill to remove their loved ones' corpses. Orphaned children were a daily scene milling about the deserted streets. Miss Drinker, writing that "the accounts . . . are many and various," began compiling lists of all those dying in the city and worried that everyone "will quickly die of this terrible disorder." The death toll and evacuations were such that the city was in the grips of chaos. Drinker summarized, "Some, 'tis said, die of fear."[2]

Mathew Carey described the "universal terror" at the site of so many sick and dying. One educator of the blind recalled, "The horrors of this memorable affliction were extensive and heart rending." The deaths suddenly skyrocketed in August such that a typical day in the city saw three people buried. Then in the days after Rush's "discovery," twelve, then thirteen, then seventeen people died.[3]

Rev. Helmuth, leader of the city's German Lutheran Congregation, was summoned on August 19 to the home of one of his flock. He recorded that the parishioner, "whose breathing was very short," seemed otherwise in fair condition. Yet, the Reverend wrote of his shock to find the man "was a corpse" the next day. The day after that, a member "of the same family was buried." Though surprised, Helmuth and his congregants did not believe a crisis was at hand. However, no sooner had he noted his thoughts about the deaths than he learned that people began dying in alarming numbers around the city. Just one day later, he changed his opinion, describing the "terrifying accounts" of "horror" coming from Water and Arch Streets.[4]

By the end of August, both those living by the wharf and his congregants began falling sick and dying in increasing numbers. "Terror," the Reverend observed," was now "visible on every face in that part of town." This was also true for those who had to travel to the waterfront. Most began to avoid Hell Town, but those who could not "would go with a trembling heart and hasten away as fast as possible." Others simply abandoned the city altogether.[5]

What alarmed Helmuth the most, though, was that the ill "usually died in three or four, some even in one or two days." "Many," he noted with disbelief, "went to bed in the evening to all appearance in the enjoyment of perfect health" only to find that "at the break of day they were often at death's door." It was, he concluded, "the most pitiable conflict of nature," causing some to "fall into fits of real madness," which, he added, "greatly augmented the terror of their relations." Death, it seemed, offered a welcome and quick relief for the suffering and even their families.[6]

The reverend and his fellow clergy and many residents worried about omens portending what was to come. On Saturday, August 24, it rained. Strong winds and lightning were recorded, followed the next day by severe thunderstorms that pummeled Philadelphia. The young diarist Elizabeth Drinker also recorded that it rained "all night, and all this day." Rush noted that water cascaded through the streets, leaving the city full of mud and puddles. Where the reverend saw evil in the weather, Drinker hoped that "this Storm may, if it please kind Providence so to order, abate the alarming fever." She could not have known that the pools of stagnant water would provide an ideal environment for the invading mosquitoes to multiply.[7]

The disease raged through the closing days of August. Ms. Drinker's family struggled to keep their shipping business open in the face of so many employees falling ill or succumbing to the fever. On August 26, Drinker shared the growing concern of many, saying, "We have been rendered very uneasy this evening by hearsays from the City of a great number of funerals."[8]

Soon, businesses closed their doors and the city government discontinued services. Even four of the five newspapers in the city shuttered their presses; only Andrew Brown's *Federal Gazette and Philadelphia Daily Advertiser* continued to be printed, providing history with a valuable chronicle of the life in the interim capital during the pandemic. Even the important and highly partisan newspaper *The National Gazette*, published by Thomas Jefferson's protégé Philip Freneau, went bankrupt and closed.

Then, as might be expected, the exodus occurred. It is estimated that at least seventeen thousand of the city's residents fled during August, a number that amounted to nearly half the population.[9] Isaac Heston, a young man who chronicled the disease in a touching letter, wrote about the evacuation: "Those who at first appeared stout hearted, are now moveing out of the city, there is now Scarsely any body to be seen in many parts of the town, and those who are seen are principally French, and Negroes."[10]

Caravans of wagons, carts, and horses filled the roads leading out of the interim capital, as residents fled to the country or to the homes of friends and family. This convoy, marked by distressed and grieving faces, was observed by Charles Biddle, a relative of Elizabeth Drinker. While traveling back to Philadelphia, Biddle heard horrific stories of a mysterious malady striking the city, yet he continued on. When Biddle arrived home, he learned that his friend Peter Aston had been among the first to die. Although Biddle bravely—or perhaps foolishly—remained, he sent his children to live with relatives in Delaware.[11]

Biddle urged his wife to leave with their children, but she insisted on staying, reflecting the dilemma so many families now confronted. However, Biddle asked his friend and physician, Dr. James Hutchinson, for advice and asked him to encourage Mrs. Biddle to evacuate. Hutchinson had never seen a disease that struck with such force and quickness. He recommended that the Biddles leave the city but noted that "as a physician he thought it his duty to remain and let the disorder be ever so bad, he would not leave." Biddle recalled that he and his wife took Hutchinson's advice and shook his hand before departing, all believing they would never see one another again.[12]

Hutchinson had originally rejected Dr. Rush as an alarmist, but was forced to reevaluate his assessment of the pandemic. Drs. Rush and Hutchinson also disagreed on whether the disease was contagious. Rush believed it was, but Hutchinson did not, prompting Rush to complain that his colleague "denied the existence of a contagious fever . . . [and] treated the report of it with contempt and ridicule." It was not contagious, but it was deadly. Ironically, years earlier, when a young Hutchinson departed Philadelphia to attend medical school in Europe, the city was in the grips of a less deadly affliction, prompting the young man to announce that his goal in going into medicine was "to expel the raging fever, to make diseases die."[13]

After advising Biddle, Hutchinson dined with Thomas Jefferson at a mansion along the edge of the city's Schuylkill River. Over a bottle of expensive wine, the two toasted to better days. The next morning, however, Hutchinson awoke with a headache and signs of the fever. The surgeon general sent an aide to notify Dr. Adam Kuhn, who hurried to see his friend. Kuhn recorded that Hutchinson "had gone to bed about 11 o'clock perfectly well and he indeed never felt better or in higher spirits." Yet, as was so often the case with the peculiar disease, he was up at three in the morning with the "most violent headache attended with fever." The situation was dire. Hutchinson was in "excruciating" pain and deteriorating fast. Making matters worse, Mrs. Hutchinson was nine months pregnant and "with great anxiety."[14]

Groping for any cure, Kuhn purged Hutchinson's bowels then ordered an elixir of water, lemonade, ripe fruit, and a tonic. Hutchinson, who weighed in excess of three hundred pounds, could not stop his bowel movements and was deteriorating by the hour. Kuhn prescribed laudanum and Peruvian bark.[15] Hutchinson ingested a total of forty-five drops of the opiate and was soon "deranged." Dr. Currie and Dr. Rush were brought to see the surgeon general and found him "much debilitated and faint," with a low pulse and "suffused with blood." Even though Hutchinson had "30 stools in three days," Rush recommended more purging, but Kuhn refused to allow it. Tensions flared, but Hutchinson fell into a coma on September 5. Two days later, his wife delivered their fifth child, a daughter, and Hutchinson died. He was forty-two. His obituary was published in papers across the nation. Panic ensued, as he was the first prominent physician to die from the plague.[16]

"Groans and Laminations"

September picked up where August left off. By the end of the first week of September Dr. Rush estimated that 456 people in Philadelphia had died from the malady. And it was getting worse. Almost half the population had abandoned the city and, of those remaining, over half were now infected, with an average of thirty people a day succumbing to the disease. There were forty-two reported deaths on September 8 alone. The next day brought a cool rain, bringing with it the hope that it would somehow wash away the infection. It did not. The heat returned and with it a perfect warm, wet breeding period for the mosquitoes carrying the fever.[17]

Isaac Heston, a twenty-three-year-old law clerk, wrote of the grave situation in a letter to his family in September, summing it up quite directly: "They are a dieing on our right hand & on our left." The ordeal was taking a toll on the city's physicians. Dr. Isaac Cathrall described caring for his patients as a particularly foul ordeal because of the constant vomiting, diarrhea, and bleeding. One entry described a patient vomiting violently: "The matter ejected . . . was of a dark color, resembling coffee grounds, sometimes mixed with blood; great flatulency; haemorrhages from different parts of the body; tongue frequently covered over with blood . . . urine very offensive."[18] Foul indeed!

Even the buoyant Dr. Rush was becoming worn down, writing to his wife Julia about his fellow Philadelphians that "dejection sits upon every countenance." A few days later in early September, Rush added ominously in a letter to his wife, "This evening I fear I shall lose a son of Joseph Stansbury, a sweet youth, a little older than our Richard.[19] It has been particularly fatal to young people. I rejoice that our boys escaped from the city."[20]

Rev. Helmuth also noted the particularly painful and stressful nature of the affliction while visiting dying parishioners. "The sick," he remembered, "complained of a great pain in the head and back; and all their limbs felt as if they were bruised." So, too, did they have "an uncommon difficulty in breathing" and "seemed to be in constant pain." The malady sweeping through his congregation was just as frightening for the families who watched their loved ones' vomit "black coagulated blood" and bleed "very much from the nose." Helmuth offered a clue to the source of the disease when he expressed shock that "most of them turned yellow during their sickness, which color they kept after their deaths, though it then became of a deeper hue."[21]

The chaos sweeping Philadelphia was, in the words of the reverend, "greatly heightened" by so many "people going mad." He described what he called daily scenes of "terror" such as some "unfortunately creatures" jumping "out of their beds" and "escaping in the night time" only to run through the city "into another street, and sometimes into a strange house if they found one open." No matter where one went in the city, "groans and lamentations" were heard coming from the homes of the afflicted.[22]

Rumors swirled of friends and family members going mad and killing one another. Whether these stories were true or not, disease and death were ever-present. Isaac Heston, wrote, "To se[e] the [hearse] go by, is now so common, that we hardly take notice of it." He resigned himself to the inevitable, "We live in the midst of Death, as we may stand in the Door and se[e] the dead Bodies carried out."[23]

Thomas Jefferson, the secretary of state, wrote to his trusted confidant Congressman James Madison on the first of September that "a malignant fever has been generated in the filth of Water street which gives great alarm." He shared the shocking news that seventy people had died in the city in the closing two days of August and that "many more were ill of it." Like the scholar he was, Jefferson described the symptoms in detail and suspected that, "at first, 3 out of 4" of those afflicted would die, but he believed that rate was "now about 1 out of 3." Although the mysterious disease appeared to be "less mortal" than when it was discovered, "it is still spreading, and the heat of the weather is very unpropitious." Indeed, the secretary's concerns were that it had spread throughout the city and could not be controlled.[24]

Jefferson echoed other accounts that residents were abandoning the city in droves, writing, "Every body, who can, is flying from the city." He was also perhaps the first senior official in President Washington's administration to raise concerns about governing. He added in his comments to James Madison that the country would soon be in the grips of "panic" such that they would have to "add famine to disease" as the problems facing the country. Jefferson sent his daughter Martha from the city but maintained that he was "obliged to go to it every day myself" from his rented home outside the city proper.[25]

So, too, did unhelpful rumors run rampant, such as sightings of ships coming to the port with "2 or 3 hundred passengers from Ireland" with "an infectious fever on board." Others warned that "several hundred French soldiers, armed, were coming" to the city, and that "5 negroes" were arrested "for poisoning the Pumps." Such unfounded, malicious gossip tore through the city like a wildfire and soon many residents believed Black residents had contaminated the wells and water supply.[26] Although such rumors were "flying" about, Drinker added that she believed "most [were] likely false."[27] The newspaperman, Mathew Carey, quipped that "the hundred tongue of rumor were never more successfully employed, than on this melancholy occasion."[28]

The rumors simply stoked fear. Anti-Black, anti-Irish, anti-French, and anti-immigrant sentiments were building. The "public panic," according to Carey, rolled across Philadelphia in stages. At first it was denial, especially among the city's religious leaders and more conservative elements of the population who questioned the severity of the situation. Then it was stoked—often by the very same people who once dismissed it—to a fever pitch as the bodies piled up and public services were interrupted. Later, however, there was less panic as a fatalistic resignation haunted those who remained in the city.[29] Rev. Helmuth described the array of emotions and stages of panic as first a "melancholy, or pain, of sadness" but then "an anxious fear," only to become a grim acceptance.[30]

Neighbors started to shut doors on neighbors, turning away both the sick and healthy alike. Elizabeth Drinker shared one story of "a young woman who had nursed one or more" afflicted individuals "who died of ye disease" but was then told by the residents nearby "to go somewhere else, as none of them chose to take her in." The poor woman had contracted the disease and was later found dead on the door of a neighbor's home. Another similar account recalled a woman who had been dropped off at a hospital in a "cart" but that "she was refused admittance." That woman was "found dead in the cart" the "next morning."[31]

Similarly, Carey described "a woman, whose husband had just died of the fever," who immediately "was seized with the pains of labour, and had nobody to assist her." Tragically, no one in her "neighbourhood" would dare to enter the house. The pregnant widow ended up alone and in "anguish" for what the newspaperman described as "a considerable time." When she was about to deliver, she "struggled" to "cry out for assistance" and her pleas were eventually heard by two men who "went up stairs; but they came at too late a stage." Nearly dead when the men arrived, she "died in their arms."[32]

One of the most compelling losses was that of a woman whose husband and two children had died in the family home, but she was too far in the grips of the disease to move them or leave the home. She was also nine months pregnant. After she gave birth alone, volunteers with the Committee for the Relief of the Sick went to her home, only to find that she and the newborn were dead from what they believed was both "her labor" and "the disorder." They removed all five dead members of the household. There was no shortage of such shocking stories, prompting an exasperated publisher to say, "To relate all the frightful cases of this nature that occurred, would fill a volume."[33]

The *Federal Gazette*, the only newspaper still publishing in the city, recorded that "acquaintances and friends avoided each other in the streets, and only signified their regard by a cold nod." Soon, family members of the deceased, anyone appearing to be sick, and "a person with a crape, or any appearance of mourning, was shunned like a viper." Carey shared stories of "parents forsaking their only children without remorse—children ungratefully flying from their parents" and both a "husband deserting his wife, united to him perhaps for twenty years, in the last agony" of her affliction and "a wife unfeelingly abandoning her husband on his death bed."[34]

Of course, these accounts just heightened the panic. People began avoiding one another and took to holding handkerchiefs and cloths over their mouths. Carey wrote that throughout the city, when residents saw another, they "shifted their course." In fact, "Many never walked on the foot path, but went into the middle of the streets, to avoid being infected in passing any houses wherein people had died." So, too, "the old custom of shaking hands fell into such general disuse, that many were affronted at even the offer of a hand."[35]

A publisher added a particularly chilling observation, writing, "The corpses of the most respectable citizens . . . were carried to the grave, on the shafts of a chair, the horse driven by a negro, unattended by a friend or relation, and without any sort of ceremony."[36] The fear impacted friendships and family. The scourge was believed to be a contagion causing even children and spouses to, in the words of Reverend Helmuth, be "shunned" by their parents and partners.[37]

No one was spared. Many of the earliest casualties were young boys and dockhands working along the waterfront, but as is the case with many diseases, the young and old would perish in disproportionately larger numbers. However, the virus visiting its wrath on Philadelphia was not limited to just the young and old, it struck down the wealthy and poor, Black and White. People were literally falling dead in the streets, and piles of unburied bodies were seen at the port. Entire families were lost. Rev. Helmuth, however, believed that men were "ravaged with more violence" than women, most likely

85

on account of men handling the majority of the labor outdoors, including at the docks and for the government, tasks that would expose them to the as-of-yet undiscovered tiny carriers of the disease.[38]

Darkness Falls

With so many people evacuating the city and perhaps a few thousand dying in September, Philadelphia had become a ghost town. But that also meant that there were now not enough workers for even the most basic of tasks needed to keep the city functioning. This included not only laborers but also nurses and gravediggers. Indeed, the presence of the mysterious disease was ever-present in the city's cemeteries, which contained so many fresh graves that locals likened them to plowed farm fields. As Rev. Helmuth observed, those who buried the dead "were not exempted from this disorder." After those living along the wharf, grave-diggers were among the next group to die in number.[39] The city soon needed gravediggers, but no one wanted to be near the infected corpses. By the end of the second week of September, the cemeteries were full, and the unburied bodies began to pile up at sites such as Potter's Field.[40]

Most families with the means to leave did so, but those that remained found themselves without domestic staff, as servants abandoned homes with the fever or fled the city. At the same time, firefighting, policing, and other essential services ceased to exist. There were not enough officers and with so many homes empty, stores closed, and properties unprotected, people began to loot unoccupied buildings and businesses. Elizabeth Drinker noted that by the end of the first week in September most of "Water St. appears to be depopulated by deaths and flight." The only people about were looters.[41]

As Philadelphia's economy collapsed, those who remained had no source of employment or income. The poor and homeless suffered the most, although everyone in the city was directly impacted by the disease in one way or another. On one street alone, thirty-eight people perished in a nine-day period, while one family lost eleven relatives in a matter of days. Farmers were unable to tend to their crops and animals. Food shortages further stressed the capital. Teachers fled or died. Schools closed. The capital ran out of medicines and other supplies.

One ominous reminder of the plague was the darkness of night. For public safety, the city had some 662 whale oil lamps that were lit at night, however with most of the lamplighters either sick or dead and the government in disarray, the lamps remained dark. One resident commenting on the dark, quiet streets was Rev. Helmuth, who wrote, "Such a deep silence reigned in the streets [at night]. . . . I perfectly recollect several visits of the sick, which I had to make, entirely alone, at that time of the night." He described "houses shut up to the right and left, deserted by their inhabitants, or containing persons struggling in death at that very time, or whose former inhabitants were all dead already." Darkness had fallen on the capital.[42]

Mathew Carey found good news in that the number of "burglaries committed" was not as high as expected, given the shortage of law enforcement, unlit streets, and desperation through the city. Plus, the city jail did not yet have an outbreak of the fever. The jail held 106 "French soldiers and sailors, confined by order of the French consul," along with eighty assorted "convicts, vagrants, and persons for trial." Amazingly, "All of whom," noted a publisher, "except two or three, remained perfectly free" from disease."[43]

Carey, who like others, did not understand that mosquitoes carried the fever, attributed the miracle at the prison to it being well run, the mandatory cold baths, and forced labor of growing vegetables in the garden on the grounds. Yet, Carey and others were confounded when Elijah Weed, the jailor, came down with the disease and died at the prison while his inmates were healthy. Moreover, in the words of a newspaper publisher, he did so "without communicating it to any of the people confined."[44]

God's Wrath

As corpses remained unburied and public services ended, Carey summarized the impact as being the "total dissolution of the bonds of society." He even likened it to the plague that struck London and concluded that, even long after the affliction had ended, he was unable to "think of these things without horror."[45]

To some, it was the plague, to others—including many of the city's faithful—it was God's wrath. From pulpits throughout Philadelphia, messages of fire and brimstone were delivered claiming the vengeance of God was "purging" the city of its "sinners." One of them was Rev. Helmuth, who preached to one of the larger congregations in the city.

Fumed the popular pastor, "I look upon the whole as a deserved punishment of a just, as well as merciful God." From the pulpit he evoked Amos III, verse 6: "There is no evil in the city, but what the Lord hath done." For the reverend and his fellow pastors, there was no shortage of judgments in the good book; the congregants of the city were reminded of Deuteronomy, Jeremiah, Isaiah, and other passengers describing a jealous and vengeful God.[46]

Helmuth's litany of charges against the residents of his city were that they "gamed, drank to excess, and frequently quarreled and fought" and partook of "drunkenness, lewdness, fraud, pride, avarice, uncharitableness" and more.[47] Moreover, "Philadelphia was the unfortunate place, where cursing, swearing and perjury had fixed their residence." One need only, he claimed, "to walk the streets on Saturday evenings and Sundays in particular to hear the most horrid imprecations from men, and sometimes from women and youths, nay even from children!"[48]

The reverend's attacks continued, as he claimed that "Philadelphia far exceeded most of the cities of North-America, in luxury and dissipation among all classes of people." He joined his fellow clergy in trumpeting, "Away with these horrid benefits and the money of sin," adding, "God knows how to gladden the heart of the widow and orphan in a better manner; he does not want for this purpose your wages of vanity!"[49]

His ire was also directed at the theater, which he saw as "vanity" and the work of the devil. The government was to blame too; after all, "Performing of theatrical exhibitions was authorized by law." Moreover, Philadelphia had gone so far as "to erect one of the largest houses upon the continent for theatrical exhibitions and engaged actors at a prodigious expence." The city already boasted a small theater, reminded the reverend, adding, "As if one house, that existed before were not sufficient to ruin our young people." So, too, were there "70 or 80 actors" employed, some of which were "imported from luxurious Europe," and wealthy, leading men in the city had "given willingly 300 dollars to obtain a perpetual right of free access with wife and children to the plays." The city's clergy pointed to the fact that the fever struck the city "the very Autumn in which the new house was to be opened" and the actors had arrived.[50]

Helmuth and other preachers saw evil and God's wrath everywhere. It was not just the theater that the faithful railed against. Philadelphia, it was said, "did not rest." Residents enjoyed "sins" such as "rope-dancing and other shews exhibited in the city." Such entertainment was so popular that "one hardly knew how to pass along" the streets "for the immense number of people, who were either going to these diversions or returning therefrom."[51]

Clergy bemoaned that "Philadelphia was the place that seemed to strive to exceed all other places in the breaking of the Sabbath." Carriages rode happily through the city even on Sundays, which he dubbed "our most sinful days." Some skipped "holy-days" to go for picnics "into the country . . . with their families." Others visited "the taverns and beer-houses in the city," where they "drank to excess, and frequently quarreled and fought." Rather than "approach the Deity in public worship," roared the reverend of his fellow citizens, "every part of their minds . . . [were] filled with these follies."[52]

And so it was, claimed the reverend, that the "Sabbath-breakers" were being sent "to their silent graves; while their souls have been obliged to appear before the tribunal of that God who himself had given the strictest command: Remember the Sabbath-day to sanctify it." Never mind that Helmuth originally denied the existence of the disease, then downplayed it, he and other clergy refused to refrain from large public gatherings as recommended by the city, and also experienced deaths among his own congregants. To be sure, Helmuth even admitted that their flock suffered "a great number" of losses, in part because he and other clergy refused to heed decrees to avoid public gatherings and many of his congregants were poor and did not leave town.[53]

The question was asked why Divine Providence did not intervene to save Philadelphia. Helmuth and others concluded, "It was God's will to visit the city." The answer is apparent in scripture: The twenty-fourth chapter of Isaiah 5 and 6 reads, "The earth is defiled under the inhabitant's thereof," reminded Helmuth, "because they have transgressed the laws, and changed the ordinances and broken the everlasting covenant." The result is also in scripture: "Therefore the inhabitants of the earth are burned, and few men live."[54]

Judgment Day was upon them, Helmuth warned. In just one week in October, 130 of his parishioners died of the disease.[55] The disease was bringing out the worst in the city's residents. Soon, however, others would rise to the occasion to confront the crisis.

CHAPTER EIGHT
PHILADELPHIA RESPONDS

Wrath has come out from the Lord; the plague has started.

—Numbers 16:46

"Callousness"

It was not just the city, but the state government that was breaking under the strain of the disease. The Pennsylvania Assembly had convened in the state capital the final week of August, but just ten of eighteen senators and thirty-six of seventy-two representatives showed up. The legislature hoped to reassure the people of the city, but after "a young man by the name of Fry," who served as the doorkeeper, was found "lying dead at the west end of the State House," they adjourned for a three day-weekend. On Sunday, September 1, the eminent Dr. Benjamin Rush was asked, in writing, by the popular former mayor of Philadelphia, Samuel Powel, whether or not the legislators were safe. The physician was so overwhelmed with patients that he simply scribbled back on the same letter the words "I know of but one certain preventative of the disorder, & that is to keep at a distance from infected persons and places."[1]

On August 29, Pennsylvania's governor, Thomas Mifflin, warned the state legislature "that a contagious disorder existed in the city" but tried to assure them that he had taken every proper measure "to ascertain the origin, nature, and extent of it." He also encouraged them to

Quaker leaders decided to hold the meeting, writing in their *Yearly Epistle*, which was published shortly after the gathering, that to change the date or location would be but a "haughty attempt" to avoid "the rod of God." Maybe, reasoned the Quakers, God had sent the disease to test their faith. To cancel the event would denote a lack of faith and perhaps invite further punishment from the divine.[8]

Once again, several members of the community became ill and some of them succumbed to the fever. One of them was John Todd, whose month-old son William, mother, and father were also lost to the disease. Todd had taken his wife and their two children to a farm in the country but traveled back to the city to attend the annual meeting and care for his parents who had also fallen ill. Family lore suggests that, near death, he raced back to the farm to see his wife. Todd's last words were purported to be, "I feel the fever in my veins, but I must see her once more." He collapsed by the entrance to the farmhouse and died a few hours later. His new, young wife, Dolley, contracted the malady but survived—and, one year later, went on to marry Congressman James Madison and eventually become the first lady in 1809.[9]

What the Quakers did do was raise funds and provide relief for those afflicted in the city. Their large almshouse on Walnut Street, another on Spruce Street, and a few other large brick homes were used for the care of the sick.[10] Similar acts of charity also flowed into the city from around the country. New York City sent aid in the form of wagons full of vegetables, chickens, and $5,000. Individuals, such as one woman in Chester, New Jersey, collected and sent large bundles of clothing. Other communities, such as Elkton, Maryland, both Springfield and Woodbury in New Jersey, and towns on the outskirts of Philadelphia announced they would accept refugees.[11]

Mayor Clarkson

Without the state and with little of the federal government still in the city, the crisis fell to Mayor Clarkson. Though born in 1733 into a moneyed family in New York City, Clarkson was orphaned as a child and, as a young man, moved to Philadelphia. He found employment as a clerk at a dry goods store on Second Street. Seeking adventure, Clarkson set out for the frontier town of Pittsburgh in western Pennsylvania, the woods of the Ohio Territory, and the Mississippi River, where he traded with French trappers and Native Americans. He returned to Philadelphia with a small fortune and parlayed it into vast wealth by underwriting and insuring development projects. He also purchased ships and invested in a new settlement in Nova Scotia.

As one of Philadelphia's most popular and important leaders, Clarkson had cofounded the Bank of Pennsylvania, helped fund the Continental Army during the Revolutionary War, and, with Benjamin Franklin, cofounded the American Philosophical Society in Philadelphia, the first of such scholarly and civic-minded organizations in the new nation, for which he served as treasurer. His political career included serving as a judge and alderman. Though elected to serve in the Congress under the Articles of Confederation, he declined the honor. Then, the year prior to the pandemic, the sixty-year-old Clarkson was elected mayor. He would turn out to be the right person for the crisis that was about to befall the city.

One of Clarkson's first actions was to meet with Dr. Rush around August 21 in the new City Hall. The mayor was greatly distraught by what he was told. Rush diagnosed the malady as yellow fever and said it was spreading uncontrollably through the city. Rush claimed the fever had originated with the filth and rotted coffee dumped at the wharf but assured the mayor that he was working on a cure. Clarkson was anything but an alarmist; rather, he was level-headed and judicious, described as "a sober, substantial, tough-minded man" by author John Harvey Powell. Clarkson knew he had to act. The very next day the mayor offered his first "public notice" about the disease.[12]

Clarkson then prepared a report for Philadelphia's commissioners describing what he had learned about the disease, called for a meeting, and ordered the streets be "cleaned and purified by the scavengers, and all the filth immediately hawled away."[13] Wisely, the mayor's next action was to meet with Philadelphia's famous College of Physicians and ask them to provide advice on how to address the fever. This marked probably the first time in the young nation's history that a leader convened a medical group for advice. The College of Physicians was the foremost medical body of its kind in the country, comprised of many of the nation's leading physicians, surgeons, and scientists.

On Clarkson's request, the College of Physicians convened on Sunday, August 25, in an emergency session. That same day, Clarkson asked the port physician, Dr. Hutchinson, who was also a Fellow of the College of Physicians and Pennsylvania's surgeon general, for his counsel. Hutchinson immediately met with the State Assembly and the American Philosophical Society to seek their advice. Even though Dr. John Redman, the president of the College of Physicians, was not in attendance, sixteen members were present, including Dr. William Shippen, the vice president and a professor of anatomy and surgery, described by one historian as "elegant, contentious, able . . . brilliant . . . and a genius." Also in attendance were officers including Samuel Griffitts, a "gentle Quaker [and] professor" who was "tireless in good works," Benjamin Say, a popular physician and leading abolitionist in the city, Adam Kuhn, a botanist and professor who had been a student in Europe of the great Linnaeus,[14] and William Currie, a former surgeon in the Revolutionary War, "Renaissance Man," and author of respected books on fevers and diseases in America. It was an impressive gathering.[15]

Philadelphia had roughly eighty physicians working at the time of the fever, which constituted a greater concentration of medical professionals than any other place in the new nation. Of course, like any city—or any period in history—Philadelphia had its share of charlatans. Medicine, at the time, was often the realm of healers, seers, and apothecaries. Unlike today, medicine was largely unregulated—outside of the College of Physicians—giving way to practitioners with such titles as "doctress," "surgeon and seer," "barber-surgeon," or "physician and bookseller." Clarkson's decision to convene and then listen to this group, when taken within the context of the times, is all the more admirable.[16]

On August 26 and 27, the College of Physicians published recommendations in the newspaper. Dr. Rush spoke on its behalf in the subsequent days, lending his considerable esteem to the report. Most importantly, they acted swiftly, stating that they believed the virus was contagious and ordering people to avoid contact with one another, including even family members. Among fellow physicians, they counseled to "use vinegar and camphor on handkerchiefs and in rooms" and that they "cannot be used too frequently upon handkerchiefs, or in smelling bottles, by persons whose duty calls to visit or attend the sick." Some residents, however, refused to cover their mouths and noses with handkerchiefs or masks, seeing them as an infringement on their rights. Their public advisory included an array of other measures, some of which were adopted; others were opposed by the public:

- to avoid "all unnecessary intercourse" with the infected;
- to "place marks on the doors or windows" of the sick;
- to "pay great attention to cleanliness and airing the rooms" of the sick;
- to provide a "large and airy hospital in the neighbourhood of the city for their reception;"
- to put a stop to the "tolling of the bells;"
- to bury those who died of the "disorder . . . as privately as possible;"
- to keep the "streets and wharves clean;"
- to avoid "all fatigue of body and mind, and standing or sitting in the sun, or in the open air;"
- to "accommodate the dress to the weather;"
- to "exceed rather in warm then in cool clothing;" and
- to "avoid intemperance, but to use fermented liquors, such as wine, beer, and cider, with moderation"[17]

The report was reprinted in subsequent days and was discussed throughout the city.[18] On August 27, Clarkson issued a similar report to the city's businesses, leading citizens, and government clerks. This was followed on August 31 with a public letter from the College of Physicians containing guidelines about the disease. It was published in the newspaper. One controversial recommendation was "burning of gunpowder" and tar in the streets as a way to cleanse the air. Soon, Philadelphia was draped in black smoke and ash from all the fires. Gov. Mifflin also believed that smoke would cleanse the air of whatever was plaguing them. He ordered troops from nearby Fort Mifflin to regularly fire small cannons placed along the city's streets.

However, Mayor Clarkson opposed the noisy "salutory preparations" that he felt only scared people, instead immediately issuing a proclamation to ban the fires and cannons in the city because they "were very dangerous, if not ineffectual." A few days later, on September 4, he outright declared such practices "forbidden." However, a newspaper noted that "almost every night large fires" were lit by concerned citizens "at the corners of the streets" in defiance of the prohibition; other residents adopted the practice of carrying a piece of tarred rope, believing it would neutralize or ward off any airborne dangers.[19]

As the infection rate grew, other controversial measures would be debated including the forced evacuation of certain neighborhoods and quartering refugees from the West Indies in supervised camps. There were two measures from Clarkson that, in hindsight, perhaps made the most sense, although neither one addressed the threat from mosquitoes. One was adopting the recommendation to ban churches from the custom of ringing bells to mark the death of a resident. The bells throughout the city had been ringing nonstop through August and into September such that the constant clamor was unnerving Philadelphians. It was thus "forbidden for several days." The bells ceased tolling, which likely calmed the panic.

The other was to order the streets, beginning at the waterfront, be cleaned "as fast as filth is laid together." Although many physicians disagreed with Rush's conclusion that the fever came from filth in the city, Clarkson had Water Street, Front Street, and then the alleys cleared of debris rather quickly, which likely helped stem the spread of other maladies. But the city ran out of funds to continue the task and members of the sanitary crews were coming down with the disease. Nonetheless, the mayor encouraged the citizens to clean their households and both walkways and gutters near their homes. Garbage was placed outside every week. Although the city no longer had the means to collect and dispose of it, scavengers, the poor, and homeless were encouraged to take as much of it as possible.

Another simple effort was to order that the doors of homes with the contagion be "marked" by placing a small red flag on them. These homes were to be avoided. The mayor also posted twenty-three "watchmen" throughout the city with orders to patrol the streets at night. After several of them contracted the disease, the watchmen either abandoned their jobs or fled the city.[20]

Nothing worked. In desperation, the city constructed special camps outside its borders, erecting tents, homes, schools, and a treatment center, where the infected could go. It was decreed that anyone at the fever camps had to wash their clothing and bedding three times a week. If not, they would be expelled. Guards were even posted to enforce the rules. The city also built a quarantine center by the port on a small island in the middle of the Delaware River known as Fisher's Island and assigned a physician to staff it.[21] Immigrants and refugees were quarantined there between two and three weeks. Eventually, with the outbreak increasing and people either evacuating the city or remaining indoors, the quarantine became unenforceable.[22]

People started avoiding one another throughout the city, many still believing the disease was contagious. The custom of shaking hands ended, people kept their distance, held handkerchiefs over the mouths, and took to walking on opposite sides of the street and sheltering in their homes. The public also stockpiled vinegar and camphor,[23] leading to shortages. It was believed they prevented airborne illnesses and the College of Physicians suggested placing these in "infected rooms," dousing handkerchiefs in vinegar and holding them over the mouth and nose and offering "smelling bottles" to "persons who attended the sick."[24]

The Committee

Clarkson, who bravely remained at his post in the city, followed the report of the College of Physicians on September 12 with another announcement about the pandemic. His warning, published in a newspaper, stated that there was "great reason to apprehend that a dangerous infectious disorder" was in the city. Importantly, Mayor Clarkson called for the organization of a "committee for relieving the sick and distressed." An announcement about the meeting appeared on September 13 in the newspaper. On Saturday, September 14, the mayor formally established the "Committee to Attend to and Alleviate the Sufferings of the Afflicted with the Malignant Fever" to address the public health crisis and to also help run the City of Philadelphia. It initially contained ten members, with Clarkson serving as chair. Other officers included Caleb Lownes, who served as the secretary, and Thomas Wistar who was the treasurer. However, it was soon expanded to twenty-six members. Several members became sick, died, or fled the city, leaving the mayor to grumble that the work was "principally conducted by twelve only."[25]

Over the next week, Clarkson would organize several additional subcommittees to assist the effort. These subcommittees covered a wide range of problems. For instance, one was charged with securing nurses and attendants to care for the sick. The city lacked the staff and funds, so the onus was placed on the subcommittee. Another subcommittee oversaw the publication of letters and announcements about the disease and was led by Caleb Lownes and Mathew Carey, the publisher. Henry Deforest headed the effort to secure food, while James Sharwood and John Connelly kept the records and account books. One of the most important subcommittees was the Committee of Distribution, which provided clothing, medicine, and other essentials throughout the city and was staffed by Israel Israel, John Haworth, James Swaine, Mathew Carey, James Kerr, Jacob Whitman, J. Letchworth, and James Sharswood.

Soon after its creation, the committee received word that fifteen-month-old twins were found alone and neglected after their parents died. The shocking story prompted the creation of another subcommittee that dealt with the growing population of orphans. The effort was headed by Israel Israel, John Letchworth, James Kerr, and James Sharswood. Israel, a forty-seven-year-old tavern keeper, assumed primary responsibility, working tirelessly to find orphans, secure homes for them, and raise funds for their care. On September 19, he and his committee "hired a house" for thirteen orphans on Fifth Street and paid a woman to care for the children. They also saw that food was delivered. Relatives were tracked down for thirty other orphans, who were then relocated to live with extended family. With the number of orphaned children growing as the weeks passed, Israel formed a new organization for orphans that ended up caring for 192 children during the crisis. Housing was a primary problem, so on October 3 the subcommittee "procured" the Loganian Library from owner John Swanwick and turned it into an orphanage. When the pandemic ended, they still had eighty children in their care, all of whom were placed in homes.[26]

There was even a subcommittee on burials headed by Samuel Benge, which oversaw the transportation of the sick to hospitals and the burial of the dead. One of the first orders of business was to secure $1,500 to purchase coffins and supplies, then hire gravediggers. They also inventoried the homes in the city to determine which were occupied and which were shuttered. Homes where the fever had claimed lives were cleaned and any children were taken to either a relative or to the subcommittee on orphans. Benge also organized a list of prominent residents who died and detailed the number of burials by the city's churches.

In the city's church cemeteries alone, the subcommittee recorded 325 burials during the month of August, 1,442 more in September, and additional 1,993 in October, and 118 in November. This covered Christ Church, St. Peter's, St. Paul's, First Presbyterian, Second Presbyterian, Third Presbyterian, Scotch Presbyterian, St. Mary's, Trinity, Free Quaker, German Lutheran, German Calvinist, Moravian, Swede, and the Universalist houses of worship. Disappointingly, they did not record Jewish burials, even though a synagogue and Jewish cemetery were built the year before the pandemic to serve the city's small but growing Jewish population. When these and other cemeteries, such as Potter's Field, became full, they requisitioned additional public areas to be used for burial. There were also mass burials in fields during the height of the outbreak, used mostly for the poor and those without families.[27]

Throughout the crisis, roughly one dozen members of the committee remained in the city and active, although four members succumbed to the fever: A. Adgate, T. D. Sargeant, Daniel Offley, and Joseph Inskeep. Like others who remained in Philadelphia, they bravely risked their lives. For instance, in the days following the formation of the committee, the death toll continued to soar. Sixty-seven died on September 16. One week later, the city recorded ninety-six deaths in just one day.[28]

The efforts of the mayor and his committee ended up being more effective than the city's physicians in comforting the dying and limiting the spread of the disease. Clarkson was a symbol of strength and resolve. The mayor went to City Hall every day during the crisis, even as municipal employees fled the city. The committee issued public warnings, helped people to evacuate, attempted to clean the city's streets, homes, and port, and distributed food, medicine, and clothing to those suffering from the disease. This small group of civic leaders showed themselves to be remarkably forward-thinking and "gradually brought the panic under control," restored a degree of normalcy to the city, and extended dignity and compassion to those dying.[29]

CHAPTER NINE
BUSH HILL

How many a wretch whom poverty had driven
From all the joys to haughty affluence given;
Whose piercing woes from pitying strangers shut
Within the humble cot, or lonely hut
In vain for aid, in baleful accents call,
Rend the sad bosom and the soul appall;
Where no rich vests the tortured body bore,
No couch could press, but an unfeeling floor

—Poem about physicians treating the victims
of yellow fever in Philadelphia, 1813

A Fever Hospital

Philadelphia's hospitals were so overrun with the sick and dying that they were forced to refuse admission to anyone with signs of the fever. This was true, at the time, even at the young nation's premier medical facility—Pennsylvania Hospital. Making matters worse, many of the physicians, nurses, and attendants that staffed the city's hospital had either fled, were sick, or had died.

A plan, however, was in place. On August 29, volunteers with Philadelphia's largest social services organization, the Guardians of the Poor,[1] met with Mayor Clarkson about the pressing need to establish a separate "fever hospital." The city's newspapers eagerly reported on the development, stating, "In consequence . . . the Guardians of the Poor resolved to sow their utmost exertions to procure such a house out of town." On the final day of August, plans were drawn up for the fever hospital and they began looking for a suitable property and hiring of physicians and nurses.[2]

The Guardians initially considered almshouses that were run by the Quakers. These community centers had a history of philanthropy and service for the poor and homeless, plus a half dozen members of the mayor's committee helped to run them. However, even these large brick homes lacked sufficient space. It was preferred to have just one large facility, but there were not enough members of the Guardians still in the city to operate both the almshouses and the new hospital. So, too, were infected, dying, and homeless individuals squatting on the streets beside the almshouses, prompting nearby residents to protest.

The Guardians then wrote to John Bill Ricketts, a well-known Scottish equestrian who operated Ricketts' Circus, which was performed in a large amphitheater on High and Twelfth Streets. It had sufficient space in its open courtyard to house a facility for those inflicted with the fever. Ricketts was away in New York City for the summer and, in the words of one committee member, the amphitheater was "the only place that could be procured for the purpose." Not hearing back from Ricketts, the Guardians commandeered the circus and began relocating the sick to its grounds. However, due to a lack of beds, patients were left lying on the floor, and the Guardians still lacked funding, physicians, nurses, and supplies. Once again, neighbors protested, alarmed by a report in a newspaper claiming one of the patients "crawled out of the commons, where he died" on the street in plain view of everyone. Those living near the circus "threatened to burn or destroy it, unless the sick were removed." So angry, claimed the article, were those living near the circus, that "it is believed they would have actually carried their threats into execution, had a compliance been delayed a day longer."[3]

The Guardians then turned their attention to Bush Hill, one of the most famous mansions in the city, one that had hosted the likes of George Washington and Benjamin Franklin and was the site of not only popular Independence Day celebrations but also a citywide event in 1787 that marked the signing of the Constitution. Just four years earlier, John Adams rented the home when he was sworn in as the nation's first vice president. Abigail Adams loved the mansion, even calling it "delicious!" Writing to her sister Elizabeth Smith in 1791, the Second Lady commented, "I am told that this spot is very delightful as a summer residence. The house is spacious. The views from it are rather beautiful than sublime. . . . We have a fine view of the whole city from our windows; a beautiful grove behind the house, through which there is a spacious gravel walk, guarded by a number of marble statues."[4]

In 1793, however, Bush Hill was vacant, as Adams had moved back to his home in Quincy, Massachusetts. Bush Hill was owned by the descendants of Andrew Hamilton,[5] one of the city's most prominent lawyers and a colleague of William Penn, the former colony's founder. Referred to as either Bush Hill, Bush-Hill, or Bushhill, the mansion was built in 1737 on 150 acres atop a hill near the present location of the Free Library of Philadelphia by Vine Street and Fairmont Avenue. It sat conveniently about 2.5 miles northwest of and well outside of the center of Philadelphia.[6]

Its size and location away from neighborhoods made it an attractive site for a hospital—it boasted three stories, eleven rooms, stables, a coach house, ice cellar, guest quarters, groves of trees, gardens, wide lawns, and even an impressive art collection. Importantly, Hamilton's heirs—one of whom served as the colonial governor of Pennsylvania—were Loyalists who fled the colonies during the Revolution. Therefore, the home was empty. The caretaker of the property, Thomas Boyles, was simply "brushed aside" and the home was commandeered without permission from William Hamilton. Mayor Clarkson approved the decision.[7]

The handful of Guardian volunteers started admitting patients even though the new facility lacked adequate staff and supplies. The effort quickly fell apart. The handful of nurses they recruited were unqualified, and the Guardians had yet to find a full-time physician. One of the volunteers was a medical student named Charles Caldwell, who described the ad hoc hospital as "limited, crude and insufficient."[8]

In September, the fever spiked and Bush Hill was overrun with roughly one hundred patients who had been dropped off there by family, friends, or the crews hired by the committee to gather the sick. Lacking care, medicine, or even adequate beds, the patients began to die, and bodies began to pile up. The Guardians even had to hire a driver to cart away the dead. This cart-driver offered a terrifying glimpse into the work, describing his effort to place a decomposing corpse in a coffin. Unable to lift it into the cart, he was approached by a little girl. The young servant girl was at the hospital, apparently to drop off her employer. She "offered her services" to the struggling worker, "provided he would not inform the family with whom she lived." He agreed and the young woman "accordingly helped him put the body into the coffin, which was by then crawling with maggots, and in such a state as to be ready to fall in pieces." The publisher, Mathew Carey, wrote about this touching and troublesome scene, adding thankfully, "It gives me pleasure to add, that she still lives, notwithstanding her very hazardous exploit."[9]

"The Pest House"

On September 10, an alarming story ran in the *Federal Gazette* stating that all but three of the remaining Guardians had either died or abandoned the city. This trusted charity had become even more vital to the city once government offices closed but had been unable to meet the demand of providing essential services to the nation's largest city and interim capital. The article went on to say that these Guardians—William Sansom, Jacob Timkins, and James Wilson—"now laboring under the prevailing malignant disorder, are almost overcome with the fatigue they undergo, and require immediate assistance." Mayor Clarkson pleaded with the public for "want of assistance" and was quoted in the newspaper as urging "those who are humanely disposed . . . to apply to the mayor" to assist with caring for the sick, performing city services, and burying the dead. The city, he said, needed "benevolent citizens" to answer the call.[10]

On September 12, Clarkson appointed a small group of leaders to essentially assume the work of the Guardians of the Poor and oversee the management of the fever hospital. One of the first items of business was to generate a report on the status of Bush Hill and its many needs. The committee sent a delegation to inspect the new fever hospital the next day. They found Bush Hill to be "in very bad order, and in want of almost every thing." The inspectors found many patients "abandoned" and the nurses and attendants unqualified and of "suspect character." The publisher Mathew Carey offered an alarming assessment: "The sick, the dying, and the dead were indiscriminately mingled together." He reported that committee members found "the ordure and other evacuations of the sick, were allowed to remain in the most offensive state imaginable." They issued their report on September 16, calling the hospital "truly deplorable" and a "wretched picture of humanity." The hospital was, they concluded, "a great human slaughter-house." The public began referring to it by an equally unflattering nickname: "the pest house."[11]

Richard Allen and Absalom Jones, leaders of the city's Black community who assisted at Bush Hill, echoed the committee, describing the neglect and lack of care to the extent that "not the smallest appearance of order or regularity existed." They concluded that the hospital was a "wretched picture of human misery."[12] Word spread quickly about its deplorable condition. "Panic-struck" residents wanted their "neighbors" to immediately be sent out of the neighborhood and to the hospital but were "much afraid of being sent to [Bush Hill]" because of its reputation. So bad was the situation at the pest house that some people with the affliction "would not acknowledge their illness, until it was no longer possible to conceal it." There was also debate among both physicians and the public about whether it was best to leave the sick in their homes during the ordeal rather than force them to suffer a wagon ride on bumpy, unpaved roads out to the hospital. Either way, the hospital needed leadership.[13]

The committee met and decided to borrow $1,500 from the Bank of North America for "procuring suitable accommodations for the use of persons afflicted with the prevailing malignant fever." Not long thereafter, donations such as bedding, medicine, firewood, and food for the fever hospital arrived from across the city and as far away as New York City and Baltimore. The committee prioritized the hiring of qualified physicians, nurses, and attendants, and procured wagons to transport the sick to the hospital and, if necessary, from Bush Hill to Potter's Field for burial. But the main concern for Mayor Clarkson was finding the right person to "superintend the business at Bush Hill, and to agree with and appoint the necessary officers at that place."[14]

Leadership

The mayor and committee made the right decision on September 15 when they hired the French-born merchant Stephen Girard to run Bush Hill. He was born Étienne Girard in Bordeaux, France, in 1750. Girard, forty-three at the time, was one of the wealthiest men in the city. As a child, he went to work in the shipping industry, working his way up to captaining his own ship while in his twenties despite a boyhood medical condition that left him blind in one eye. Restless and entrepreneurial, the young man established a trading charter that ran between Saint-Domingue and New York City. In 1776, while sailing to the American colonies, a British warship forced Girard and his crew ashore in Philadelphia. He decided to stay and opened a shipping and trading office in the city. Two years later he became a naturalized citizen.

Girard married Mary Lum, a few years his junior, who is believed to have had a mental illness and was later institutionalized. He never remarried but maintained long-term relationships with Sally Bickham and other women. Never having children of his own, Girard devoted himself and his considerable fortune to charities, children, and the care of those in need in his adopted city. Such was his wealth that when the charter of the First Bank of the United States, located on Third Street in Philadelphia, expired in 1811, he purchased much of its stock and helped his country finance the War of 1812.

During the yellow fever outbreak, Girard expressed that he was "touched by the wretched situation of the sufferers at Bush Hill" and willingly volunteered to supervise the hospital. He proved to be resourceful, compassionate, and tenaciously committed to his work. Even though he contracted the fever in late August, he remained in the city and emerged as a tireless, natural leader of the hospital.[15]

Peter Helm, a native Pennsylvanian, agreed to assist Girard. A kind and caring man, devout member of the Moravian Church, and resourceful barrel maker who was once hired by George Washington as a carpenter, Helm oversaw the construction and repairs at the property. The two men would end up doing more to alleviate the suffering among the sick than anyone.

They did not waste time. The two managers visited Bush Hill on September 16 and, mindful of the scathing report by the committee, developed an inventory of all the supplies they needed and changes to be made in its operation. The list was daunting. The two managers agreed that, to save money, they would volunteer their time "for that benevolent employment." One of the first priorities, Girard noted, was that "the sick may probably be reduced for want of suitable persons to superintend the Hospital." They needed quality, caring physicians and nurses.[16]

That same day, Girard and Helm also found four young physicians: Michael Leib, who was also a prominent political figure in the city; Philip Syng Physick, who had studied in Scotland and was only twenty-seven; Isaac Cattrall, who had also studied in Scotland and throughout Europe; and William Annan. They agreed to spend part of their time at the hospital, taking time away from their own practices. On September 17, they hired nine female nurses, ten male attendants, a woman named Mary Saville, who functioned as the head nurse and overseer of the staff, and Ann Beakly, a maid charged with cleaning and organizing the hospital. Girard, recognizing the importance and difficulty of cleaning the hospital, later agreed to pay the staff an impressive three dollars a day.[17]

The two administrators continued their frenetic pace improving the hospital and its operations. They rented a horse, cart, and driver to begin bringing the sick to the hospital, obtained the necessary supplies, converted a barn on the property to a convalescence center, ordered that male and female patients would have separate rooms, and pledged that, never again, would patients be on the floor. To that end, Helm set about building and repairing beds. He also located a natural spring on the grounds and proceeded to construct a system to pump water into the hospital.

Ultimately, eighteen men and women would operate the hospital, taking over the work of the overrun and understaffed Guardians. This included two carpenters who repaired the old mansion and built additional items needed, including furniture and coffins, one mechanic, and even a schoolteacher for young patients. The two administrators and the committee wisely invited young physicians and medical students to offer their services as often as they could, which would alleviate the load on the four overworked, part-time doctors and also assure that all the patients were being attended.

Devèze

The administrators also made one of their best hires in Jean Devèze, a thirty-nine-year-old Frenchman who had practiced medicine in Saint-Domingue and thus had ample experience with the horrors of yellow fever.[18] Born in Rabastens in southwestern France on December 4, 1753, Devèze studied medicine in Bordeaux before moving to the French West Indian colony of Saint-Domingue in 1775. While practicing medicine there he contracted yellow fever and was forced to return to France for treatment. After recuperating, Devèze remained in France to continue his education but appears not to have completed his medical degree—an indication of this is that he would later refer to himself as a "Master of Surgery" rather than a doctor or physician. In 1778, he returned to Saint-Domingue.[19]

Devèze became the chief surgeon for the National Troupe of the Northern Province and also helped open a hospital in the large port city of Cap Français. Even though those who contract yellow fever are generally immune from future afflictions, Devèze appears to have again fallen ill with the disease or a similar affliction. However, this experience and time on the island would not only provide him with the eventual protection of immunity but offer him insights into the fever that his colleagues in Philadelphia did not have. Yet nothing could have prepared him for the revolution that struck the island fifteen years after his arrival in 1778.[20]

The slave uprising began on June 21, 1793, after a force of a few thousand "free Blacks" and former slaves, known on the island as *"gens de couleur libre"* or "free people of color" seized Cap Français. Amid the bloodshed and burning of the city, Devèze remembered that he and other White colonists "were forced to take refuge on the ships lying in the harbor." With the city and their homes aflame and death at hand, they had no choice but to flee Saint-Domingue, which he called his "greatest misery." The refugees were crowded into a sailboat and soon fell ill and began to die. Devèze recalled that "during the whole voyage, [they] breathed the foul air in the hold of the vessel." The refugees took turns going above deck to breathe fresh air, but each night the captain "forced" them back into the holds, described by the French physician as "a kind of infested dungeon."[21]

Not only did the refugees suffer from the fever, cramped conditions, and bad weather that tossed the small craft to and fro, but they were robbed by pirates. "I thought myself fortunate to rescue a little money" before fleeing Saint-Domingue, remembered Devèze, "but my good luck was of short duration." Sailing a merchant ship without military escort, "we were captured by English corsairs, and it was only after having been plundered in the most barbarous way, and in violation of all personal rights, that we were allowed to continue on our journey to Philadelphia." Devèze and his fellow passengers finally arrived in the interim capital, but with little more than the clothing on their backs. So, too, were many of them suffering from an ailment that Devèze suspected was yellow fever.[22]

When disembarking in Philadelphia, Devèze realized that, cruelly, he and his fellow refugees had fled the specter of death in Saint-Domingue and yellow jack aboard the ship only to be greeted by them both at the American port. "Many persons" living near the port, the French physician learned, "had lost their lives in consequence of a sore throat." Even though he had just lost his house, livelihood, hospital, and homeland, he wrote that he waited only two weeks "before I had an opportunity of inspecting into the nature of this complaint." He went back to work, seeing patients living by the port and in the most blighted part of the city, noting that he felt it the responsibility of physicians to "give themselves up to the care of the diseased, live in the midst of them, and breathe the same air."[23]

Devèze, a refugee having only recently fled the bloodshed on Saint-Domingue, was still in "most serious misfortunes." Yet Girard was impressed when Devèze showed up at Bush Hill to volunteer, remarking that the fellow Frenchman "appears to be a professional character." Others knew of his important work in Saint-Domingue and vouched for him, prompting Girard to comment, "From the information . . . received of his abilities and practice in Cap Francais, from persons who were intimately acquainted with him at that place" he was hired. Helm also believed Devèze to be "well qualified." The French surgeon explained his interest in helping, stating, "In an epidemic disorder those who continually touch the sick . . . listen only to their courage and love of humanity."[24]

The admiration was mutual. Devèze was equally as impressed with Girard's compassion, commenting that "he visited the apartments of the sick: the unfortunate persons in the greatest danger were those who first attracted his attention." Devèze observed one patient covered in black blood "run[ning] from both mouth and nostrils, and feeling about with a bloody and tremulous hand for a vessel" because he had to vomit. Girard "ran to his assistance" and held out a vase but not before the patient vomited a foul bile everywhere, including on the administrator, who continued helping as if nothing had happened and led the sick man to his bed.[25]

So, too, did the French surgeon recognize Girard's thoroughness and dedication, writing that the hospital director's "first care was not only to direct, but to inspect into the provisions and arrangements of the house." Devèze remarked that although his new friend was exhausted, he and Helm "went every morning to the hospital." They did not stop working even when they were hungry.[26] The committee had the right team for the difficult job at hand.[27]

On September 20, Dr. Physick met with Girard, Helm, and the committee and proposed the medical work at Bush Hill be split—he would supervise half the patients, Dr. Devèze the other half. They both agreed to defer any payment until after the crisis ended.[28] Not only was the idea behind Bush Hill rather novel at the time, but physicians in Europe rarely tended to the poor. In fact, it was somewhat common to simply observe the decline in poor patients in order to advance scientific understanding and then devote time to the autopsies. At Bush Hill, every person was given medical treatment.

"Heroic Conduct"

The fever continued to spread, and funds and supplies remained difficult to obtain. Yet the co-administrators remained undeterred. They worked an astonishing sixty straight days at the facility, dividing up the work. Helm oversaw the admission of patients, construction needs, including coffins and additional housing for the staff, and assured that recovering patients were moved away from those in the worst condition. Girard saw that the building was cleaned daily, organized the rooms according to the severity of the illness, assigned a nurse to each room of patients, and even hired a doorman for security—and to make sure none of the delirious patents attempted to leave the hospital.

Carey said of Girard and Helm that they worked "without any possible inducement but the purest motives of humanity." Their "sacrifice" and "heroic conduct" inspired others, as they toiled "uninterruptedly" caring for their patients while also handling all the administrative aspects of the hospital. Moreover, the work was of the "most irksome" variety, given the horrific nature of the disease.[29]

The transformation of Bush Hill under the capable leadership of Girard and Helm was such that individuals contracting the disease no longer protested being taken there. In fact, quipped, Dr. Annan, "No sooner was a Person affected with a headache, than he became anxious to be removed to [Bush Hill] Hospital."[30]

Still, the effort was not without obstacles. One arose from professional jealousies, rivalries, and the bitter political feud that would soon engulf the city. Devèze and the four American physicians hired by Girard agreed on the basic origins of the disease, in that they rejected Rush's claim that it was miasma and the foul coffee at the port. So, too, did they disagree with their famous colleague's cures, feeling Rush's aggressive purging and bloodletting were too violent. As the city and medical community erupted in debate over how to address and treat the disease, these physicians maintained their opposition to Rush. However, an anti-immigrant and anti-French mood swept through the city, sparked not only by concerns about the refugees from Saint-Domingue, but from the passions surrounding the French Revolution, French interference in American domestic politics, and Congress's impulsive decision to suspend repayment of French loans incurred during the Revolutionary War. President Washington wisely charted a path of neutrality in response to the spreading war in Europe and simmering tensions in his own country.[31]

The four American physicians volunteering at the hospital grew tired of their French colleague and his increasing clout at Bush Hill. After realizing that the four young physicians, who came and went sporadically, were often giving patients differing advice and diagnoses, Girard put Devèze in charge and allowed him to hire assistants, who also happened to be French. Girard appointed his fellow Frenchman as medical director of Bush Hill. The surgeon moved into a room at Bush Hill and ended up replacing the other physicians as the primary doctor on site.[32] The mayor, committee, and, importantly, Girard sided with Devèze. Importantly, the French surgeon became a leading proponent for the theory that the disease was not contagious, which, to a degree, helped calm the city. He pointed no further than Girard. "What man could be more exposed to the danger of catching this disease than Mr. Girard," he asked. Accordingly, "We may very reasonably conclude it was not contagious." The surgeon also pointed to the nurses and attendants at the hospital, all of whom were in direct daily "proximity" to the patients, yet only two died during the scourge, and one was believed to have been from "intemperance," that is, alcohol.[33]

Furthermore, "To all these undeniable proofs against the opinion of those who have advanced that the disease was contagious," continued Devèze, "I will add another fact, which of itself must be a perfect conviction of the truth of my assertions." He pointed to Bush Hill taking care of "many persons attacked with diseases totally different to the epidemic" who were often "at the same time and in the same apartments with those infected with the reigning malady." Yet Devèze noted the other patients "recovered," whereas those with the fever often died. They both "received into their lungs the same air that had repeatedly passed and re-passed through those of the other sick." He called it obvious and "remarkable" that "I have not seen one example of those patients [contracting] the epidemic" despite "circumstances to favourable contagion."[34]

Girard and Devèze also opposed Rush's "pernicious treatment" which, they felt, did nothing more than "send many of our citizens to another world." Girard also supported Devèze's more "gentle" approach to care. Rather than extensive purging and bloodletting, Devèze prescribed quinine,[35] a bit of wine (which he thought would stimulate the blood), and a diet of chicken broth and creamed rice or tapioca.[36]

Like Rush and others, Devèze believed he "had fallen upon the true indications of the cure." He had some "success" in the "management of the disease." Yet, unlike Rush, he recognized his limited abilities in treating the malady. Devèze admitted, "It was very seldom medicine had sufficient power . . . to save the patient."[37] Indeed, Rush estimated that about half of the patients brought to Bush Hill died.[38] The publisher Mathew Cary echoed Rush, estimating, "Most of those who went to Bushhill . . . died there."[39]

In the face of failure, the French surgeon was willing to attempt "various methods." He described his treatments "in general unfavorable, but more or less consoling." Therefore, he stayed with what worked, but was always adapting his efforts depending on "the number and malignity of the symptoms" as well as their "constitution, the sex, and age of the patient, the manner of living, state of the humours, and complication of other diseases, etc." Indeed, lacking Rush's zeal and overconfidence, he was humbled by the disease and did what physicians and scientists are supposed to do: experiment, test, and adapt. Devèze even called yellow fever "one of the most destructive that the human race can be afflicted with."[40]

The two rival physicians did share a trait: Devèze also felt it was his "duty" to remain in the city and attempt to treat the disease. "An hospitable and generous people," he wrote, "cannot be inhuman." Also, like Rush, the Frenchman recognized the risk and had also contracted the fever. He, too, struggled under the weight of despair, writing, "Affectionate wives! Unfortunate mothers and orphans! Your fate overwhelms me with heart-felt distress." Tenderly, he added, "Would to Heaven I could assuage your sorrows, by accumulating them in my own breast." Unlike Rush, however, Devèze understood his limits, noting "Alas! My wishes are useless."[41]

Even though Girard, Helm, and Devèze made many remarkable improvements at Bush Hill, it was nearly an impossible situation. In response to some criticism, Devèze pointed out that "the patients were not carried to the hospital till reduced to the last extremity." Therefore, "Many expired six, eight, or twelve hours after their arrival, some even did not live two hours." He also did not miss the opportunity to address Rush and his other critics, reminding that "many" of his patients at Bush Hill had previously been in their care and thus, through their "use of very fatal medicines, such as drastic purges, composed of jalap or gumboage, and calomel" came to him in a deteriorated condition.[42]

The hospital remained crowded through September and October, housing roughly one hundred patients at any given time, despite having a capacity for just sixty patients. They toiled with upward of 140 patients during the worst of the outbreaks. To attempt to alleviate the problem, effective on Sunday, October 12, the committee started requiring a letter from a physician attesting to the patient having yellow fever in order to be admitted to Bush Hill.

The important work at Bush Hill alleviated some of the suffering but did not address the underlying problem of the disease-carrying mosquitoes. The death toll remained high; for instance, 82 died on October 7, 90 on the eleventh, and 111 the next day. So, too, Devèze never achieved Rush's fame, although his efforts were vastly more humane and effective in alleviating the suffering. With great tragedy, it was Rush's approach rather than Devèze's that ended up being the more widely accepted. But then, Devèze was a refugee from the West Indies, whereas Rush was a signer of the Declaration of Independence.

Historic charter of "Colonial undertakings in Sierra Leona and the Island of Bulama"

Map of Bulama Island

Slave revolt in Saint-Domingue

Arch Street Ferry, Philadelphia, by W. Birch, 1800, Library Company of Philadelphia

Old cartoon depicting yellow fever

Old cartoon depicting the 1793 fever in the City of Philadelphia

Bush-Hill, the seat of William Hamilton, near Philadelphia, Library of Congress

Benjamin Rush, 1812, Library of Congress

Matthew Clarkson, Library Company of Philadelphia

Mathew Carey, publisher, Philadelphia

Stephen Girard, by Albert Newsam,
1832, Library of Congress

Absalom Jones, by Raphael Peale,
1810, Library of Congress

Richard Allen, first AME Bishop, by C.
M. Bell, 1873, Library of Congress

Washington's 1793 Inaugural at Philadelphia, by J. L. G. Ferris, Library of Congress

CHAPTER TEN
THE PHYSICIAN'S WAR

As for the bodies of my disciples, the contagion will be banished
and the illness will quickly leave and they will be healed.
My disciples, now devote yourself to the three treasures—
burn incense and prostrate, and practice this incantation of the various
Buddhas.

—Sutra from the monk Shōei, ninth century

Confusion and Misinformation

Not only was the disease that struck Philadelphia deadly, but
there was no known cure. Medicine and science had yet to even
determine the cause of yellow fever. In addition, the medical
community disagreed over how to respond to the crisis, and the result
was that Philadelphians were bewildered, confused, and felt vulnerable
to the fever. The scholar, Martin Pernick, writing in the publication
The William and Mary Quarterly, contends that there were three big
questions that faced the capital city: What caused the fever and how
did it spread? What to do about the sick and infected? Should the city
be evacuated? Unfortunately, there was little consensus among the city's
physicians.[1]

Ironically, Philadelphia was the undisputed "medical capital of the
United States." It boasted more physicians than any other city, the

finest hospital, birthplace to the American Philosophical Society, the nation's first learned society, and was home to the "Dean of Philadelphia Medicine" and most famous physician in the country—Benjamin Rush. Yet the city found itself utterly unprepared for the outbreak, initially paralyzed with inaction, and unable to find consensus on any of the questions it raised. As Pernick reminds us, there were "scores of conflicting causes, preventives, and cures, each presented as gospel by its learned advocates."[2]

Moreover, the sheer variety of implausible treatments circulating in the city from both medical professionals and charlatans would be laughable if the situation had not been so deadly. For example, Dr. Duffield, who proved helpful as an assistant to Dr. Devèze at the Bush Hill hospital, suggested throwing fresh dirt on the floor to a depth of two inches. This should be done every day, he said, as it was the "most comfortable and sure antidote." Others suggested warm baths, myrrh, black pepper, and tar. People took to carrying tarred ropes around their waists or necks. One patient who tied a rope around his neck, reported the publisher Mathew Carey, forgot that tar restricted the fibers of the rope, and nearly strangled himself. "He may with justice," Carey quipped, "be said to have nearly choaked himself to save his life."[3]

Even some of Rush's medieval cures came from well-intentioned sources. One of the famous physician's medical books offered cures from the 1665 Great Plague of London and another outbreak in Marseilles in 1720. It claimed that gravediggers and pallbearers avoided death by chewing garlic, smoking tobacco, and covering themselves in vinegar! These were adopted in Philadelphia.[4]

To make matters worse, everyone in the city seemed to have an opinion. People were getting their information on the disease not from their leaders or physicians, but from newspapers, politicians, and preachers. Newspapers regularly published cures that did not come from physicians. For instance, Dunlap's *American Daily Advertiser* published seven different cures, from ingesting herbs to spreading dirt on the floor to igniting gunpowder.[5] On August 23, an editorial in the *Federal Gazette* signed "A.B." suggested smoking tobacco or . . . "having plenty of smoke nearby" would help fend off the disease. Ironically, mosquitoes usually avoid thick smoke, so there may have been something to the advice. A.B. also suggested "a sprinkle of vinegar, carrying tarred rope, hanging a bag of camphor around the neck" as treatments.[6] A few days later, the *Federal Gazette* published another editorial from "A.B.," this time recommending the church bells be silenced. As has been mentioned, too many funerals and the constant clanging of bells were distressing the public.[7]

Another anonymous editorial appeared under the initials "W.F." and suggested inhaling camphor in the nostrils and mouth. The writer also borrowed a popular recipe from the *Town and Country Almanac*: "Take of Rue, Wormwood and Lavender, of each one handful; put these altogether with a gallon of the best vinegar into a stone pan, covered over with paste, and let them stand within the warmth of a fire, to infuse for eight days." This, mixed with liquid in a "quart bottle" would prevent the disease, the writer claimed.[8]

Another citizen wrote an anonymous editorial in the *American Daily Advertiser* that occasioned quite a stir. It would be reprinted, including as late as 1802 in the *Philadelphia Gazette*. Under the heading "Recollections relative to Egypt," the author claimed to have an idea some time ago "concerning the yellow fever, plague, &c. I have long been of the opinion those diseases were produced by minute insects depositing their eggs in the pores of the human body." Subsequent editorials listed the "facts" to support the anonymous author, including that lamplighters did not catch the disease because they were covered in oil. Scripture, after all, called for "the practice of anointing with oils," which had the corresponding benefit of deterring insects![9]

Yet there were some surprisingly enlightened or lucky proposals. Prophetically, on August 29, "A.B." was again offering advice in the newspapers, this time in Dunlap's *American Daily Advertiser*. The editorial observed, "As the late rains will produce a great increase of mosquitoes in the city, distressing to the sick, and troublesome to those who are well, I imagine it will be agreeable to the citizens to know that the increase of those poisonous insects may be diminished by a very simple and cheap mode." The anonymous author then offered the best advice of anyone during the entire ordeal: "Whoever will take the trouble to examine their rainwater tubs, will find millions of the mosquitoes fishing about the water with great agility, in a state not quite prepared to emerge and fly off." Citizens should simply "take up a wine glass full of the water, and it will exhibit them very distinctly. Into this glass pour half a teaspoon full, or less, of any common oil, which will quickly diffuse over the surface, and by excluding the air, will destroy the whole brood." This author had stumbled onto the origins of the outbreak.[10]

All but one of the newspapers stopped publishing during the outbreak, which likely prevented further misinformation and fear. Yet the damage had been done and the only newspaper still defiantly being published began featuring quack advice on how to deal with the disease. The situation was such that some citizens took measures into their own hands. On September 3, the diarist Elizabeth Drinker commented that, with the government no longer providing most services, people were left to shelter in their homes, rely on homemade cures and treatments, and pray. Drinker provides one such remedy when she wrote that she gave a sick relative "a small spoonful of Daffy's Elixir, and Vinegar in a sponge, and a sprig of wormwood," which she said were effective "precautions."[11]

Debates

The debate still swirled as to the origins of the disease, prompting Rev. Helmuth to ask, "The first question now naturally was 'from whence did this dreadful disorder take its origin'?" Although the disease was ravaging the West Indies and spreading to other coastal communities in the United States, Helmuth echoed others in wondering if "this dreadful fever" was "generated in Philadelphia itself." The capital city was hit far worse than any other community in the country and, although it had suffered other earlier outbreaks of yellow fever and similar maladies, the 1793 ordeal was worse.[12]

Helmuth added, "The opinions of our citizens were much divided." Some thought the disease was generated in Philadelphia. But where? Some thought "it had been imported by some vessel from abroad," while others figured it came from Water Street. Still others thought "the originating cause of this fever" was "the weather." The reverend admitted that "how it found its way to us, has as far as I know, never yet been ascertained." He was only certain that God was exacting retribution on the sinful city from some source.[13] In her diary, Drinker also wrote about the debates surrounding the mysterious disease, pondering, "Some say it was occasioned by damaged Coffee and Fish . . . others say it was imported in a Vessel from Cape Francois, which lay at our wharf or at ye wharf back of our store." Either way, she added that it was agreed that the affliction was "of ye malignant kind."[14]

Those who believed the disease came from the port noted that the great preponderance of "afflicted" living there and the first known outbreaks came from the Hell Town neighborhood near the river. Helmuth wrote that those who believed it was a miasma or foul air maintained that "less quantity of tar" was "being burnt therein" than elsewhere. Relatedly, many blamed bad air and hot weather, "Some ascribing the originating cause of this fever to be the weather." Helmuth said simply, "This disorder is the offspring of another climate." Yet others who backed the miasma theory also claimed the cause was the "vessel [that] arrived here with some damaged coffee." It was said that a few members of the crew of that ship were already dead and "some onboard that ship . . . died soon" after.[15]

The publisher, Mathew Carey, also described the confusion, writing, "On the origin of the disorder, there prevails a very great diversity of opinion." Carey claimed, however, that it "is the opinion of most of the inhabitants of Philadelphia" that it is an "imported disorder." Yet there was even disagreement among the refugees from Saint-Domingue who had seen the terrors of yellow fever but assumed that, if it did not kill them in the West Indies, they would be safe in America.[16]

Once again, a variety of opinions existed. "Some assert," Carey wrote, "that it was brought" aboard the ship *Ill Constante* "which arrived here from Ragusa and Martinico."[17] He pointed out that it docked at a place in the city which "was free until the disorder spread there." However, "Another opinion is, that it was introduced by the *Mary* . . . which arrived here on the 7th of August, with some of the French emigrants from the cape." Still others pointed at a ship from Tobago "which arrived here in July, lost nearly all her hands with a malignant fever." There was even an argument that the city "had two disorders . . . introduced about the same time," one being "the yellow fever, from the West Indies," and the other "a species of pestilence from Marseille."[18]

Carey shared his own opinion that it was most likely brought by "the privateer *Sans Culottes*,[19] with her prize, the *Flora*, which arrived here the 22nd of July [and] introduced the fever." His justification was that the ship "was in a foul, dirty condition—her hold very small—and perhaps as ill calculated for the accommodation of the great number of people that were on board, as any vessel that ever crossed the ocean." The ship "emptied" her "filth" at the wharf by Arch Street, which included "a dead body, sewed up in canvas." There were rumors in the city, he claimed, that several other corpses were secretly unloaded at night.[20]

Carey also chronicled the lack of consensus among the medical community. On one hand, Dr. Hutchinson, the state's surgeon general, did not initially believe the disease was "important." He felt the minor outbreak, which he dismissed as a "disorder," likely "originated from some damaged coffee, or other putrefied vegetable and animal matters." Captain Falconer, a health officer at the port, agreed, noting "a little above Arch-Street, there was not only a quantity of damaged coffee, extremely offensive, but also some putrid . . . substances."[21]

Dr. Hutchinson appears to have identified "two circumstances," but then stated that one was "mistaken." He disagreed that the disease was related to the sailors coming to the port, claiming that "no foreigners or sailors were infected" in August and "that it had not been found in lodging houses" that lined the waterfront. Hutchinson was wrong on both accounts. Carey disagreed with the surgeon general, reminding him that the disease first "made its appearance" at lodging houses such as Denny's and that "some of the earliest patients were French lads."[22]

The one consensus that many agreed upon was that the disease struck Philadelphia during the "sickly season" of late summer. Yet this outbreak was far different than the usual illnesses that sprang up during that time of the year. Helmuth also wrote that there was also a fair amount of agreement among Philadelphians that its origins were at the port by "Water-street," which was littered with garbage, rotted fish, and open sewage. The neighborhood had "a great deal of dirt and filth and even real ordure in it."[23]

Rush's Guide

Ironically, one of the problems in treating the outbreak was Rush himself. Dr. Rush's reputation was such that he stood head-and-shoulders above any other physician in the country. But it was precisely this celebrity status and Rush's personality that often worked against treating the disease: he was both overly confident to the point of not questioning his own abilities and theories and thin-skinned to the extent that he would not tolerate anyone who questioned his work. His reputation alone limited debate on the disease—at least initially. Much of Rush's advocacy about the disease was "self-justification" and as much about *him* as it was saving lives, just as his claim of "scientific" research was not and his "wonder drug" for the disease ended up being poisonous.[24]

Rush correctly identified the disease as yellow fever, but once he offered his view on its cause and his prescribed treatment, he was unwilling to consider other perspectives and was petty in attacking dissenters. As the death toll continued to rise, so did frustration and tensions. The struggle for a treatment quickly turned into a highly public feud among the city's physicians. Even members of Philadelphia's hallowed College of Physicians started accusing Rush—and then one another—of misconduct, malpractice, and even murder. Meanwhile, people continued to die.

Rush released his guide for treating the outbreak on September 10. Officially known as "Dr. Rush's Directions for Curing and Treating Yellow Fever," the "guide" immediately became the standard for confronting the disease. Of course, the problem was also that Rush got much of it wrong, starting with the idea of miasma—that the disease came from bad air and originated with the rotten coffee dumped at the port around the time of the outbreak. Rush's aggressive protocol of "purge and bleed" ended up doing more harm than good and would later become a point of debate among the medical community. Rush, dogmatic and uncompromising, pushed back. Once, while speaking to a large crowd in the town of Kensington, two miles north of Philadelphia, someone from the audience yelled out, "What? Bleed and purge everyone?" To which Rush is said to have replied loudly, "Yes! Bleed and purge all Kensington!"[25]

The surgeon had a preferred potion for purging, referred to as "ten-and-ten." He would give his patients a pill containing one-third of an ounce of calomel (mercury) and ten grains of jalap (a poisonous root from Mexico). Of course, this elixir was killing his patients and caused severe vomiting and diarrhea. When it failed to cure his patients, he increased the dosage. On the other hand, if he saw improvements, he assumed it was working and increased the potency of both ingredients, even administering his elixir three times a day. Many patients were in a constant state of "evacuating" and had such inflamed and raw throats that Rush had to force the medicine down them. He followed the same logic with bloodletting. The average human had roughly 1.2 to 1.5 gallons of blood (usually measured in milliliters or ounces), about 10 percent of an adult's weight, but Rush was draining an alarmingly dangerous amount of blood—eight to ten ounces at a time—by cutting veins and leeching. He often bled patients until they passed out. Ignoring details of all the patients who died, he focused on the few who lived, writing in early September to his wife that eight of twelve patients "seemed" to recover. Days later, he boasted, "I now save 29 out of 30 of all to whom I am called on the first day" of illness. It is, of course, doubtful that those numbers were accurate.[26]

Rush followed his protocol aggressively and regularly, to the extent that patients were in a constant state of vomiting and diarrhea. Many became so weak that they were comatose and had severe stomach distress. Autopsies performed by physicians like Physick and Cathrall found that Rush's patients suffered damage to the stomach, esophagus, and colon. Patients' bowels were emptied by a poisonous elixir administered (he often used a "Mercurial Sweating Powder") "every six hours, until they produce four or five large evacuations from the bowels." Likewise, his prescribed regimens of heavy doses of calomel, cream of tartar, and salts left patients dehydrated as well as weak and delirious. Despite the heat and humidity of the season, he wrapped his patients in hot blankets soaked in vinegar.[27]

In one astonishing admission, Rush recorded that "between the eighth and the 15th of September I visited and prescribed for, between an hundred and an hundred and twenty patients a day." On top of that, he allowed three of his medical students—Coxe, Fisher, and Stall—to board at his home and had them visiting another twenty-five patients a day. The sheer number of patients harmed or killed by Rush was staggering![28]

Rush bravely but defiantly carried on, even after sending his wife and children out of the city for their protection and despite the passing of his beloved sister, who died on the afternoon of October 1 in the height of the panic. Her loss devastated the surgeon who relied on her serving as his nurse. Writing that she was "my whole heart." He was also racked with guilt because she had remained in the city.[29]

Rush commented that her loss was so distressing to him that the only way he found "comfort" was to work. But the loss took a toll. "From this time," he confessed, "I declined in health and strength." He also started suffering from "frightful dreams" where he was haunted by "grave-yards." Besides losing his sister, Rush also lost close friends Rev. Fleming and former mayor Samuel Powel, whom he tried to treat and save.

Another friend and fellow physician, Dr. Penington, who Rush described "was to me dear and beloved, like a younger brother," was also lost. The surgeon always maintained that, had his friend "lived a few years longer, he would have filled an immense space in the republic of medicine." Dr. Penington had already, despite his few years, penned important medical books.[30]

One positive aspect of Rush's prescribed treatment was that patients should drink plenty of fluids. He also suggested that, once they were recovering, they consume "gruel, sago, tapioca, tea, coffee, weak chocolate, wine whey, chicken broth, and white meats," depending on "the weak or active state of the system." Furthermore, "The fruits of the season may be eaten with advantage at all times." Another wise recommendation was that families should maintain a separate "sick room" and that it should be kept "cool." It helped, the famous physician counseled, that a lot of vinegar be "sprinkled" on the floor from time to time.[31]

Hamilton

Despite Rush's standing in the profession and his many political ties at the highest level, there were dissenters. In fact, the city was quickly embroiled in what might properly be seen as a "physician's war." Doctors attacked one another, aired their views in the press, sought support from politicians, and, as the plague coincided with the nascent rise of political parties, even resorted to partisan extortions. Soon, anonymous appeals were being published in newspapers asking the city's physicians to stop their bickering and begin working "in concert" to address the crisis.[32]

The public feud pitted doctors Adam Kuhn, Isaac Cathrall, William Currie, and Edward Stevens in opposition to Rush. The aforementioned physicians called for a less harsh treatment or abandonment of so much forced purging. Kuhn and Stevens even published letters in the newspaper, sharing their views and mentioning their own "successful" treatments. One of the national leaders who joined the debate was Alexander Hamilton. The famous founding father was a voice to be reckoned with and used it to write in support of both Kuhn and Stevens, crediting them with saving lives. All three men contacted Mayor Clarkson about their concerns with Rush. But then Rush immediately announced he had found a cure. News of his discovery overshadowed the criticisms. Still, however, letters on both sides of the debate appeared, none more effective than those penned by Hamilton.[33]

Rush had a history with Hamilton. He ardently opposed Hamilton's politics and openly criticized the secretary's financial system.[34] Hamilton had emerged as the leader of the Federalist faction, while Rush supported the anti-Federalists, led by his friend Thomas Jefferson, which formed the basis for the first political parties the year prior to the yellow fever outbreak.

The record shows that Hamilton had contracted the fever and, on September 6, was too ill to attend an emergency cabinet meeting called by the president. His wife, Eliza, also fell ill but lived and ended up taking the children to her family's home in Albany, New York, as a wise precaution. The secretary of the treasury moved to a summer home a few miles outside the city under the care of a childhood friend from the Caribbean island of St. Croix named Dr. Edward Stevens, who had recently moved to Philadelphia.[35]

Stevens, like Devèze and other physicians from the West Indies, had either heard about firsthand accounts of yellow fever in the islands or had previously treated the disease. One of the Hamilton family servants had earlier fallen ill from the fever and lived while in the care of Dr. Stevens, buoying the secretary's confidence in his boyhood friend and bolstering his concern about prevailing treatments. Hamilton's public efforts were designed to stem the outbreak that threatened both the city and fledgling national government and to oppose the harsh and counterproductive treatment advocated by Rush. It is also possible that politics played a role, as Rush had publicly supported Jefferson's efforts to obstruct the treasury secretary's policies. Rush and other Jefferson allies such as Philip Freneau, editor of the *National Gazette*, had begun politicizing the disease.[36]

To that end, Rush went so far as to suggest his cure was more "republican," in that it was in line with democracy; in other words, *his* faction addressing the disease, and not the Washington administration. Rush also claimed to be putting power in the hands of the people. "It is time to take the cure of pestilential fevers out of the hands of physicians," argued Rush, "and to place it in the hands of the people." He even advocated that children ought to be able to draw blood and that patients could care for themselves. Rush even attacked his colleagues, arguing that "knowledge of what related to the health and lives of a whole city, or nation, should not be confined to one, and that a small or a privileged order of men." Yet, hypo-critically, Rush was, at the same time, forcing his own treatments on the entire city, criticizing anyone who disagreed with him, and inadvertently, killing more patients than he saved through his methods.[37]

It was also around September that Edward Brown, publisher of the widely read *Federal Gazette and Philadelphia Daily Advertiser*, ended any pretense of objectivity or political neutrality when it came to the fever. The newspaper endorsed Rush, Jeffersonian Republicans, and Rush's treatment, then joined the partisan fray with its own allegations against Washington, Hamilton, and the Federalists, marking a troubling low point in terms of politicizing the disease. Brown and his paper went so far as to attack Bush Hill and the volunteers staffing the important facility and, in an ugly precursor of the yellow journalism of the next century, claimed the Rush-Jefferson faction were the ones who truly cared about curing the sick.[38]

As early as late August, Hamilton began publishing in newspapers his concerns about Rush's treatments. On September 11 he reached out to the College of Physicians to share his disagreements.[39] In his letter, Hamilton expressed his interest in saving lives and the importance for all of them to stem the "undue panic which is fast depopulating the city, and suspending business both public and private." He added that the "motives of humanity and friendship to the Citizens of Philadelphia, induce me to address to you in this letter, in the hope that it may be in some degree instrumental in diminishing the present prevailing calamity."[40]

Hamilton had a number of outlets willing to publish his work, not only because of his reputation, but because there were newspapers sympathetic to the Federalist cause and concerned by Rush's politicization of the disease. One of them was the *Gazette of the United States*, published by John Fenno. A native of Boston, veteran of the Revolutionary War, and fellow Federalist, Fenno willingly published Hamilton's letters, including one he had written to Dr. John Redman, the president of the College of Physicians. This infuriated Rush, who even angrily confronted Hamilton over the matter.[41]

Trying to find a balance between recommending residents leave Philadelphia, while trying to prevent a panic and mass evacuation, Hamilton wrote in New York City's *Weekly Museum*, "I have serious thoughts of removing out of town, if I can get a place for my family, — I do not wish to alarm them, but it is very certain there is great danger from a species of

Yellow Fever, very infectious." He encouraged them to heed the advice of the College of Physicians, adding, "I do not like the idea of flying, and not unless things are much more alarming then they now are. As your city can be so easily guarded, I should support you would find it proper to examine passengers in the stage, before you admit them — This precaution, as a time when there are so many strangers travelling, may be useful."[42]

In a letter to the *Daily Advertiser*, Hamilton shared his personal experience with the disease, writing that the "motives of humanity and friendship to the Citizens of Philadelphia, induce me to address to you this letter, in the hope that it may be in some degree instrumental in diminishing the present prevailing calamity." Continuing his goal of reducing the panic, he added, "It is natural to be afflicted not only at the mortality which is said to obtain, but at the consequences of that undue panic which is fast depopulating the city, and suspending business both public and private." Hamilton then pivoted to his other objective—advocating a different approach to treatment. "I am now completely out of danger," he shared. "This I am to attribute, under God, to the skill and care of my friend Doctor Stevens, a gentleman lately from the island of St. Croix." Hamilton lauded Stevens's approach to the fever, saying his "whole medical opportunities have been of the best" and that, having worked in the West Indies, Stevens "has had the advantage of much experience."[43]

Hamilton continued to put his formidable quill to work, writing also to newspapers in Boston and elsewhere about the "putrid fever" and offering alternative treatments. Writing in Boston's *Independent Chronicle* in third person, he noted, "We have good authority to assure the Public, that the recovery of the secretary of the treasury, and his lady is confirmed, and that a servant girl in the family, who attended Mrs. Hamilton, having been afflicted with the complaint, and having had the same treatment for it, is also in a fair way of recovery." Hamilton then got to the point: "This is a strong confirmation of the goodness of the plan, pursued by Dr. Stevens, and ought to recommend it to the serious consideration of our Medical Gentlemen." He added a direct attack on Rush, pointing out, "In such a case, the pride of theory ought to give way to fact and experience."[44]

In the *Daily Advertiser*, he opened with an admission that he contracted the disease, "But I trust that I am now completely out of danger." Hamilton again credited Dr. Stevens for an effective and enlightened treatment of baths, wine, inhaling herbs, and other more humane approaches than Rush's excessive purging, bleeding, and reliance on leeches and dangerous powders. The famous founding father also advocated cold baths, proper hygiene, and drinking hot brandy and Madeira wine.[45]

"Poisons and Purges"

What followed was a bitter, public feud among the city's medical community. In the newspapers, Dr. Kuhn referred to Rush's aggressive purging and dangerous elixirs as a "murderous dose." Devèze deemed Rush's treatment "a scourge more fatal to the human kind than the plague itself." Of Rush's use of "poisons and purges," Dr. Currie said they only bring "certain death." Of course, Rush took all this personally, bristling that his work was being questioned. He lashed out, "Besides combatting with the yellow fever, I have been obliged to contend with the prejudices, fears and falsehoods of several of my brethren, all of which retard the progress of truth and daily cost our city many lives." He was, however, undeterred, and his zealousness and confidence did not wane.

Currie was born in Pennsylvania, the son of an Episcopal clergyman. He had served as a surgeon during the Revolutionary War and had written extensively about the yellow fever outbreak. Unlike the more famous Rush, however, Currie was not a professor at the medical college or a prominent public figure. However, like Devèze, he was open to new ideas and treatments, and was an adherent of the fever classification system developed by Dr. Cullen of the University of Edinburgh.

Like Dr. Devèze and Hamilton, Currie boldly disagreed with the conclusions of Rush, writing, "To suppose that the air in the streets can be contaminated by the contagion so as to communicate the disease through that medium, is contrary to, and is contradicted by, the observations and experience of the learned of the faculty of every age and country." Currie then took off his gloves so to speak, announcing, "Any apprehension of an infectious disease from that source, can only be excused in those who have not had suitable opportunities for better information."[46]

Even if a few physicians disagreed with Rush's treatment, some supported his argument that it was contagious. Dr. Currie, for instance, believed the disease was contagious. However, like Devèze, he recognized that many people that should have contracted it did not, adding that there is "much consolation" because "the disease under consideration, though certainly infectious is nevertheless only communicable under particular circumstances."[47] Currie added that "the only circumstances" for communicability are threefold: "Confinement for any length of time in the bedchamber of the sick, especially when the apartment is not large and freely ventilated . . . coming in immediate contact with the patient, his body, or bedclothes . . . or by receiving the breath, or the scent of the several excretions of the sick." Currie tried to calm Philadelphians by assuring them that "people in walking the streets, are by no means in any danger of infection, as the miasmata, or contagious exhalations from the bodies of the diseased have never been known to be conveyed by the air many feet beyond the chamber of the sick."[48]

He also disagreed with Rush's advocacy for burning tar and firing cannons, arguing that "burning heaps of odorous and noisome substances in the streets is therefore not only useless, but injurious."[49]

Another disagreement was with Rush's other treatments such as "camphor," "tarred ropes," and excessive use of "vinegar." He also weighed in against treatments being proposed in the newspapers such as "amulets of dried frogs."[50] Similarly, Dr. Kuhn, who studied medicine at the University of Uppsala in Sweden, tried Rush's "remedies," but found they did not help. At the same time, Rush stuck with his own cures because he claimed that he tried the treatments advocated by Kuhn, Dr. Stevens, and his other critics, but that they did not work.[51]

Such was the state of the physician's war. Ultimately, many of Rush's views were not only popular, but they had also been around since the time of Hippocrates, over two millennia earlier. It is no wonder the public did not know who or what to believe. Of the bewildering array of treatments being debated in Philadelphia, Currie set about trying to compile an exhaustive list that included: calomel; purging; shaving patients' heads; having them wear linen turbans soaked in cold vinegar and dipping their hands and clothes in cool vinegar and water; pouring cold water over a patient's head and shoulder; exercise and encouraging perspiration; consuming Madeira wine, vinegar, salt, lime juice, and a mix of barley water or gruel; changing bed linen regularly; placing the patient's bed in the middle of the room; keeping the doors, windows, and curtains open; relocating patients to high ground and nearby hills, if possible; and using elixirs made of tartar emetic mixed with peppermint or cinnamon and drops of laudanum or drops of ammonia and opium. Ultimately, Currie was not confident in any of these treatments, but continued to experiment with cures and kept an open mind.[52]

Like his colleagues, Currie visited patients by the docks and suspected that location was the origin and cause of the outbreak, reasoning that in August it "raged with great violence" along Water Street and "occasioned a much greater proportion of mortality than in any other part of the city." Here he agreed with Rush, but unlike his rival who pronounced the name, source, and treatment for the affliction, Currie felt that further research was needed, and that the disease was far from being understood.[53]

Indeed, he took a measured view in calling for further study before determining an exact cause and preferred treatment. He asked, "How the disease was introduced into the city, whether imported from some other country, in consequence of the contagion adhering to goods or to the apparel of diseased persons . . . or generated in the low and filthy apartments of some of the inhabitants of Water-street, can only be determined by a collection and faithful statement of facts, and must be left for future investigation." Although a wise position, the city was in the grips of a crisis and needed answers and a response.[54]

Voices of Calm and Humility

Diametrically opposed to Rush on many aspects of the fever was Devèze, who early on realized that patients who recovered "owed their convalescence to the goodness of their constitution, and the little effect the malady had upon them." He realized medicine had little to do with it.[55] Devèze was also a voice of calm and reason regarding the origins of the disease and, in particular, the fear regarding the waterfront and immigrants. Many in the city pointed angrily at the brig *Mary* and other ships such as the *Hankey* and *Sans Culotte*, which arrived from the West Indies. The *Mary* had docked in Philadelphia after a harrowing sailing from Cape Francois with many passengers on board. Rumors immediately circulated that many of those on board died of the disease. Yet he reminded the public that he was one of those passengers and the charge was "without foundation."

Only one person, noted the French surgeon, died on the crossing. Three were ill, but one was a woman who suffered a miscarriage at sea and later died at Bush Hill. The other two recovered and were in "good health" during the outbreak. Other condemnations of the passengers were because they were in a "most pitiable state" and "ill-cloathed." But Devèze pointed out that it was because they had just fled a revolution, barely making it out of Saint-Domingue alive, and lost their homes and livelihoods. They were then plundered by English pirates who treated them with much "cruelty." It was to be expected that the passengers on the *Mary* arrived with "grief depicted on our countenances."[56]

Rush's other critics likewise called for more humane treatments. For instance, Dr. Stevens recommended less intrusive approaches, preferring cool baths and plenty of fluids.[57] Dr. Kuhn suggested "weaker wines, such as claret and Rhenish; if these cannot be had, Lisbon or Madeira diluted with rich lemonade." Like Devèze, Currie, and others, he opposed aggressive treatments, saying of any treatment, "The quantity is to be determined by the effects it produces and by the state of debility which prevails." Kuhn also favored "throwing cool water twice a day over the naked body" to cool down the fever. Advice that is timeless in its applicability, Kuhn stressed to his patients, in all cases, "cleanliness" along with "moderate and frequent exercise in the open air when dry and serene," while, "above all," avoiding the "monstrous and abominable vice of getting drunk."[58]

Devèze was magnanimous during the "physician's war," even acknowledging his differences with Rush but stating, "I now, once and for all, declare that I renounce all controversy." Rush was not as gracious for forgiving. He also wrote that he understood the public's fear and frustration, commenting, "An ill-directed public often acted contrary to what was efficacious." Too many people were "misinformed," which "added" to the "dangerous" state of affairs in the city. Instead, he directed his frustration at "the public papers" because they "inspired you with terror" by making false claims and reminding the public of the daily death toll. However, unlike Rush, Devèze did not take to the newspapers to make his points or assail his critics; nor was he politically connected.[59]

All the while, however, the highly public feuds among the city's physicians and their competing arguments and contradictory proposals simply confused and frustrated the public and their patients. And the bodies kept piling up.[60]

III

TURNING POINTS

CHAPTER ELEVEN
UNLIKELY HEROES

Star of Heaven, who nourished the Lord
And rooed up the plague of death which our first parents planted;
May that star now deign to hold in check the constellation
Whose strife grants the people the ulcers of a terrible death

    —"Stella Caeli Exstirpavit," Gregorian chant during the plague

Free African Society

During an outbreak of the fever in Charleston, South Carolina in 1742, Dr. John Lining, a prominent physician, studied the casualties. An early pioneer in American medicine and science, he compiled a record of the African community during the contagion: "Though many of them were as much exposed as the nurses to the infection," he observed, "yet I never knew one instance of this fever among them." It seemed that African slaves had a far lower rate of death than White people, leading Lining to surmise that they may, therefore, be "wholly free" from yellow fever. "There is something very singular in the constitutions of the negroes," wrote Lining, "which renders them not liable to this fever."[1]

Dr. Rush had studied Dr. Lining's observations of the 1742 epidemic and shared the physician's belief in the natural immunity of Africans. Therefore, Rush penned a much-read editorial for newspapers under the name "Anthony Benezet," claiming to be a Quaker who taught Black people and suggested they were immune. He then appealed to the Black community "to offer your services to attend the sick to help those in distress."[2]

The idea of African immunity was widely accepted at the time. Interestingly, such ideas were premised on the disease striking in the hot months or being more prevalent in Africa, although the medical community at the time never made the link that yellow fever may have been imported from Africa by way of insects. Rush shared his personal opinion, noting, "A great number of the blacks were my patients. Of these not one died under my care." Yet he once again contradicts himself, adding, "This uniform success among those people, was not owing altogether to the mildness of the disease, for I shall say presently, that a great proportion of a given number died under other modes of practice." Therefore, maybe he doubted whether Black people were immune.[3]

Rush was, however, quite devout and believed that God would not abandon people in times of crisis. God, Rush reasoned, must have given humanity some protection. The egotistical and zealous Rush felt it was his duty to find that answer—and he now believed he had done so: he would get Philadelphia's "free Blacks" to help with the disease by collecting bodies, burying the dead, and assisting in the care of the afflicted. Thousands of White residents had fled the city, but most of the Black community, lacking the means to leave and likely not being welcomed by other communities, remained in Philadelphia. Rush's appeal would be directed at the leadership of the city's Black churches.

Interestingly and admirably, Rush was a committed abolitionist. Philadelphia was the hotbed of abolition at the time and Rush, like many Quakers and other enlightened Philadelphians, supported Black clergy when they were attempting to build their own houses of worship.[4] His beliefs and actions were honorable, even if the appeal to the Black community seems a bit condescending by present standards.[5]

And so, despite the enlightened leadership at Bush Hill and Herculean efforts from the staff, the fever hospital was still overrun with cases and a constant stream of new patients; likewise, the capital city had largely come to a standstill in terms of public services. Help was needed. In response, on September 2, Rush published an appeal for help in the newspaper, requesting the assistance of Philadelphia's free Black community, based on his stated opinion that those of African descent were, at the least, partially, if not fully immune from yellow fever. On Dr. Rush's recommendation, Mayor Clarkson reached out to the city's Free African Society for assistance.

The African and West Indian community in Philadelphia dated to the 1600s, many of whom were enslaved and taken to the city in colonial times. The Black population reached its height in Philadelphia in the 1750s and 1760s when an estimated one hundred to five hundred enslaved people per year were brought to the city. Philadelphia was the hotbed of abolition in colonial times and Pennsylvania officially ended slavery in 1780. Yet even though it was the first state to do so, some Black Americans were still in bondage in the ensuing decades. Moreover, even after abolition, the "small but robust community" of roughly three thousand free Black people faced disenfranchisement and discrimination in Philadelphia. The ironic reliance on the Black community to keep the nation's capital functioning reflected the desperation of the city, but in a larger sense was yet one additional troubling instance of the history of race in America.[6]

The Free African Society was founded in the city in 1787, the first organization of its kind by and for Black people. Philadelphia also hosted the nation's first Black newspaper, the *Freedom Journal*. Most of the Society's membership were former slaves who organized to offer food, clothing, and other assistance to the poor, orphans, and widows in their community. Even though the Society was desperately in need of funds for the construction of Black churches and few White people had come forward to help with either the yellow fever or the needs of the Black community, on September 5, the leadership of the Society met in a home on Fifth Street near Walnut Street for the purpose of discussing the appeal by Dr. Rush and Mayor Clarkson. They knew the city and Bush Hill needed attendants for the sick and gravediggers but were assured by Rush that God had made Africans immune from disease.

Tragically, as we shall soon see, it was discovered that individuals of African and West Indian heritage were not immune to the disease. The Black relief workers that responded to the crisis walked into a furnace. As one account described, "The hospitals were in a horrible condition; nurses could not be had at any price: to go into a house in which nearly every bed contained a dead body, and the floors reeked with filth, was courting death in its most dreadful form." Ultimately, Black people ended up dying in rates similar to the White population, with an estimated 240 succumbing to the disease.

Allen and Jones

The appeal was answered. It was led by two prominent Black preachers, themselves former slaves. The plan was simple: they would propose the need for essential services to the members of the Free African Society and encourage them to tend to the sick, serve as nurses, staff the newly opened fever hospital, collect and distribute goods and supplies, and bury the dead for the besieged capital. It was a dangerous but noble decision and would end up alongside those who staffed Bush Hill as being one of the great examples of heroism during the outbreak.

The news that the Free African Society had agreed to fulfill the request was met by Clarkson, Rush, Girard, and many others with relief and hope. Rush could not keep up with the demands of the disease and had lost three of his assistants. He needed help. The situation was so dire that at one point he had to teach his eleven-year-old servant Peter how to cut veins and bleed patients. The assistance from the Black community was seen as a godsend, prompting Rush to write to his wife on September 6, buoyed by some long-awaited good news, that our "African brethren . . . furnish nurses to most of my patients." He immediately began instructing his new assistants how to serve as nurses. The diarist Elizabeth Drinker noted that all of Philadelphia was following the development, writing, "'Tis remarkable that not one Negro has yet taken the infection—they have offered to act as nurses to the sick."[7]

The effort was led by the Reverends Richard Allen and Absalom Jones, two of the city's most prominent Black leaders. They agreed to help, seeing it as their Christian responsibility. Interestingly, both men had only recently gained their freedom, had roots in Delaware, and had been members of the same church in Philadelphia.

Richard Allen was born into slavery in 1760 in Philadelphia and suffered the horrors of enslavement, including being known as "Negro Richard" as a boy and young man. The slave owner, Benjamin Chew, sold Richard and his family to a man named Stokley Sturgis, who owned a plantation in Delaware. When Sturgis faced financial losses, he sold the family to another plantation. Before the sale, however, Sturgis had pushed his slaves to embrace religion, which young Richard did, attending a Methodist service that changed his life. It led the teenager to attend a sermon in 1775 given by the Rev. Freeborn Garrettson, an itinerant Black preacher. Emboldened by the experience, Richard vowed to teach himself to read and write; he even started preaching at seventeen. Garrettson encouraged slave owners to reject slavery, prompting Sturgis to allow Richard and his family to purchase their freedom. In 1786, he finally saved enough money to gain his freedom. One of his first actions was to change his name to Richard Allen; he then moved to Philadelphia.[8]

Allen traveled as a circuit preacher and in Philadelphia began speaking in public at the city's famous commons, where he quickly attracted a following known as the "Allenites." He joined St. George's Methodist Church and led prayer meetings for the Black congregants. However, the White clergy and congregants forced the Black congregants to sit in the balcony, prohibited them from kneeling at the main altar, and placed limits on those permitted to attend Allen's prayer meetings. Frustrated, Allen left the church in 1787 and began efforts to build a new church.

Reverend Jones was born in 1746 on a slave plantation in Delaware. Small, frail, and frequently ill, Jones was unable to work in the fields, so he became a house servant. It was while caring for the plantation library that he taught himself to read and write and developed his lifelong passion for books. But at age eighteen his family received the devastating news that they were being sold. However, only his mother, sister, and five brothers were sent away, leaving Jones alone. Soon thereafter, his owner moved to Philadelphia and opened a store where Jones was required to work as a clerk.

An opportunity arose in the new city when he was permitted to attend a school in the evening that was founded by abolitionist Quakers. The opportunity nurtured his interest in both books and theology. At twenty-four, Jones married a slave named Mary. Working long hours at various jobs, he finally saved enough money to purchase her freedom. All the while, he was attempting to free himself, but his owner refused to allow him to purchase that right. Even though Pennsylvania ended slavery in 1780, he was not permitted by his owner to gain his manumission until 1784.[9]

Like Allen, he was attracted to the message of racial tolerance at St. George's Church but grew disillusioned that the message did not go far enough. Ironically, at the same time the Framers were gathering close by in the building known as Independence Hall, Jones knelt in a nearby pew to pray. However, a White preacher removed him from the church, so Jones joined Allen in leaving the church for good. In April of 1787, the two men convened a meeting of Black congregants and announced their plans to build their own church.

Allen and Jones obtained an old blacksmith shop on Sixth Street near Lombard and turned it into the first Black church in the nation.[10] Allen was assisted by his wife, Flora, whom he married in 1790, and Jones. Together, they advocated for equality, promoted charitable works, and organized literacy classes on behalf of the city's Black community. With the support of the city's Quakers and Philadelphia's Episcopal bishop, the church they built in 1792 became the Bethel African Methodist Episcopal Church, known in the city as "Mother Bethel."[11]

Only one year after their new church opened, Allen and Jones received the appeal for help from Dr. Rush and Mayor Clarkson. As they recollected in their memoir, "Early in September, a solicitation appeared in the public papers, to the people of colour to come forward and assist the distressed, perishing, and neglected sick; with a kind of assurance, that people of our colour were not liable to take the infection." It was a dangerous endeavor. However, they met with "a few others" and "consulted how to act on so truly alarming and melancholy occasion." After praying and "some conversation," the two preachers announced that they had "found a freedom to go forth, confiding in Him who can preserve in the midst of a burning fiery furnace." Believing "it was our duty to do all the good we could to our suffering fellow mortals," Allen wrote, "we set out to see where we could be useful."[12]

"Scenes of Woe, Indeed!"

Allen recalled the first assignment for him, Jones, and the Free African Society. They were sent to see "a man in Emsley's alley, who was dying, and his wife lay dead at the time in the house." They discovered, "There were none to assist but two poor helpless children." Allen and Jones remembered, "We administered what relief we could, and applied

140

to the Overseers [Guardians] of the Poor to have the woman buried."
Their work was only beginning. "We visited upwards of twenty families
that day . . . [and] found them in various situations . . . some laying on
the floor as bloody as if they had been dipt in it . . . others laying on a
bed with their clothes on as if they had come in fatigued and lain down
to rest. Some appeared as if they had fallen dead on the floor." The two
preachers described the experience, writing, "They were scenes of woe
indeed!" However, their faith imbued them with confidence. As Allen
described, "The Lord was plentiful to strengthen us, and removed all fear
from us."[13]

"In order the better to regulate our conduct," wrote Allen, "we called
on the mayor the next day, to consult with him on how to proceed, so as
to be the most useful." Mayor Clarkson was thankful for the assistance
from the Free African Society and began a close working relationship with
the two preachers, who recorded, "The first object he recommended was a
strict attention to the sick, and the procuring of nurses. This was attended
to by Absalom Jones and William Gray; and, in order that the distressed
might know where to apply, the mayor advised that upon application to
them they would be supplied."[14]

The mortality rates continued to increase through September and
October such that it was difficult to keep up with the task of removing so
many corpses. Most of those who performed these tasks, along with the
gravediggers, had either died, fled the city, or were no longer willing to
perform the work unless "offered great rewards." The work thus fell to the
Free African Society, who, day after day, collected bodies around the city,
some that had been decomposing in sweltering homes for several days.
The accounts are gruesome. Some homes they entered contained both
the deceased and living—although barely—family members. But the most
stressful for the Society volunteers was when they found "innocent babes"
in the house. Indeed, too frequently they discovered "little children . . .
wandering" around the house asking where their parents had gone. Day
after day of rescuing, burying, or taking children to "the orphan house"
impacted the workers such that some "almost concluded to withdraw from
our undertaking."[15]

One particularly troubling day the Society workers were sent to remove the body of a woman who had died. But "on our going into the
house and taking the coffin in, a dear little innocent accosted us, with,

CHAPTER TWELVE
A NATION WITHOUT A GOVERNMENT

You will not fear the terror of night,
Nor the arrow that flies by day,
Nor the pestilence that stalks in the darkness,
Nor the plague that destroys at midday.

—Psalm 91

Tensions

Even before the yellow fever pandemic struck, Philadelphia was in the throes of crisis. One of the more sensitive and potentially ruinous issues that year involved relations with France, which would, in a roundabout way, end up impacting the arrival of the pandemic at Philadelphia's docks and the public response to it. Like Congress, the public was divided on the matter of the war then raging between Britain and France. Only four years prior, the bloody French Revolution had begun, and in January of 1793, King Louis XVI was beheaded in public. Thomas Jefferson, the secretary of state, advocated for intervention on behalf of France, while Alexander Hamilton, the secretary of the treasury, favored neutrality. There was the very real possibility of the nascent American republic being pulled into another conflict. Ultimately, however, Washington, whose second term in office began that year, chose neutrality, a more prudent course of action, and issued his "Neutrality Proclamation" on April 22, stating, "The duty and interest of the United States require that they should with sincerity and good faith adopt and pursue a conduct friendly and impartial toward the belligerent Powers." It was the only reasonable course of action but seemed to please few. France, after all, had aided the American Revolution by sending troops and supplies.[1]

Both British and French privateers were visiting American ports, a situation that raised concerns both in the city and across the country, as noted by Philadelphia resident Elizabeth Drinker, who described commercial and private vessels being harassed including when an English ship with American passengers was "taken by a French Frigate, and brought back." She added, "'tis not yet determined whether she is a lawful prize or not."[2] This incident further heightened tensions at home, as did the fact that both the British and French wanted the United States to avoid trading with the other power. President Washington acted by drafting eight rules to regulate the presence of foreign privateers and warships in US ports and territorial waters, which he announced on August 3.[3]

The president attempted to resolve the growing tensions by diplomacy, meeting with George Hammond, the British minister, and with Edmond Charles Genêt, the French minister, but was unable to deescalate the situation. The problem had less to do with any failures of Washington—or even congressional divisions and diplomatic sensitivities—than with Genêt himself. In what became known as "The Citizen Genêt Affair," the French minister, who had just been appointed that spring, challenged America's neutrality, began attempting to unduly influence domestic politics, encouraged French privateers in American ports to attack British shipping, and went so far as to threaten war with Spain by advocating the liberation of Louisiana from Spanish rule. Even the unabashedly pro-French Jefferson became "increasingly distressed" by Genêt's actions and was unable to convince him to moderate his position or behavior. Ultimately, Washington, though wanting to support France on account of its earlier support for his colonial army, was forced to demand that the French government recall Genêt in August.[4]

The American public was becoming bitterly divided over whether to support France or Britain and the stories of savagery and bloodshed inflicted by privateers off American waters did little to help the matter. American ships and Americans continued to be the target of the opportunistic privateers. Ships, money, food, and possessions were looted, and Americans threatened. One of the ships sacked was the American brig *Mary*, caught after sailing from Cap-Français for Philadelphia—one of the ships that, as was mentioned earlier, was believed to have brought yellow fever to the capital city.

Soon, such groups as the Pennsylvania Democratic Society sprung up. The pro-France, pro-Republican (anti-Federalist), pro-Jefferson organization stoked the flames of partisanship with their criticisms of the Washington administration, despite the fact that France chose to go to war with not only Britain, but Austria, Holland, and Spain, was destabilizing Europe and the West Indies, and had begun a "Reign of Terror" in their own country. American newspapers joined the fray, with John Fenno's *Gazette of the United States* supporting the Federalists' neutrality and the Washington administration, and Philip Freneau's *National Gazette* siding with France and the Republicans. Other papers, such as Andrew Brown's *Federal Gazette*, published objective stories on the issue as well as a few dozen essays on both sides of the debate, including Hamilton's anonymous "Pacificus" letters for neutrality and James Madison's anonymous "Helvidius" editorials on behalf of France.[5]

Frustrated by the Neutrality Proclamation and his ongoing debates with Hamilton, while also seeking to launch his own bid for president, Jefferson announced on July 31 that he would resign by the end of the year. Amid this chaotic backdrop, other ships started arriving in Philadelphia from the French port of Saint-Domingue, fleeing not only privateers but also revolution and the yellow fever.

In July and August, Philadelphia absorbed approximately two thousand French refugees and their slaves from the troubled island. The new French presence further inflamed sentiments, as some stores catered to the new arrivals, while many of the refugees were aristocrats who demanded an unabashedly pro-French response by the Washington administration. Large, unruly pro-France, pro-Republican demonstrations were held in the streets of the city and near Washington's rented residence, prompting Vice President John Adams to deem it "French Madness" and complain that there were "ten thousand people in the streets" who "threatened to drag Washington out of his house, and effect a revolution in the government or compel it to declare war in favor of the French Revolution." Ironically, quipped Adams, maybe only the outbreak prevented complete chaos over the subject.[6]

How to Govern?

When the fever struck, the federal government, like the nation, was just four years old. Both were still finding their footing, and the experiment in popular governance was still very much a work in progress. It remained uncertain as to whether or not it would long endure. Moreover, the "French crisis" had divided the nation, Congress, and the administration. Add to this volatile situation a full-blown pandemic, and the nascent government was about to face its first crisis.[7]

The disease impacted the government and President Washington in intimate ways. One of Washington's neighbors and friends, Dr. Caspar Wistar, contracted the fever in early September, as did his treasury secretary and most trusted aide, Alexander Hamilton. "With extreme concern I receive the expression . . . that you are in the first Stages of the prevailing fever," Washington wrote to his aide. "I hope they are groundless, notwithstanding the malignancy of the disorder." The president, trying to remain positive, invited the Hamiltons to dine with him when they were recovered, adding that he anticipated it "would be a very pleasing circumstance." Although Wistar and Hamilton recovered, one of the city's foremost physicians and the state's surgeon general, Dr. Hutchinson, died from yellow fever, and all this was at the same time—the first week of September. And there were many others in the government who were stricken with the fever.[8]

After that alarming first week, President Washington wrote to Henry Knox, his war secretary and trusted friend from the Revolution, "I think it would not be prudent either for you or the Clerks in your Office, or the Office itself to be too much exposed to the malignant fever, which by well authenticated report, is spreading through the city." Washington expressed concern for his friend and wished him well: "The means to avoid it your own judgment under existing circumstances must dictate."[9]

Both Jefferson and Madison, then serving as a leader in the House of Representatives, were aware of and concerned about the fever's impact on the government. In a letter to his close friend and political confidant, Jefferson wrote, "The yellow fever increases." He was tracking the cases that first week of September: "The week before last about 3 a day died. This last week about 11 a day have died; consequently from known data about 33 a day are taken, and there are about 330 patients under it." Jefferson then warned Madison, who was away while Congress was on recess, "They are much scattered through the town, and it is the opinion of the physicians that there is no possibility of stopping it."[10]

So, too, the government lacked experience dealing with a health crisis. In addition, the prevailing interpretation of the new Constitution was such that it was believed the federal government had no authority to intervene in what was seen as an issue for the state of Pennsylvania and the city of Philadelphia. Even if action was warranted, Congress was not in session—since June—although President Washington had continued to meet with his cabinet through the fever months of August and early September. Still, civil society and the fledgling government were at a breaking point.

President Washington had planned to return to his home on September 10, a date that coincided with the height of the outbreak and put into question the matter of whether the cabinet and federal employees should remain and, if not, how to govern the nation. Jefferson described the quandary in another update to Madison: "The Presidt. goes off the day after tomorrow as he had always intended. Knox then takes flight. Hamilton is ill of the fever and is said he had two physicians out at his house the night before last. His family think him in danger."[11]

It was beyond time to consider whether the federal government should join half the city's residents in evacuating the capital. "The fever spreads faster," Jefferson warned Madison. "Deaths are now about 30 a day. It is in every square of the city. All flying who can." On September 8, Jefferson pondered the unthinkable—evacuating the city—writing, "I would really go away, because I think there is rational danger, but that I had before announced that I should not go till the beginning of October, & I do not like to exhibit the appearance of panic." There was more than the concern about illness, there were concerns about governance. "Besides . . . I think there might serious ills proceed from there being not a single member of the administration in place."[12]

However, on September 12, the secretary of state made his decision: "Most of the offices are shut or shutting. The banks shut up this day. All my clerks have left me but one: so that I cannot go on with business. I shall therefore set out in 3 or 4 days & perhaps see you before you get this."[13]

Washington Leaves the City

In mid-September, the situation became so dire that Washington gave the order: evacuate! He had no option but to encourage all nonessential federal employees to leave. Residents and government employees joined the exodus filling the roads leading out of Philadelphia. The president ordered his staff and family to leave and begged his friends the former mayor Samuel Powel and his wife Elizabeth to evacuate. The Powels, however, remained in the capital city. Mrs. Washington also initially refused to abandon her husband or the city. Soon, however, neither one had much choice but to leave. Joined by his wife and her two grandchildren—Eleanor "Nelly" Parke Custis and George Washington Parke Custis—they traveled to Mount Vernon.

Even though he had made plans before the arrival of yellow fever to depart Philadelphia for a vacation at Mount Vernon, the president worried about both the appearance of abandoning the capital and the impact on governance. Washington would end up very uncharacteristically putting the onus on his wife. In a letter to his longtime aide, Tobias Lear, the president wrote, "It was my wish to have continued there longer; but as Mrs. Washington was unwilling to leave me amidst the malignant fever wch. prevailed, I could not think of hazarding her & the Children any longer by my continuance in the City." On one hand, Mrs. Washington was dutiful—she did not like being separated from her husband. For example, she had bravely traveled to his winter encampments every year of the war. Therefore, she may have bravely remained. Yet, on the other hand, she was something of a hypochondriac who had buried all four of her children. It is not a stretch to imagine her concern about a deadly disease.[14]

Lear, who lived at Mount Vernon, would have been well aware of Washington's planned departure date, so it is almost certain the president was trying to put himself in a more favorable light by writing this letter and others sharing Mrs. Washington's worry. Moreover, he wrote the letter over two weeks into his vacation. However, Washington was a practical man who had been urged to leave and noted that he was "blocaded" in his rented home in the city "by the disorder" that "was becoming every day more and more fatal." Whatever the reason and perceived response, he was wise to abandon the city and avoid catching the fever. Although his party was stopped while traveling near Baltimore by authorities warry of Philadelphia's contagion spreading to their communities, the presidential party was permitted to pass—in part because they were not planning to stay. Washington arrived safely back home with his family and servants on September 14.[15]

The publisher Mathew Carey took note of the president departing "with his household," and added that "most, if not all of the other officers of the federal government were absent." Likewise, he commented that the governor claimed to be ill and retired to his country house and "nearly the whole" of the state workforce in the city had left.[16] Washington's trusted aid, Tobias Lear, wrote to the president, "Inexpressibly happy is it for our Country that you left the unfortunate City of Philadelphia before the malignant disorder had seized upon your valuable life." He then shared the alarming truth that "for at all times since we have been a nation your life has been considered by the good Citizens of America as essentially necessary for the prosperity of our public affairs—At the present juncture our existence as a united people is thought to depend upon it."[17]

However, in a shocking omission, the president did not transport his official papers to Mount Vernon, relying on Knox to tend to them. But none of Washington's aides or anyone else dared to go back into the fever city to fetch them. Likewise, other senior officials were away, but their papers and work remained in the capital. During this time, the British ship *Roehampton* was seized by Genêt's privateers and sailed into Baltimore harbor. The British demanded an answer, and the French insisted the ship was rightfully theirs. The governor of Maryland, uncertain as to the jurisdiction, wrote to Washington. Remarkably, the president admitted in a letter that "I brought no public papers of any sort (not even the rules which have been established in these cases) along with me; consequently I am not prepared at this place to decide points which may require a reference to papers not within my reach."[18]

State agencies and the Pennsylvania Assembly had already fled the city along with many city employees. The city, state, and federal government would largely cease to function. There was limited policing, no soldiers at the ready in the capital, court closures, and the shutting down of State Department offices. Congress was not scheduled to return to session for over two months. The sole remnants of the federal government were a few postal employees and a handful of Treasury clerks who collected customs. These brave public servants remained throughout the outbreak. Philadelphia became a ghost town. Eerily silent, the only thing on the streets according to one observer was "the doctor's carriage."[19]

Hamilton returned to New York when he was healthy enough to travel. However, when stopping in Trenton, New Jersey, the family was "refused" entry and was "compelled" to leave. Jefferson, despite earlier pledges to the contrary, headed home to Virginia.[20] Before departing, Jefferson sent the president a report on the fever: "Having found on my going to town, the day you left it, that I had but one clerk left, & that business could not be carried on, I determined to set out for Virginia as soon as I could clear my own letter files," he wrote. The secretary of state also pledged to stop to see the president while on his way home to Monticello, noting, "I shall hope to be at Mount Vernon on the 5th day to take your orders." He also provided an update on their colleagues: "The fever here, is still diffusing itself. It is not quite as fatal. Colo. Hamilton & mistress Hamilton are recovered. The Consul Dupont[21] is dead of it. So is Wright."[22]

It had become a matter of either remaining in Philadelphia and dying or leaving and living. Madison expressed the concerns of others in a letter to Jefferson: "I have long been uneasy for your health amidts [sic] the vapors of the Schuylkill.[23] The new & more alarming danger has made me particularly anxious that you were out of the sphere of it," admitted the congressman. "I cannot altogether condemn your unwillingness to retire from your post under the circumstances you describe," but he then added a slap to Washington and others, "but if your stay be as unessential as I conceive it to be rendered by the absence of the [president] and the fever does not abate, I pray you not to sacrifice too much to motives which others do not feel." It should be noted that Madison did not come back to the capital and that Jefferson was also on his way out, despite their repeated criticisms of others for precisely the same thing. Likewise, Jefferson had tendered his resignation a few weeks earlier and was merely biding his time.[24]

The death toll continued to rise, and the disease swept through the ranks of physicians, government employees, and even political leaders.

Last Man Standing

In a day and age of limited communication and rudimentary transportation systems, the president's order meant that not only neighbors and friends, but political leaders and government employees, generally had little idea of one another's whereabouts. Many had fled in panic, with little planning or advance notice. It was not a simple matter or reconvening the entire government, cabinet, or Congress should another threat or emergency arise. However, the president arranged for his cabinet to meet at a later date in Germantown, a few miles outside of the city.[25]

Washington placed his trusted friend and war secretary, Henry Knox, in charge of the city and government. In doing so, important questions were raised regarding the extent of Knox's powers and nature of his role in the city and as interim custodian of the federal government. The president requested his friend to make weekly reports to him. These pressing issues became academic when Knox's aides feared the disease and soon joined the stream of evacuees, leaving him as virtually the only senior official of the US government in the city. There was little Knox could do—and ended up doing—other than collect the mail and messages for the government and dispatch reports to Washington.

In a letter to Washington on September 15, Knox reassured his old friend that Alexander Hamilton and his wife "are both recovered" from the disease and have set off for New York. Washington's close friend, Samuel Powel, the former mayor of Philadelphia, and his wife are "well," added Knox, knowing how close the couples were. There was bad news, however. Knox informed Washington that several friends were either sick or had died. This included Dr. Warner Washington and Colonel Timothy Pickering, both of whom were ill.[26] Knox also reported that the fever "made great havoc" since the president departed.[27]

The fever, Knox added, "at present seems to be from 2d to 3d street, and thence to Walnut streets. Water street however continues sickly. But the alarm is inexpressible. Every body who could, has removed into the Country." Accordingly, Knox stated that there was no choice but to make plans to abandon the city. "I hope to be able to set off hence eastward on the 19th or 20th," he informed Washington. "All the public offices of the State and of the U.S., are shut I believe, or at least that very little is done in them, excepting the war office—But as all my efficient clerks have left me from apprehension, mine will be as the others. According to my view however nothing will suffer during my absence as I shall put into train of execution, all the preparations directed."[28]

With virtually no staff, the military dispersed, and government offices abandoned, Knox rode out of the city on the nineteenth. He was joined by Oliver Wolcott Jr., the comptroller. By the end of September, nearly all public services in the city ceased to exist and the United States was without a seat of government or a functioning national government. At the same time, public papers as well as national treasures such as the Constitution and Declaration of Independence were not fully secured.[29]

Knox's travel to his home in New England was harrowing. He described to Washington several "inconveniences" such as hostile checkpoints, crowded roads leading out of Philadelphia, and widespread panic among the people. To be sure, anyone traveling at the time risked roving bands of angry citizens. Cities and states established patrols to prevent entry by anyone from Philadelphia. Quarantine centers popped up. On September 12, the governor of New York issued a proclamation banning Philadelphians from traveling to his state. Days later, Maryland did the same, followed by others. Some residents from the capital city were, for instance, forced into tent cities on islands on the rivers around New York City and northern New Jersey.

Knox traveled to New Jersey, then to New York City, but was denied entry to Manhattan. Instead, he was sent by local authorities to an ad hoc quarantine facility in Elizabeth, New Jersey. The new protocol was that anyone from Philadelphia would be quarantined for "14 days" and then demonstrate that they were "in perfect health" in order to "be admitted" to the city. Despite protesting and reminding officials who he was, the secretary of war was stuck there for two weeks. From his quarantine, Knox informed the president of the situation and noted the dangers of state militias enforcing roadblocks.[30]

Knox was forced to continue making his official reports to the president from the quarantine center in New Jersey. Frustrated, the rotund former general even contemplated an escape, but mused, "I am too bulky to be smuggled through the Country." He was not alone. Hamilton also encountered "inconveniences" while trying to get into New York City. He abandoned his plan and traveled instead to his in-laws' home in Albany. A bigger problem was the lack of reliable intelligence and reports on domestic and foreign affairs. Until his departure, Jefferson sent Washington and Madison updates. His main focus, regrettably, seems to be a list of who was dead or dying, such as in one letter written in mid-September where he mentioned the names of diplomats, government employees, prominent merchants and bankers, and other notable Philadelphians lost. Jefferson added another concern to the ongoing fever: hunger. "Everybody who can, is fleeing from the city," he noted, adding, "and the panic of the country people is likely to add famine to the disease."[31]

Later that month, Knox sent the president one of the requested reports. It, too, contained grim news. "The mortality in the city where I was yesterday is excessive. One has not nor can they obtain precise information but the best accounts of the 14th 15th and 16th which were warm days the numbers buried were not short of an hundred each day—some average much more, and some much less." The nation's largest and once-most vibrant city was a shell of itself. "The streets are lonely to a melancholy degree—the merchants generally have fled," observed Knox. The city and port were also empty. "Ships are arriving and no consignees to be found. Notes at the banks are suffered to be unpaid." The war secretary concluded with a military reference, "I find the stroke is as heavy as if an army of enemies had possessed the city without plundering it."[32]

At the end of that fateful month, Knox shared more disturbing news with the president. "The alarm of the people . . . on account of the prevailing fever is really inexpressible. The militia are posted at Trenton Brunswick and Newark and New York. . . . At New York reason appears to been entirely lost." The war secretary shared horror stories, about the mobs and quarantine centers "frightening some Philadelphians to death." He discussed one incident where a "Mob" stopped a ship full of passengers arriving from New Jersey at New York's port. A local man named Mercier who was not a passenger and who "had not been out of New York for a long time," was grabbed and "forced" aboard the ship "with persons whom he believed to be infected with the plague."

Another individual that Knox called "Poor [Richard] Courtney the Tailor," who used to make clothing for President Washington in Philadelphia, was a hypochondriac and felt what he believed to be "the symptoms of an intermittent or yellow fever." The man "took Rush's medicines so frequently that he really became ill." When the public heard of his condition, they "ordered his coffin in his presence." Nosy crowds also "came into the sick man's room . . . to see the curious fever." Those same crowds, however, threatened to kill the man, who Knox claimed "has been so worried that his life is in great danger." The country was boiling over in panic.[33]

And for good reason. By October, the fever had spread well beyond the capital city and was infecting communities up and down the East Coast. Rev. Helmuth recalled, "The infection spreading in a few weeks not only through the whole city, but likewise filling the suburbs with terror." He mentioned nearby communities such as Kensington, Campington, and "the Neck," a community in between the Schuylkill and Delaware Rivers.[34] The result was that "our frightened inhabitants pursued their flight into more distant parts." Dr. Rush concurred, "The disorder . . . began to spread among others" and listed nearby cities up the Schuylkill and Delaware Rivers. Knox informed Washington that he attempted to "get a passage to Rhode Island." But no one would take him there because it was not "worth" their "lives." Alarmingly, "it was reported at Newport that the yellow fever, or plague killed in New York 40 people a day."[35]

Knox continued, as much as was possible, his updates on the spread of the disease. "The Weather yesterday and today is quite cool," he noted in latter September, optimistically, as he believed cooler temperatures to be "favorable to checking the disorder." Knox even updated Washington on Dr. Rush, writing, "Everybody whose head aches takes Rush." He even reported on Rush's much-discussed cures, sharing the story of a mutual friend who "took upon an alarm 20 grams of calomel and as many of Jalap. Although it cured him," pointed out Knox, "it has nearly killed him." Most importantly, perhaps, Knox let Washington know that it was not safe for him to return to the capital city. "From the present view of the subject," he advised, "the earliest period at which would be safe for you to return would be the first of November."[36]

CHAPTER THIRTEEN
GHOST TOWN

Have pity upon us miserable sinners,
who are now visited with great sickness and mortality;
that like as thou didst then accept of an atonement,
and didst command the destroying Angel to cease from punishing us,
so it may now please thee to withdraw from us this plague

—*Book of Common Prayer*, seventeenth century

Beyond Philadelphia

I t is estimated that at least twenty thousand residents of Philadelphia had evacuated the city during the disease. This constituted nearly anyone with the means to do so. Given recordkeeping at the time, the number was likely a bit higher and, therefore, ended up amounting to almost half the city's population. Accordingly, the death toll in the city was even higher as a percent of the population, given that nearly half the city had fled. Consequently, the streets of the nation's largest city and capital were empty, houses sat unoccupied, markets remained closed, weddings were canceled or delayed, and even the usually bustling port was avoided by incoming ships. Schools, theaters, taverns, boardinghouses, bakeries, and jails were all shuttered. Mail delivery continued, although only sporadically. As was mentioned earlier, all but one of the city's several newspapers ceased publishing.

Church services continued through August and most of September, as preachers refused to follow recommendations from the city and physicians to avoid large public gatherings in the event the disease was contagious, as many had thought. Many preachers and congregants openly defied—even flouted—these public health measures. Many refused to cover their mouths and noses with handkerchiefs. At worst, they rejected the existence of the disease or claimed they would pray it away; at best, however, some provided solace for their frightened and grieving congregations. Ultimately, however, with their congregations sick or dying, by October even the most dogmatic preachers discontinued services.[1]

Rev. Helmuth, who remained in the city to tend to his flock, wrote, "The streets of the city looked quite empty; most of the stores and a great many houses were shut up; many of those, who remained in the city kept themselves pent up in the back part of their houses, and even cut off all communication with the neighborhood." Helmuth bravely continued to visit his congregants, writing of these distressing calls that he was "intirely alone, at that time of the night. . . . Houses shut up to the right and left, deserted by their inhabitants, or containing persons struggling in death at that very time, or whole former inhabitants were all dead already." When out in the city, he remembered that "in two or three squares hardly a living soul was to be met with." He was also haunted by "such a deep silence" that "reigned" at nights. It was, he described, a "melancholy scene."[2]

The only carriages and wagons on the streets were those departing the city or those collecting the dead. Philadelphia was used to slower, quieter Augusts, because of the "sickly season" that periodically struck in the hot, humid months. The heat and humidity were "unbearable," and many longtime residents could not remember such an inclement time in their city. It would get even worse in October, and the panic spread throughout Philadelphia and beyond. Isaac Heston, a young law clerk, worried about the possibility of lawlessness in Philadelphia. The sheriff, he noted, was among the sick. Heston worried about vigilantism. "They have it in New York . . . they have it in Derby," he began. Now "the governor of New York . . . have published their proclimations, injoining the strictest search to be made of ever[y] person that arrives from Philadelphia." Heston was rightly concerned.[3]

On September 11, the mayor of New York City announced an "alarm" when a few cases of the fever were discovered. Physicians throughout the city were to report who had arrived and their health status. The city acted quickly, building a fever hospital and quarantine center. The next day, the governor of New York issued a similar proclamation "to prevent the bringing in, and spreading of infectious disorders." It banned any ship from Philadelphia from entering its waters within a two-mile distance.[4]

Such orders snowballed. On September 12, the governor of Maryland issued a proclamation "subjecting all vessels from Philadelphia to the performance of a quarantine, not exceeding forty days, or as much less as might be judged safe by the health officers." The state also subjected any resident traveling to Philadelphia to undergo a health examination. The next day, Baltimore appointed health officers to enforce yellow fever protocols, including the establishment of patrols outside the city and bans on "sheltering" anyone from Philadelphia. They later took "possession of a pass on the Philadelphia Road" outside of Baltimore "to prevent the entrance" into their city. On September 13, the towns of Trenton and Lamberton, New Jersey, organized patrols outside the city and enacted bans on entry, while also discontinuing the ferry service across the river between the cities.[5]

Then, on September 17, Virginia joined other states in banning both Philadelphians and anyone from the West Indies, while also establishing a quarantine center. Alexandria posted guard boats by its docks and Winchester organized units of armed guards blocking every road into town. That same day, New York announced it would "cease intercourse" with Philadelphia and ordered "guards" be placed at ports and roads "with orders to send back every person coming from Philadelphia."[6]

The prohibitions continued in late September and October, with Havre de Grace and Hagerstown in Maryland banning Philadelphians. As far away as Massachusetts, the state legislature "passed an express act for guarding against the impending danger." It directed that city officials are authorized to stop and "examine any persons, baggage, merchandise, or effects, coming, or supposed to be coming into the towns" from Philadelphia. In the days to come, Boston, Rhode Island, North Carolina, and Georgia joined them.[7]

Soon, cities around the country were denying anyone from Philadelphia admission. Roadblocks appeared, often with armed patrols. In Trenton, New Jersey, a "total stop" was issued. In Winchester, Virginia, not only people were stopped but packages arriving in wagons as well. Stagecoaches were stopped. Authorities in Lancaster, Pennsylvania, printed and posted handbills warning citizens of "the present alarming State of the Malignant Fever, which rages in the City of Philadelphia." A ship from Philadelphia was fired upon; another was sunk. Notices were either posted or published in newspapers across the country, including in the cities Charleston, Elizabethtown, New York City, Norfolk, Princeton, Trenton, and Woodbridge warning of the plague. Other cities established committees of health to inspect anyone coming from Philadelphia. Stage-coach operators were told that their passengers from Philadelphia cannot "pass through the town." A mixture of practical and fearful measures spread across the country; some communities in Pennsylvania and New Jersey generally allowed family members to return home.[8]

As a result, violence ensued. In Milford, Delaware, a woman and her Black servant arrived outside the city in a wagon. She was stopped and all her belongings were seized and set aflame. The woman was even stripped and "tar and feathered." Her servant managed to run away.[9] Another resident of Philadelphia named Major Christian Piercy attempted to flee after contracting the disease and his son paid a stage-coach driver to transport him and the family to Camden, New Jersey. However, as Piercy's condition worsened, the stagecoach driver and other riders stopped the coach and threw him out. The family continued on to Camden. Piercy managed to make it to a farm along the road, but was again turned away, eventually finding and dying alone in an abandoned cabin. A headstone was erected, reading[10]

> Stay Passenger see where I lie
> As you are now so once was I
> As I am now so You shall be
> Prepare for Death and follow me[11]

"The Patriotic Mayor"

One of those who contracted the disease was America's celebrated artist Charles Willson Peale of Philadelphia, who chose to remain in his city with his wife, Betsy, and their six children. As was recommended, they regularly doused the interior of their home in vinegar and even took to firing a "musket with the House" six times "each day." It did not help. Betsy contracted the fever and Peale's family physician died, as did the replacement physician. Both Peale and his wife fell violently ill but lived and became even more "vigilant" about remaining inside. So many of Philadelphia's leading citizens were now either sick, dead, or outside of the city, that it undermined the efforts of Washington, Hamilton, and Jefferson to give assurances to the residents not to panic. Not just the city's celebrated artist, Peale, but Philadelphia's foremost hero from the Revolution were now among the casualties of the disease.[12]

The former mayor of Philadelphia and Pennsylvania state senator, Samuel Powel, a widely admired politician known as "The Patriotic Mayor" because of his stoic leadership during the Revolutionary War, had, like Peale, remained in his beloved city. Powel had the distinction of being the last mayor of the city under British rule and then was elected the first mayor after independence was gained. Mayor Powel was joined by his wife, Eliza Willing Powel, the premier *salonista* of Philadelphia. The Powel's were arguably the city's most famous permanent residents— Mrs. Powel's great-grandfather, Edward Shippen, was appointed by the colony's founder, William Penn, as the first mayor of Philadelphia. Mrs. Powel's father, Charles Willing, and brother Thomas Willing were also mayors of the city and Thomas served as the first president of the Bank of the United States.

They were also abolitionists and social reformers, representative of the progressive city and leaders in Philadelphia's philanthropic causes, one of which included Mrs. Powel's generous donations to Reverends Allen and Jones in support of their AME church.[13]

The Powel's were also close friends with George Washington, who encouraged them to join him in returning to the safety of Mount Vernon. The Powel's refused, insisting on remaining in their city, in part because of the need to assure their fellow citizens and also because, in the words of Mrs. Powel in a letter to the president, they "thought there was no propriety in the citizens fleeing from the one spot where doctors were conversant with the treatment of the fever." Moreover, the outbreak was now a pandemic, spreading to other coastal communities and port cities. Likewise, the Powel home on South Third Street in the Society Hill section of town enjoyed an elevated height, both socially and physically. The Powels believed the location might keep them safe, as it was not located on the blighted waterfront, which sat at sea-level. Their decision inspired the remaining residents and gave people hope. Even though Congress had adjourned a few weeks earlier, President George Washington had stoically remained in the city through August and early September, offering a calm public face. He had ordered his cabinet to continue to work—for the time being—and he nearly changed his travel plans to remain in the city because of his deep admiration for the Powels, but they urged him to leave.[14]

Mayor Powel begged his wife to depart and join Washington at Mount Vernon. She would hear none of it and was planning her grand fiftieth birthday celebration. It was around that time that Mayor Powel contracted the fever; he was noticeably ill on September 25. The Powels were also friends with Dr. Rush, so a coachman was sent from the Powel home to retrieve his friend. Rush sent a young physician who lived near Powel to treat his friend with aggressive calomel purges and bleeding. The patient wrote to Rush, most likely on the twenty-fifth with good news: "I certainly don't feel worse for the operation. The discharge from my bowels are exactly as you described them."[15]

Rush visited Powel the next day and noted that his friend's condition had not changed. However, two days later on the morning of the twenty-eighth, Powel's nephew, Dr. Samuel Powel Griffitt, arrived at Rush's home in a panic. He reported that Powel was dying. The patriotic mayor passed the next day.

On President Washington's request, Rush agreed to escort Mrs. Powel to Chester or Mount Vernon, writing to her, "Your affectionate & friendly Attention to me, at this awful Moment, filled my Heart with so much Sensibility as rendered me incapable of expressing my Feelings on the Subject of our Conversation, and when my amiable Friend, the President, renewed his Invitation to me to accompany you to Virginia." She declined, noting that her husband "wished me to follow my own Inclinition and the Dictates of my own Judgement in a Matter that may eventually affect my Life and his Happiness—this has thrown me into a Dilemma the most painful." Ultimately, Mrs. Powel chose to remain in the city, but then moved to her brother's home in nearby Chester. "The Conflict between Duty and Inclination is a severe Trial of my Feelings," she informed Rush, "but as I believe it is always best to adhere to the line of Duty, I beg to decline the Pleasure I proposed to myself in accompanying you to Virginia at this time."[16]

Mrs. Powel also wrote to her friend, the president, saying, "Death has robbed me of many Friends." The passing of the celebrated mayor, a hero to Philadelphians, alarmed the city and set off further panic, causing even more people to leave. As for Rush, although he courageously remained to care for the sick, he blamed the physician he had sent to treat Powel. Even though the young man employed Rush's treatment and Rush had also tended to Powel, he criticized him for "the neglect of a 4th bleeding."[17]

"Mass of Contagion"

The disease continued through October with no signs of ending. In early October, over one hundred people per day were dying in the city. That first week of October, the defiant Rev. Helmuth lost 130 of his parishioners. Even he finally decided to suspend large services. The public's resolve received yet another shock when Dr. Rush collapsed while visiting a patient on October 4. His orderlies had to carry him back to his home and even the brave but zealous Rush had trouble working, fainting again in public just five days later. He was forced to remain bedridden for six days.[18]

Philadelphia had become a ghost town and was teetering on complete chaos. Yet the situation continued to worsen, as outbreaks hit their most alarming level in the middle of October. Rush and other physicians were unable to meet the growing requests for their services. It was reported that 111 died in the city on October 12, followed by 103 the next day, and the numbers remained above the century mark, forcing the city to start burying the dead in mass graves, some of which were dug in public squares because all the cemeteries were full. On the fourteenth, articles appeared in New York City newspapers announcing that Philadelphia had completely shut down. The city would likely remain unsafe, claimed the papers, who then encouraged Congress and the federal government to relocate back to New York City.[19]

The worsening of the disease in October prompted another exodus, as "thousands of the inhabitants fled away." The alarming sight was made all the worse because "some of these carried the infection along with them" and furthered the spread of the fever to other communities. Rev. Helmuth added that some of those who abandoned the city "were brought back to us dead."[20]

One of those leaders encouraging people to leave was Dr. Rush. Soon after the "fever made its appearance," Rush had encouraged his wife and children to go to New Jersey, a family tradition each summer. Back on August 25, they wisely headed out of Philadelphia along with Rush's mother, one of his sisters, the family's Black servant, a "mulatto boy" that lived at the home, and several of Rush's students. One can understand the surgeon's concern about his family—he and his wife had eleven children, but four of them passed in infancy. His worry was also prompted by cases of the fever appearing in his Walnut Street neighborhood and because, among the Rush children, was a two-year-old son and nine-month-old daughter. Even his teenaged sons were told to go to New Jersey, as Rush had observed that there seemed to be a larger proportion of teenaged boys and young men contracting the disease—most likely because they worked the docks and performed outdoor manual labor, thus exposing them to mosquitoes.

Rush again advised: "All that can move, to quit the city"; but still he remained. He advised those in this second wave of evacuations not to see or speak to anyone from Philadelphia because the city had turned into a "mass of contagion." He also wrote to his wife of his despair, "You can recollect how much the loss of a single patient in a month used to affect me. Judge then how I must feel, in hearing every morning of the death of three or four!" He was soon losing far more.[21]

So many people hurried out of the city in October that roads were again blocked, making it difficult to travel. The author Lillian Rhoades said simply of the vacant city, "The hearse and the doctor's carriage were the sole vehicles on the street."[22] It had been rough since the outbreak appeared, but there were now not enough workers to keep Philadelphia functioning. Most abandoned their jobs or the city altogether. The few remaining gravediggers were digging dozens of graves per day. The main cemetery had two employees, but "both were laid up with the disease," remembered Rev. Helmuth, and soon "one of them died." Likewise, "the number of attendants at a funeral was greatly diminished," added the reverend. In fact, "Frequently nobody but the driver of the hearse . . . accompanied a coffin."[23]

Typically, dozens if not hundreds of people walked behind the deceased in a funeral procession. In the eighteenth century, funerals were large, public reaffirmations. People both gave gifts and wore special cloth-ing—not only mourner's black but gloves, rings decorated with a skull or skeleton, and other symbolic items. However, Philadelphians now "retired at the approach of a hearse," noted Helmuth, who added that "windows and doors were shut as they passed." Historically, funerals were also announced by an individual known as "the inviter,"[24] a kind of town crier who went door-to-door as a messenger of death, dressed in black, and inviting the public to attend the service and procession. The role was so important that the inviter was sometimes accompanied by a "weeper," who was there to cry at the grave news. Even the inviters and weepers stopped attending funerals.[25]

The publisher Mathew Carey returned to the city to assess the crisis, which he, too, found to be at its worst in mid-October. By then, newspapers had stopped being printed and the city's sole remaining paper refrained from publishing obituaries. Carey found Rush recovering and determined to return to his practice. Only a few other physicians and preachers were still alive and active, he reported. A sad mixture of fear and hopelessness gripped the city. Those still present walked in the middle of the near-empty streets to avoid any other pedestrians and diseased homes, and fires again burned on street corners in hopes that the smoke would mitigate the diseased air. People desperately soaked their clothing in vinegar, carried pouches of camphor, and chewed on cloves of garlic all day. "Acquaintances and friends avoided each other in the streets and only signified their regard by a cold nod."[26]

The only hope was that it rained on October 12, then again on the fifteenth, prompting Rush to proclaim, "The appearance of this rain was like a dove with an olive branch in its mouth." Everyone hoped the waters would wash away the disease and they awaited the cooler weather. It was not to be. Unseasonably warm weather returned, and a gloom fell across the city. There was no sign of relief.[27] The diarist Elizabeth Drinker, who by then had lost many friends and family members, summed it up, "Desolation, Cruelty and Distress have of late resounded in our ears from many quarters." She feared that "nothing but the power of the Almighty could stop it."[28]

CHAPTER FOURTEEN
THE FALL FROST

A yellow fever burns with anger.
Mothers fill with a sense of danger.
As towns die and graveyards grow,
A carpenter's child waits for snow.

—"Yellow fever 1793"
Meghan Letson, 2012

Cornerstone

E ven though the president and most of the federal government had
departed the capital city by mid-September, there was an important date and event approaching. The cornerstone of the Capitol
was to be placed on September 18 in the future federal city, which was
then under construction and scheduled to open in the year 1800. A grand
ceremony had been planned. However, the city that would later be named
in Washington's honor was but 150 miles from Philadelphia, and the
boggy area on the banks of the Potomac River was also ripe for the fever.

Washington understood the importance of this milestone—years of
bitter political fighting had erupted over the location of a capital city.
States and cities jockeyed for the obvious economic and political advantages that would come from hosting the federal government. Political factions emerged over the issue and many Southerners had been demanding

the location be in the South. In fact, it took from the start of the Revolutionary War in 1775 until 1790 before Congress finally approved a site for the capital and only after a close vote.[1] The debate did not end, but rather shifted to arguments about New York and Philadelphia functioning as the interim capital while a permanent seat of government was being built. So, too, did questions (and concerns) over the composition, size, and actual building of the capital erupt.[2]

Even though yellow fever was not present along the Potomac, many people were avoiding travel, especially along coastal and marshy regions. Yet within that divisive and ongoing debate, Washington wanted to assure that his vision of a "city for the ages" would become a reality. The ceremonial laying of the cornerstone could not be postponed, and he needed to preside at the event. He therefore rode from his Mount Vernon home in Northern Virginia into the planned city, and on September 18 set the cornerstone for a new Capitol in a future seat of government. It was a grand ceremony in the Freemason tradition, of which Washington was a member. However, once the cornerstone was laid, the president and others in attendance departed, and Washington returned to Mount Vernon.[3]

This event highlighted the questions of how and when the president and federal government should return to Philadelphia. No one knew how long the yellow fever would last, although it was hoped that rain and cooler weather would drive the disease away, as had often been the case with lesser outbreaks during the "sickly months" of late summer.

In addition to concerns over whether Philadelphia would be safe, there was the matter of whether, in the interim, Congress should—or even could—convene in a location other than the interim capital city. Washington and other senior members of the administration did not know if Congress could legally convene elsewhere; the Constitution was not clear on the topic and the nation was barely into its fourth year. Jefferson, Madison, and other Southerners who fought so hard to prevent a capital north of the Mason-Dixon Line worried that, should Congress meet in another location, it would reopen old feuds about the location of the capital. The disease was now threatening the future location of the capital city.

Washington's Letters

While awaiting updates on the status of the disease in Philadelphia from Timothy Pickering, the postmaster general, Dr. Rush, and others, Washington reached out to his cabinet for advice on when and where to meet and the related issue of Congress reconvening. The deliberation began on September 25, when the president wrote several important letters.

In one, Washington congratulated Hamilton and his wife "very sincerely on your recoveries from the malignant fever," then turned to the topic of returning to the capital city. Washington mentioned that he heard alarming reports from Jefferson and Knox and concluded that "under the most favourable change that can reasonably be expected, the first of November is as soon as business can, with safety, be transacted" in Philadelphia. The president then broached the legal matter of meeting in another city, something he favored because of the urgent need to reconvene the federal government. Yet he received counsel from Jefferson and others suggesting it would be unconstitutional to do so. "But it appears necessary, at all events," wrote Washington, "that the heads of Departments should assemble—if not at that place, yet in the vicinity of it (say German Town)."[4] He wanted Hamilton's advice on the constitutional question.[5]

The president also wrote to Knox that same day, reiterating his concern that the cabinet needed to meet soon and "in Philadelphia or the vicinity of it." He also stressed that "I shall make it a point to be present." Washington informed his war secretary that he was consulting Hamilton and Jefferson on the constitutionality and logistics of the decision. Jefferson had also visited Mount Vernon and the two discussed the topic in person.[6]

It would seem that Washington was bothered by any legal and political problems resulting from a meeting in a location other than Philadelphia and was also growing impatient with the hesitancy from Jefferson. After all, it was now mid-October, a full month since the cabinet or federal government was functioning. On October 11, he again wrote Jefferson requesting a "time & place" to meet. Jefferson had apparently not been answering Washington's requests—or perhaps there were delays in the mail or that the secretary was purposely dragging his feet so as to avoid the possibility of the government reconvening in another location or, worse yet, in the north. Even when Jefferson wrote, he was short on details and evasive as to reconvening the government. Washington noted that his attorney general, Edmund Randolph, also expressed concerns about meeting in Germantown or elsewhere, but maintained that events "may make a change of *place* necessary," then added, "but I shall wait further advices before this is resolved on."[7]

Jefferson would have been aware of the president's impatience and that he was seeking Hamilton's counsel, something that would have worried him. Washington shared that Jonathan Trumbull of Connecticut, who had just stepped down as Speaker of the House, also voiced concerns about meeting anywhere but Philadelphia.[8] He then put Jefferson on the spot, writing, "You were of opinion when here (visiting Mount Vernon) that neither the Constitution nor Laws gave power to the President to convene Congress at any other place than where the Seat of Government is." It had been several days since Jefferson or Randolph had answered his requests on the issue, so Washington continued to prod, wondering what they would do "if German town is affected, with the malady." He also noted that Wilmington and Trenton were "equidistant, in opposite directions from Philada," while floating the idea of Annapolis, Reading, or Lancaster as possible sites for a meeting. Still frustrated, the President confessed that he faced a "serious and delicate decision" that would be "equally obnoxious" to Congress and worried that "Southern members" would again complain. It was clear that Washington felt they must gather soon, even if Jefferson and others opposed it.[9]

Three days later, the president again wrote to Hamilton. He got right to the point: "The calamity which has befallen Philadelphia & seems in no ways to abate renders it more essential than ever for the heads of Departments to Assemble." He added another reason to meet as soon as possible, so "that proper measures with respect to the public offices & Papers may be adopted." Washington always recognized and appreciated his aide's brilliant legal mind, and again solicited his assessment of the constitutional question. "It is time also, if the President can with propriety interpose, to decide something with respect to the meeting of Congress," Washington wrote in the third person with urgency. "But what, is difficult; some being of opinion that there is no power vested in the Executive under any circumstances to change the place of meeting although there is power to call Congress together upon *extraordinary* occasions." Washington also obviously prompted Hamilton, writing, "The exigency of the case would warrant the measure."[10]

Washington pondered the "delicate situation," asking, "If to call Congress together, where, for the ensuing Sessions? The Public Offices & Papers being difficult & expensive to remove to any distance—and the delicate situation it would throw the Executive into by naming a place far from the present establishment. My wishes would be German town, if the place is free from the fever, for the reasons I have mentioned." He concluded the letter affirming his confidence in his treasury secretary, "None can take a more comprehensive view—& I flatter myself a less partial one on the subject than yourself."[11]

Clearly frustrated and worried, the next day the president again wrote to Knox. Washington knew the advice from Jefferson and his faction was against convening anywhere other than Philadelphia, but surely knew he could count on Hamilton and Knox, who were always loyal to him and shared his political views. "The violence with which . . . the contagious fever in Philada continues to rage," worried the president, "makes it still more necessary than ever that the meeting of the Heads of Departments which I requested you to attend." Seeking Knox's support, Washington wrote that, if the meeting should "fail to take place by the first of November that, among other things measures may be taken for security of the public offices & Papers." He had already made up his mind: "I shall set out from this place in order to meet you & the other Gentlemen in the vicinity of Philada at that time."

"Should the continuance of the fever in the City of Philada render it unsafe & improper for the members of Congress to assemble there the first of December (& indeed there seems to be no hope of its disappearance by that time)," Washington asked, "what in that case is to be done?" Washington spelled out the legal debate between Jefferson and Hamilton on the issue: "Altho; the President has power to call Congress together in extraordinary cases, it is denied that power is given to change the fixed place of convening." He added, "By others it is thought the exigency of the present case wd justify the measure. Indeed it has been made a question by some whether even Congress themselves have this power." The president closed by again reminding Knox he preferred to meet in Germantown.[12]

While Washington was gathering opinions from Hamilton and Knox to proceed and, by all intents, had made his decision but simply wanted to secure the necessary legal advice and allow for a full vetting of the options, he received a much-awaited letter from Jefferson. Writing on October

17, the secretary of state uncharacteristically got to the point, writing that he had "carefully considered the question Whether the President may call Congress to any other place than that to which they have adjourned themselves, and think he cannot have such a right unless it has been given him by the Constitution or the laws, and that neither of these has given it." Jefferson added that the president can only "alter" the "time" that Congress meets, by requesting "an earlier day . . . but no power to change the place is given." He also noted that Madison agreed with him and advised Washington to show "particular caution." Jefferson then reopened the old and bitter debate about the location of the capital, reminding Washington that "the Residence law has fixed our offices at Philadelphia till the year 1800" and recommended the decision be up to Congress.[13]

Jefferson, Madison, Randolph, and others maintained their concern about too much power in the hands of the executive, but also masked much of their debate behind their overarching priority—that Philadelphia should remain the interim seat until the permanent seat is built in the South. They even worried whether Congress would get a quorum in another location and went so far as to suggest that the body would have to actually meet in Philadelphia in order to agree to then meet elsewhere. Hamilton raised the far more practical concern of the need to govern. What if, he reminded his critics, an enemy captured the capital? Would they not meet elsewhere?

The Decision

Hamilton gave Washington the constitutional cover he needed to reconvene the government. Writing on October 24, he laid out the argument: "As to the right of the President to convene Congress out of the ordinary course, I think it stands as follows—'he may on *extraordinary occasions* convene both houses of Congress or either of them'—These are the words of the Constitution." Hamilton added, "Nothing is said as to *time* or *place*—nothing restrictive as to either—I therefore think they both stand on the same footing." He turned Jefferson's argument around: while the document does not expressly allow the president to act (Jefferson), not does it expressly forbid him from acting (Hamilton), and the Framers took the effort at the Constitutional Convention to spell out limits on power. So why did they not expressly mention the current issue as a limit?

"The discretion of the President," concluded Hamilton, "extends to *place* as well as *time*." The treasury secretary even gloated playfully, what should be done if the capital was "swallowed up by an earthquake."[14]

Hamilton offered a civil and bipartisan solution, adding, "And I know that there are respectable opinions against the power of the President to change the place of meeting in such a case." However, he counseled Washington to "take the next step," noting, "but the President may *recommend* a meeting at some other place, as a place of preliminary rendezvous for the members of the two houses, that they may informally concert what further the exigency may require."[15]

So, for Washington and Hamilton, "The question then would be, what place is the most eligible?" Hamilton again suggested an olive branch. "Obvious reasons render it desirable that it should be as near Philadelphia as may consist with the motive for naming such a place," and that would be "the safety of the members." It would be a temporary, emergency decision in order to govern amid the crisis. Hamilton added, therefore, "Innovation upon the existing arrangement with regard to the seat of Government, ought to be avoided as much as possible."

Washington's decision was made, and his rationale was solid. By October 28, he was focused on the details for the return of the government. Then, in late October, Postmaster Pickering wrote that the fever appeared to be in decline in the capital city. However, Comptroller Wolcott wrote with news that deaths in the city again spiked at the end of the month. It was typical of the conflicting reports and lack of reliable information. Who to believe? Randolph agreed that Philadelphia was still unsafe, as "we have not yet learned, that any radical precautions have commenced for purging the houses and furniture" of the infection. Complicating the matter was that, with the fever raging, the delivery of mail—which was dipped in vinegar in hopes of diminishing communicability—was slow to arrive.[16]

Nevertheless, there were undeniably encouraging signs. *The Federal Gazette* reported that "the malignant fever has very considerably abated."[17] After averaging over one hundred deaths a day during the first half of October, there were only fifty-five reported burials on the twentieth. The diarist Elizabeth Drinker wrote that October 21 was met by "a delightful, cool, frosty morning." She exclaimed, "Tis generally agreed that the fever is very much abated" then added a comment: "cold this evening."[18] On the twenty-fourth she wrote with excitement, "We have heard of no death this day," adding, "Tremendous times!"[19]

On October 25, some residents began to return, and a few stores were reopened. A ship from London arrived and "once more enlivened" the docks.[20] The next day, the publisher Mathew Carey proclaimed was "the day the fever expired." The day after that—October 27—only thirteen burials were recorded in the city and the temperature was a crisp forty-four degrees. The next day, the weather turned even cooler for a day. Then, on the last day of the month, when overnight temperatures dipped into the twenties and thirties amid a cool rain, a white flag was seen flying above Bush Hill—an indicator that no new patients had been admitted with the fever. The *Federal Gazette* reported the meaning of the flag as "no more sick persons here."[21]

Washington sent letters to the cabinet with his request that they meet in Germantown, located a convenient ten miles from the center of Philadelphia. The governor of Pennsylvania, Thomas Mifflin, had fled to Germantown and was still there. The "public business," said Washington, must go on. And so, on October 28, Washington set out for Germantown with his longtime aide Tobias Lear. He stopped en route in Baltimore, where he met with Jefferson, likely to smooth over any sensitivities. Jefferson could be famously fragile and petty about political disagreements but respected Washington, a point of which the president was well aware. On November 1, as scheduled, the cabinet met in Germantown, the site of a major battle in October 1777 during the Revolutionary War that pitted Washington against his British nemesis General William Howe.[22]

As expected, Jefferson complained but was at the meeting. His surviving letters reveal his mood: he grumbled about the road being too dusty, that the weather was too hot (it was not), and he had difficulty finding a coach to transport him and then had to pay too much for the one he obtained. He even used the word "fleeced." Germantown was overrun with refugees, and Jefferson could not find an inn or boardinghouse and had to settle for an unfurnished room in nearby King of Prussia. It was pouring salt in an open wound. He continued to complain. Jefferson's allies, Madison and James Monroe, resorted to sleeping on benches at a crowded tavern. Washington had wisely made arrangements in advance to stay at the home of an acquaintance named David Deshler. Conveniently, the Deshler mansion would be the site of the controversial cabinet meeting.

Jefferson's whining continued, although he attempted damage control. Placing himself in a more favorable light, he claimed, "It has been determined that the President shall not interfere with the meeting of Congress." He may have lost the first debate to Hamilton but was still holding out that Congress would affirm his reading of the Constitution. Venting to Madison, Jefferson reminded his friend that he advised Washington against meeting in Germantown and against asking Congress to reconvene there or elsewhere. But Jefferson does share the good news that "the fever in Phila. has so much abated as to have almost disappeared. The inhabitants are returning."[23]

Back in Philadelphia

Hamilton was still recovering from the fever but wrote to Washington on November 3 from the town of Fair Hill, roughly three miles outside of Philadelphia on the road from Germantown. "Not having been in condition to attend you yesterday, and (though free from fever) yet not being well enough to go abroad immediately," he apologized for his absence. But Hamilton affirmed his belief that the Constitution was respected through their decision to meet. "I believe it will be altogether safe for the ensuing session of Congress to be held at Philadelphia, and that the good of the public service requires it, if possible." He brilliantly suggested that not just Washington, but Jefferson, too, submit "circular letters"[24] to both newspapers and Congress explaining the need to meet in Germantown. The controversy surrounding Congress was ended by the cool weather that mitigated the disease as much as by Hamilton's read of the Constitution or Washington's eagerness to get back to governing.[25]

Washington initially had planned to remain at Mount Vernon for fifteen to eighteen days but was forced to extend his visit back home by several days because of the fever. Mindful of the morale in the capital and of the symbolism of his own travels, the president visited Reading and Lancaster in eastern Pennsylvania on November 10. Then, the next morning, Washington mounted his horse and rode alone—without aides or his valet—into Philadelphia. He was done waiting for secondhand reports. He inspected the city, politely greeting nervous residents with a tip of the hat as he rode by. His solo visit was signaling to the public and Congress that it was safe to return. Afterward, he returned to Germantown to the shock of his staff with news that all seemed to be satisfactory.[26]

Jefferson swallowed his pride and shared the good news about the capital with Madison, writing, "The stages from Philadelphia to Baltimore are to be resumed tomorrow." It was on November 13 that the stagecoaches stopped at Philadelphia for the first time since August. Jefferson added that he had heard the fever had almost disappeared and "the Physicians say they have no new subjects since the rains." Most importantly, "The inhabitants, refugees, are now flocking back generally." The city welcomed the president and federal government with open arms. Mayor Clarkson was there to greet everyone. Governor Mifflin also returned to the city and, slowly but surely, the business of governing returned to the interim capital city.[27]

Mathew Carey documented the event with excitement, writing that, with the cold weather and rains, "a viable alteration" had occurred in the city. "Our absent friends return in crowds," he added, noting that with every hour more people arrive in Philadelphia. Market Street was again filled with wagons and carriages. The city was abuzz from the visit by President Washington and residents hoped Congress would return soon. While the prevailing view was that the danger "is entirely done away," wrote Carey, there are still some who go out with caution.[28]

That same week, Elizabeth Drinker recorded more good news: "When we arose this morning, it was snowing fast . . . houses and trees covered." Her diary had an entry saying simply, "Most of ye Philadelphians are returned to ye City."[29] As on cue, Congress announced it would convene in Philadelphia for their next session in early December.

It was not just Washington that brought both the government and life back to the capital, it was the weather. Physicians and residents alike noted that cooler weather or the storms of fall tended to "blow away" contagions. All had hoped for the return of cooler weather. In November, the weather complied, turning decidedly cooler. The first frosts brought an end to the one hundred days of terror. The state of science and medicine at the time did not know why, but the fall frost killed the mosquitoes that transmitted yellow fever.

CHAPTER FIFTEEN
OF PESTILENCE AND POLITICS

Let those, then, who have remained,
Regard their long absent friends,
As if preserved from death by their flight,
And rejoice at their return in health and safety—
Let those who have been absent,
Acknowledge the exertions of those who maintained their ground.
Let us all unite in the utmost vigilance to prevent the return of the fall
    destroyer,
By the most scrupulous attention to cleaning and purifying our scourged city—
And let us join in thanksgiving to that Supreme Being,
Who has, in his own time, stayed the avenging storm,
Ready to devour us, after it had laughed to scorn all human efforts.

—Mathew Carey's "On where to go from here;
forgive and work together," Philadelphia, 1793

Racial Allegations

The prominent Irish-born publisher Mathew Carey penned two histories of the deadly yellow fever pandemic, one during the outbreak and the other rushed out months later at the close of 1793. The latter book, dedicated to the American Philosophical Society headquartered in Philadelphia, was an instant success. Carey was a well-known leader and

Republican activist in the city. Among the book's selling points was that the author compiled a list of names of the deceased. Carey claimed he was prompted to produce that second book because of "the favourable reception given to the imperfect account of the fever which I lately published" and in order to offer "a more satisfactory history of it." In *A Short Account of the Malignant Fever*, Carey also offered an "apology" of sorts, writing that "many" of his "conclusions" were preliminary and could now be recorded "with more propriety" thanks to hindsight.[1]

Carey should have offered another apology. In the book, which he began in October during the outbreak, he was critical of the Free African Society and other Black residents who came to the assistance of the city during the fever. Carey's central claim was that they profited off the plague. These allegations clearly had racist undertones and, owing to the success of the book, were, along with other criticisms and conspiracies that piggybacked off Carey's book, printed in newspapers and spread throughout the city and beyond. The most specious and tainted of which was that Black people[2] caused the outbreak.[3]

Black workers, it was claimed, took advantage of those in need, gouged needy families by charging or overcharging for their services, were often of no help, and even stole from the houses of the dead and dying. Specifically, Carey leveled his pen at those caring for the sick at private homes and at Bush Hill who, he claimed, "extorted two, three, four, and even five dollars a night for attendance" (a steep fee in 1793). Yet, grumbled the publisher, the demand for nurses and help was so great that the people had no choice but to put up with the "vilest" of Black people, who took advantage of them.[4]

The result was that "extravagant prices were paid" by sick and dying White patients. Carey goes so far as to suggest that "blacks alone" were guilty of the "selfish" opportunism and profiteering, "having taken the advantage of the distressed situation of the people."[5] Yet Carey also accuses landlords of greed, noting the many cases of them evicting dying, convalescing, and unemployed tenants out of their homes and onto the streets. That allegation was true. Of course, the landlords in the city were all White. Elsewhere, he lauds the courageous behavior of prominent White citizens such as Joseph Inskeep, a member of the mayor's committee, who helped needy families and tended the sick, yet when he contracted the fever, those same families declined to help him. Inskeep died. But Carey failed to mention the families who did not return the kindness were white. He also conveniently overlooked the many acts of bravery and selflessness by Black nurses, attendants, and gravediggers.[6]

In 1794, Reverends Richard Allen and Absolam Jones immediately came to the defense of their community and the work of the Free African Society, releasing their own pamphlet titled *A Narrative of the Proceedings of the Black People*. In it, they refuted each allegation and offered a detailed chronicle of the contributions to the city from the Black community. It also marked the very first publication by someone of African ancestry in America and itself both enjoyed a measure of success and caused Carey to revise his accusations in the subsequent edition of his book.[7]

Allen and Jones opened their pamphlet, explaining, "In consequence of a partial representation of the conduct of the people who were employed to nurse the sick, in the late calamitous state of the city of Philadelphia, we are solicited, by a number of those who feel themselves injured thereby, and by the advice of several respectable citizens, to step forward and declare facts as they were." The authors realized that Carey was influential, and his words would end up framing the memory of the pandemic. Their pamphlet corrected the record.[8]

Correcting the Record

One of the central points raised by Allen and Jones was to remember that it was Dr. Rush and Mayor Clarkson (both aided, ironically, by publishers such as Carey), who solicited the help of the Black community. Black residents stepped in when no one else would and during the most critical weeks of the pandemic. Moreover, many of those first nurses and attendants were volunteers who performed some of the worst and most dangerous jobs without pay.

The members of the Society were, argued the Black preachers, "virtuous" in helping complete strangers and doing so in deplorable working conditions and at a great threat to their own lives. Indeed, the work performed was wretched and took a toll on them. "We have buried *several hundreds* of poor persons and strangers," Allen and Jones remembered, "for which service we have never received nor never asked any compensations." Many members of the Free African Society fell ill, others died, and the work took them away from family and jobs. "Truly, our task was hard," the reverends admitted, "but through mercy, we were able to go on."[9]

The preachers offered numerous examples of the selflessness and dedication by the Black community, such as when they encountered a "poor man" in the grips of the disease who needed a "drink of water." Numerous White residents "passed by . . . and hurried as fast as they could out of the sound of his cries." A neighbor even offered money to anyone who would help but was still "refused by every one." However, a member of the Society approached him, saying, "Master, I will supply the gentleman with water, but surely I will not take your money for it." He fetched the man water and then rendered assistance.[10]

They offered other examples such as Sarah Bass, a "poor black widow" who helped "several families, for which she did not receive any thing" in return. Then there was Mary Scott, who cared for a White man named Richard Mason and his son. Both members of the Mason family died, and the widow offered Ms. Scott money for her services during the family's illnesses. However, the Black nurse only accepted a "half dollar per day," which Mrs. Mason said was not nearly enough. She again offered more money, but it was again refused. Later, the Mason widow established "an annuity of six pounds a year . . . for life" in thanks of the heartfelt service.

It was the same for Caesar Cranchal, a Black resident who, throughout the months-long ordeal, helped the afflicted at the dangerous waterfront, but always announced, "I will not take your money; I will not sell my life for money." He contracted the fever and died, unpaid and unthanked. Another case at the wharf involved a shipping company whose owner, a Mr. Gilpin, died. All the workers had either died or fled. The desperate widow instructed their Black servant to unload the merchandise from a ship and guard the shipping warehouse during the outbreak. The servant did as told throughout the outbreak and despite the dangers of remaining at the docks.[11]

In their rebuttal, Allen and Jones conceded, "That there were some few black people guilty of plundering the distressed." They added, "we acknowledge." However, they pointed out that only these few cases are "made mention of," while ignoring the vast majority of selfless and helpful acts. The allegations, they claimed were only "partial and injurious." The preponderance of the evidence supports Allen and Jones, who added, "We know as many whites who were guilty of it; but this is looked over, while the blacks are held up to censure."[12]

Did members of the Society receive money or demand payment? Yes, but many volunteered free of charge, while others were paid very minimally for life-threatening and essential work. "Our services," wrote the two preachers, "were the production of real sensibility—we sought not fee nor reward, until the increase of the disorder rendered our labour so arduous that we were not adequate to the service we had assumed."

Jones and Allen did place announcements in the newspapers that members of the Society were available to hire. This included for the task of carting away the dead and burying them. The two preachers also hired and paid five Society members (two being Allen's brothers) to remove and bury the dead. Defending the small fee they charged, they reminded the critics that roughly half the city's population—including the government— had fled and that "it was very uncommon, at this time, to find any one that would go near, much more, handle, a sick or dead person." Similarly, families who lost their maids and servants hired the members of the Society, but often times as the economy collapsed were unable to pay them. Regarding those that were paid, they were typically paid less than the White maids and servants working before the outbreak.[13]

Relatedly, "The great prices paid did not escape the observation of that worthy and vigilant magistrate, Matthew Clarkson," noted Allen and Jones. "He sent for us, and requested we would use our influence to lessen the wages of the nurses." The real problem, they pointed out, was "people over-bidding one another." Clarkson did not regulate rates; rather, "it was left to the people concerned," but Black people were generally paid less than their White counterparts . White nurses, wrote Allen and Jones, were paid far more and stole from patients. "We know that six pounds was demanded by and paid to a white woman, for putting a corpse into a coffin; and forty dollars was demanded and paid to four white men, for bringing it down the stairs." Yet some Black people were never paid for similar work. "A poor black man, named Sampson," they recorded, "went constantly from house to house where distress was" to offer "assistance without fee or reward. He was smitten with the disorder," and died. After his death his family were neglected by those he had served.[14]

The rebuttal also asked Carey, had he been requested to perform such wretched labor, "what would he have demanded?" The publisher was selected for the mayor's committee to help with relief. "Yet," the *Narrative* asked, he was helping with organization and fundraising, not nursing and gravedigging, and "quickly after his election, left them to struggle with their arduous and hazardous task, by leaving the city." Allen and Jones, who remained behind, agreed that Carey "had the right to flee, and upon his return, to plead the cause of those who fled." However, he "was wrong in giving so partial and injurious an account of the black nurses." Ironically, Carey went on to make "more money by the sale of his [books] . . . than a dozen . . . black nurses."[15]

The *Narrative* reminded history of the thankless and dangerous jobs performed during the yellow fever scourge. Moreover, "two thirds of the persons, who rendered these essential services, were people of colour." During the outbreak, it was the AME congregants and Society members who became some of the primary caregivers in Philadelphia.[16] The White resident Issac Heston concurred, explaining, "Indeed I don't know what the people would do, if it was not for the Negroes, as they are the Principal nurses." Mayor Clarkson echoed the praise, saying of the Free African Society that "their diligence, attention and decency of department, afforded me, at the time, much satisfaction."[17]

Carey wisely changed his assessment in the third edition of the book, writing that Black people were adequately "remitted as a reward for their peaceable, orderly behavior" and "voluntarily offered themselves as nurses to attend the sick at Bush-hill; and have, in that capacity, conducted themselves with great fidelity, &c."[18]

These brave workers were, as Allen and Jones wrote, "the instruments, in the hand of God, for saving the lives of hundreds of our suffering fellow mortals." Many died. As Allen and Jones noted in a letter to Rush regarding his assurances that those of African descent were immune to yellow fever, "Happy would it have been for you, and much more so for us, had this observation been verified by our experience."[19]

Partisan Politics

In a case of bad timing, the disease struck just as political factions were beginning to formalize into parties. The political rift dated to the beginning—during the struggle to draft and then ratify the Constitution. Various issues served to further divide the nascent parties, such as the hostilities between Britain and France, with Hamilton and the Federalists decrying the "anarchism" of the bloody French

Revolution, and Jefferson and the Republicans decrying English "monarchism."[20] Observers of present-day politics would not be at all surprised to note that the parties were not above fabricating allegations or taking cheap shots, such as when Jefferson and Madison referred to the Federalists as "the Anglican Party" or when Madison sneered in a letter to Jefferson in September of the outbreak, that their opponents are "busy as you may suppose in making the worst of every thing, and in turning the public feelings against France, and thence, in favor of England." He went so far as to call the party of Washington, Adams, and Hamilton "poison," alleging that they "inflame the evil," when, it must be stated, the lion's share of such rhetoric came from his own side of the aisle.[21]

Likewise, Philadelphia's history of abolition and religious tolerance was seen as a threat by southern conservatives, while the flood of refugees from Saint-Domingue simply heightened pro- and anti-French sentiment, racism, and concerns over immigration. Regrettably, but perhaps not surprisingly, in that same vein the fever was seen through partisan eyes and became a tool for both criticizing opponents and promoting a partisan agenda. At the same time, newspapers were highly partisan, often little more than mouthpieces for party leaders and often on the payroll of wealthy partisans. The alarming outbreak became fodder for their readers. Case in point: the papers did not publish all treatments and perspectives on the fever; rather, they suppressed dissenting opinions. Andrew Brown, an Irish-born publisher, for example, used his newspaper *The Federal Gazette* to promote Dr. Rush, a fellow Republican, and his approach to the fever.[22]

Brown, supported by Rush, even sought out government contracts that would cover and print the business of Congress and the administration. He ultimately received a contract from Jefferson and proceeded to hire James Thomson Callender, one of the most notorious practitioners of sensationalism and yellow journalism at the time. On the other hand, newspapers such a John Fenno's *Gazette of the United States*, which relocated from New York City to Philadelphia, were unabashedly pro-Federalist, neglecting to print recommendations from Rush if it disagreed with them.

Both local and national newspapers began, what the scholar Martin Pernick writing in *The William and Mary Quarterly*, termed a "barrage of political-sounding attacks" either for or against Rush's cure. Pernick also summed it up as follows: "Many Philadelphians persisted in the conviction that there was a 'Republican cure' and a 'Federalist cure.'" Rush later sued his critics for libel and even went after newspapers and their publishers that likened his aggressive bloodletting to the French Revolution![23]

The two fledgling parties squared off over the causes of and treatments for the disease, with the Republicans supporting Rush's foul air ("miasma") theory and his advocacy of aggressive purging and bleedings. The Federalists lined up in opposition of these approaches, pondering whether the disease had been imported from the islands and adopting more moderate treatments using herbs, baths, and hygiene. Although several physicians aligned politically and medically with these positions, such as Isaac Cathrall, William Currie, Adam Kuhn, and Edward Stevens, they tended to be apolitical. Whereas Rush was a national celebrity and very political. He did not just advocate his views, he attacked and "belittled" his opponents, including those who believed in the "importationist" source of the disease. Unfortunately, physicians and the public often felt as if they had to "choose" sides.[24]

Of the partisan bickering over treatments, Rush complained, "I think it probable that if the new remedies had been introduced by any other person than a decided [Republican] and a friend of Madison and Jefferson, they would have met with less opposition from Colonel Hamilton." Typical of Rush, he made everything personal and placed himself at the center of all debates. Rush's anger with Hamilton for disagreeing with him in the newspapers was such that he wrote to General Horatio Gates, the traitorous officer who bad-mouthed and even tried to supplant George Washington's command during a critical moment in the Revolutionary War, complaining, "Many of us have been forced to expiate our sacrifices in the cause of liberty by suffering every species of slander and persecution."[25]

Rush also mixed political views and medicine. When criticizing Hamilton's support of a less aggressive treatment for the fever, Rush gushed to Elias Bodinot, a congressman from New Jersey, "Colonel Hamilton's remedies are now as unpopular in our city as his funding system is in Virginia or North Carolina," a reference to Hamilton's debt plan that, although opposed by Republicans and Southerners, put the nation on firm financial footing and erased the large war debt. Rush then highlighted the disappointing merger of politics and medicine at the time, noting the "unkind and resentful association of my political principles with my medical character." Even years after the outbreak, Rush was harboring resentment, yet was always willing to get political.[26]

Jefferson rarely missed an opportunity to put his poetical pen to work criticizing the Federalists, even during the crisis. He delighted, first and foremost, in going after Hamilton, even when the treasury secretary and his wife were ill with the fever, blaming his rival for conjuring his illness. Claimed Jefferson, "He puts himself so by his excessive alarm." Jefferson then dismisses Hamilton as worrying excessively about the fever and lacking courage: "A man as timid as he is on the water, as timid on horseback, as timid in sickness, would be a phenomenon if the courage of which he has the reputation in military occasions were genuine. His friends, who have not seen him, suspect it is only an autumnal fever he has." The irony was that the treasury secretary was renowned for his bravery on the battlefield, whereas Jefferson was frequently gossipy, shy, and easily offended; he also did not serve in uniform during the war. Neither did the frail and weak Madison, who shared in Jefferson's criticisms of Hamilton.[27]

Similarly, both sides argued over quarantines, with the Federalists favoring them and limits on arrivals from the West Indies, while the Republicans worried about trade restrictions and the impact on the economy and plantations; they also fretting about the impact of the slave uprising in Saint-Domingue on other islands and the American South. Rush opposed the quarantines, as he believed the disease originated in foul air, not from the West Indies. Rush went on the attack against anyone supporting "useless" quarantines, such as when he exaggerated, "Thousands of lives have been sacrificed, by that faith in their efficacy, which has led to the neglect of domestic cleanliness." More so, quarantines "extinguished friendship, annihilated religion, and violated the sacraments of nature, by resisting even the loud and vehement cries of filial and parental blood."[28]

Some leaders, such as President Washington and Mayor Clarkson, despite their Federalist leanings, and Governor Mifflin of Pennsylvania, tried to stay above the partisan fray. Yet, ultimately, efforts at bipartisanship failed, prompting Freneau to gripe, "No circumstance has added more to the present calamity" than partisan bickering, even if he was a prime source for it."[29] The young law clerk Isaac Heston, recorded that "poleticks . . . run so high lately" and that the main pastime in the city is the physicians "now differing about the Disorder, and the methods of Cureing." Similarly, Jefferson bemoaned the loss of Dr. Hutcheson, a fellow Republican. In a letter to Madison, however, his focus was on the politics of the disease. He wrote, "Poor Hutcheson dined with me on Friday . . . was taken [by the disease] that night on his return home, & died the day before yesterday. It is difficult to say whether the republican interest has suffered more by his death or Genêt's extravagance."[30]

Accusation and Conspiracy

One of the ways politics was used was by the anti-Federalist faction—later the Democratic-Republicans or just Republicans, which largely represented southern slave-owning interests and opposed a centralized or active role for government—was to attack Federalists who evacuated the capital city. Yet they themselves fled in equal numbers. The *National Gazette*, for instance, a newspaper published by the ardent Jeffersonian, Philip Freneau, opined, "It is not the day of the battle that the officer ought to fly. A physician, if he was certain of falling a sacrifice to the disorder, ought to remain at his post and learn how to die." The criticism was leveled at physicians who disagreed with Dr. Rush and other Jeffersonians in their approach to the disease.[31]

Freneau even penned a satirical poem that attacked Federalists for leaving the city. Never mind that Jefferson and other Republican leaders also evacuated.

Orlando's Flight
On prancing steed, with sponge at nose,
From town behold Orlando fly;
Camphor and Tar where'er he goes
Th' infected shafts of death defy –
Safe in an atmosphere of stink,
No doctor gets Orlando's chink.[32]

Freneau's newspaper often failed to cover the fever, even though it was the most pressing issue facing the capital city and, when there was coverage, it even tried to downplay the fever. Freneau was too busy promoting France, criticizing Washington and Hamilton for the Neutrality Proclamation, and even defending the traitorous Genêt. Ironically, the issue of the *National Gazette* that criticized Federalist-leaning physicians and those who evacuated the city ended up being the very last issue of the paper published before it closed.[33]

Another example was Benjamin Franklin Bache's *General Advertiser*, another Republican newspaper. It shamefully suggested the Anglophobic notion that the disease had come from the *British* West Indies. The disease was, therefore, a foul "present" from the British. Rumors circulated claiming the British, others claiming the French, were behind the troubles and that Dr. Hutchinson kept news of outbreaks on the *Sans Culotte* and other ships quiet on purpose.[34] There were other conspiracy theories, including one that circulated about the fever being a plot by the government. The *National Gazette* went so far as to publish an article in September that listed over one dozen theories about the disease, but never mentioned the possibility of it being imported.[35]

Another conspiracy was that the fever was designed to undermine Philadelphia serving as the interim capital. This came from both sides, as some Jeffersonians worried it was to prevent the capital from moving south to warmer climates (their great concern was to prevent a capital in the north and, with it, a shift in political, economic, and abolitionist power). Meanwhile, Federalists worried about Jefferson's ongoing hostility to large cities such as Philadelphia in favor of his "agrarian ideal." Rush even felt compelled to defend himself, writing on October 28, "A new clamor has been excited against me in which many citizens take part. I have asserted that the yellow fever was generated in our city," and not by a plot. "This assertion they say will destroy the character of Philadelphia for healthiness, and drive Congress from it." National political debates became localized in Philadelphia, while at the same time the crisis in Philadelphia drove the larger political issues around the country.[36]

Eventually, once all treatments continued to fail and the disease had run its course, the city's hallowed College of Physicians released a report on November 26 taking the side of Cathrall, Currie, Kuhn, Stevens, and others, concluding, "No instance has ever occurred of the disease called yellow fever, having been generated in this city, or in any other parts of the United States . . . but there have been frequent instances of its having been imported." The report was written by Drs. John Carson, Samuel Griffitts, and Thomas Parke and, with difficulty, was released over the objections of the Republicans in the College of Physicians on party-line voting. In a fit of anger, Rush resigned from the College of Physicians.[37]

Predictably, many clergy and the religious communities both in Philadelphia and around the country continued to suggest the infliction was a judgment from God. The condemnation of not only fellow citizens, but the city's leaders, and its theater grew as did the deaths and frustrations. Even the Quakers, long the bastion of the city's tolerance and abolitionist tendencies, joined with the pious Christians in demanding the city and state legislature prohibit theatrical productions and entertainment. It had been banned, after all, during part of the Revolutionary War and had only recently been permitted, thus contributing to their argument that it was a cause of the fever.[38]

Preachers' target was the "Synagogue for Satan," their anti-Semitic name for the large Chestnut Street Theater. The new theater featured fluted marble columns and was described in newspapers as "palatial." Therefore, to many residents it was the pride of the city, a showcase of culture missing in the young republic. As soon as the fever ended, sixteen preachers in the city along with Quaker leaders and devout Republicans issued a petition stating, "We conceive that the solemn intimations of Divine Providence in the late distressing calamity which has been experienced in this city, urge upon us in the most forcible manner the duty of reforming every thing which may be offensive to the Supreme Governor of the Universe." That, apparently, included the theater.[39]

That debate was also covered by the newspapers. One of those voices pointing the finger of blame was Freneau, the Republican publisher of the *National Gazette*. Dovetailing on the theological debate about the wrath of God and the city being punished, Freneau ran articles criticizing the "pride" of Federalist leaders, suggesting they caused the fever. Of course, this put Rush, Jefferson, Madison, and others in a pinch, because they were professed men of science and enlightenment, yet their party was delving into conspiracy. Freneau and others even took cheap shots at President Washington. One such example was in a letter to Mathew Carey, where Freneau wrote, "I agree with you in deriving our physical calamities from moral causes. . . . We ascribe all the attributes of the Deity to the name of General Washington. It is considered by our citizens as the bulwark of our nation. God would cease to be what He is, if he did not visit us for these things."[40]

On the heels of the fever, rather than come together, public discourse was boiling over into blame and finger-pointing. Some Republicans, even pointing to the timing, claimed the fever appeared right after actors arrived from England to perform at the city's new theater. Fortunately, after vigorous debate, the legislature voted against closing the theater and banning such forms of entertainment.[41] Still, the rancor and rumors were such that one of the sad impacts of the fever was that it solidified political parties. In the words of one scholar, the 1793 crisis "became an integral chapter in the history of the first party system."[42]

Reforms

The impacts of the fever were not all negative. There were some positive and needed political reforms. One of them occurred as soon as the disease dissipated. On November 14, Mayor Clarkson's committee released a report on how the people should purify their houses, clothing, and bedding and laid out the steps necessary for the city to return to business as usual. Their advice was to open all windows and doors for a few days and that "lime should be thrown into the privies and the chambers whitewashed." A crew of 150 volunteers were assigned the task of inspecting homes throughout the city and taking away beds, bedding, and other items to be "fumigated" or destroyed. They also outlined a ten-day moratorium before nonresidents could enter the city. Not waiting for the report, as soon as the weather cooled, many residents threw their furnishings and clothing out the windows and doors in hopes of disinfecting it.[43]

The city continued with an array of health reforms, including efforts to mandate cleaning the streets and wharfs. Houses that were thought to have been infested were inspected and torn down. Governor Mifflin supported these municipal policies, but ordered that the state, while pursing programs to clean such public sites, would not enforce mandatory inspections at the ports or on ships arriving at the docks from the West Indies. These reforms went so far as to attempt to address landlords who gouged and evicted the needy and sick. Philadelphia established funds to subsidize the rent with small cash payments for those who could not afford to remain in their homes. It was likely, in part, attributed to not only the sheer number of Philadelphians who became homeless during the crisis but to a cruel irony. William Hamilton, the descendent of the family that built Bush Hill, finally returned from Europe to reclaim his mansion. He also happened to be the owner of the home where Dr. Rush resided. Hamilton raised the price of Rush's rent, even though the surgeon had risked his life to treat the city's residents free of charge.

The reforms came not only from the city and state, but from Philadelphia's physicians. From his experience at Bush Hill, Devèze wrote a treatise on yellow fever and needed reforms. "First," he noted, "that the interior part of the city be cleared of tan-yards and starch manufactories." His second recommendation was to enforce cleanliness "of the quays and streets to prevent the water stagnating in the ditches" as well as along construction sites and unpaved roads. Next, he added that the markets be regulated "to prevent green and bad fruit being sold."[44]

Although not fully in agreement with Rush on the theory of "foul air," Devèze did make a point of targeting "another cause, which in my opinion acts infinitely more on" causing contagions. That was the "prodigious number of burial places," some in the downtown and near residential areas. He worried that "vapors" and diseases from the decomposing bodies may "infect the air." Likewise, given the unlined caskets and open burials, the rain might work its way into the graves and then "with it into the wells." The city's wells were sometimes built near cemeteries. Devèze caught the public's attention by using the analogy that when drinking a "glass of water . . . I am about to feed upon a being like myself, to swallow particles from dead bodies." He recommended instead, a "fire-pump" be built on the Delaware River "to raise water into the city," along with a canal and pumps on the Schuylkill River, thereby providing an abundant source of fresh water for the city. Most practically, Devèze called for bathing regularly in summer and washing one's mouth "every morning and after each meal with water and vinegar."[45]

The city called for big projects as well, such as constructing a massive public water system. It was designed by the famed architect Benjamin Henry Latrobe, who worked on the US Capitol. Latrobe's waterworks moved water by steam engine pumps from the Schuylkill River to a central pumping facility located at Broad and High Streets. Another steam pump then moved the water to large wooden reservoirs. From there, gravity could deliver it to area homes.

Perhaps most importantly, Philadelphia built a new hospital and a municipal water system, the first and most advanced of its kind in the country. Other cities followed suit, and quarantines and sanitary reforms spread across the country, mostly in the northern states. There were other impacts. The future growth of the city was impacted, as people moved away from the waterfront and also to rural areas outside the city border. Even though the Residence Act—locating the national capital along the Potomac River in what today is Washington, DC, after a ten-year interim in New York City and Philadelphia—was signed into law in 1790, there were still those who either wanted or expected the capital would permanently return to Philadelphia. The fear generated from the pandemic all but ended such ideas.

EPILOGUE
One Hundred Days of Terror

Fever makes my body
A bit like the mind—
Tender.
Sensitive.
Flushed.
Pain clogging throat, ears
Be like chapters
If you focus, you read and learn
A thing or two.

—Jumelia's "Yellow Fever," 2020

Death Toll

Mathew Carey suggested that perhaps twice as many men died as women from the yellow fever in Philadelphia. If he was correct, it was likely on account of men being more likely to be working outside at the docks, the site where the outbreak started. He and others also wrote that other groups suffered higher death rates, including the old, weak, and poor, along with "tipplers and drunkards" and "filles de joie." Government reports, burial records, and newspaper articles point to higher losses of life along the wharf and waterfront. Certain streets such as Pewter Platter Alley, which had only thirty homes, lost thirty-two people. On the other hand, a similar number of people died on Market Street, despite it boasting over 170 homes. Likewise, far fewer people died in rural communities with "country air" than in the city itself. What is certain is that the entire city was affected and people of all backgrounds and neighborhoods succumbed to the fever.[1]

Carey initially estimated that people died in Philadelphia, but in a later edition of his book revised the number upward to 6,000. These figures amount to roughly 10 percent of Philadelphia's population. Other sources offer similar numbers, suggesting that, at a bare minimum, at least five thousand people died in the city and at least 20,000 evacuated, constituting at least one-third of the population. Carey put the number who fled at between 17,000 and 23,000, while Mayor Clarkson guessed that 21,000 residents abandoned the city. The official government records on the disease estimate that from August 1 to November 9, 5,000 Philadelphians died. The numbers do not include all the government workers or members of Congress, who were not permanent residents, and they do not consider the many more who fell ill but lived. So, too, the counts based on burials in church and city cemeteries do not fully reflect the poor who went unburied or were interred in unmarked mass graves. Nor do they consider bodies on ships that were simply thrown overboard or people living on the outskirts of the city in rural areas. Yet, the official count is all the more staggering when one considers that the plague raged only from early August to early November, or roughly 100 days. Ultimately, it is likely far more people died from the yellow fever than were ever reported.[2]

For perspective, the loss of one-tenth of the capital city's (Washington) population today would put the figure at over 70,000 people, whereas one-tenth of Philadelphia's population today constitutes over 158,000. In addition, the fact that the yellow fever outbreak of 1793 spread to New York, Baltimore, throughout New Jersey, as far south as Charleston, South Carolina, and elsewhere, means that likely tens of thousands of lives in the new nation were lost that summer and fall. It must be remembered that the nation's population at the time was just shy of four million people. It was therefore one of the worst epidemics in American history, comparable only to the Spanish influenza outbreak in 1918 and the COVID-19 pandemic of the 2020s.[3]

The city lost ten physicians: Drs. Hutchinson, Morris, Linn, Pennington, Dodds, Johnson, Glentworth, Phile, Graham, and Green. This is an alarmingly large number, given how few professionally trained physicians were practicing in the new nation at the time. Moreover, many of those members of Philadelphia's medical community who did not die either fell ill or evacuated the city. Likewise, the city buried many of its members of the clergy: Alexander Murray (Episcopalian), F. A. Fleming and Laurence Graefsl (Roman Catholic), John Winkhaufe (German Reformed), James Sproat (Presbyterian), William Dougherty (Methodist), Daniel Offlye, Hufon Longstroth, and Charles Williams (Quaker), and others. As was the case with physicians, many other members of the cloth contracted the disease, including R. Blackwell, Joseph Pilmore, William Rogers, Christopher V. Keating, Frederick Schmidt, Joseph Turner, and others.[4]

Fortunately for history, Mayor Clarkson's committee, the publisher Mathew Cary, and several physicians and preachers all compiled lists of the deceased. The committee even released a full report in March 1794.[5]

Legacy

In 1792, the naive but noble abolitionists who set sail from England aboard the doomed ship *Hankey* intended to provide an example to the world of an expedition that would help end slavery. Their "ship of death" would end up impacting the world, just not in the way they intended. It ended up bringing mosquitoes and a pandemic of yellow fever across the Atlantic to the West Indies and United States. The ship inadvertently unleashed death at every port where it docked, which may have been as many as one dozen. As historian Billy Smith, concluded, "Until the *Hankey's* voyage . . . the conditions that were to detonate the yellow fever bomb had never been present in so many places at the same time and with such ferocity."[6]

In an ironic and roundabout way, the *Hankey* did contribute in small measure to the eventual demise of the "peculiar institution." The transatlantic slave trade existed long before the United States was a major economic power and source of colonization and development in the western hemisphere. Slavery was woven into the fabric of American society throughout the South. There were many long-standing and powerful forces that contributed to the ubiquity of slavery and its longevity on the continent. A number of forces and new mindsets ultimately contributed to its demise, including the bloodiest war ever fought on American soil, but another factor was the spread of disease often brought aboard slave ships.[7]

Bird flu, swine flu, SARS, Ebola, HIV, West Nile virus, COVID-19, and other diseases originating in far-off places have wreaked havoc on populations around the world, including in the United States. They have decimated entire communities, impacted the outcome of wars, changed the patterns of future growth, prompted advances in medicine, led people to find God, and much more. Something as small as a mosquito, a nearly invisible stowaway on sailing ships, was behind the first pandemic to strike the new nation, one that would impact the development of political parties, patterns of growth in cities, the location of the capital city, a revolution in the West Indies, the selling and purchase of the Louisiana Territory, the building of public water works, creation of public health departments and municipal sanitation programs, and much more, including the end of slavery, as Americans and Europeans began to see Africa as "a white man's graveyard."[8]

Long before globalization and the modern era, the world was becoming interconnected and interdependent in profound and not always positive ways. The yellow fever outbreak in 1793 is but one, albeit tragic, example of a chain of circumstances in the United States. The threat of a return of this dreaded disease remained for a century afterward, as generations remembered the "Great Philadelphia Plague" as one of "the worst, the most frightening" diseases in American history. As historian J. M. Powell summarized, "It was the most appalling collective disaster that had ever overtaken an American city" at the time.[9]

Rush

Dr. Benjamin Rush was at the center of the yellow fever outbreak, as he was the face of the young republic's medical community. After he resigned in a huff from the College of Physicians, Rush helped to establish a new medical organization and, in 1798, was appointed as the head physician of a new fever hospital.

Rush continued to profoundly influence the practice of medicine in America. He also played a role in future outbreaks of yellow fever in 1794, 1797, and beyond, often commuting from his new home outside the city into the fever's furnace each day to once again care for his patients. His courage remained, but he did alter his treatments somewhat. Rush continued purging and bleeding his patients, but perhaps due to the criticism he received, he was less aggressive in purging his patients, realizing excessive evacuations weakened those already ill.

Although he was frequently wrong in his diagnoses and treatments—and at times to the point of endangering the lives of those in his care—Rush's reputation survived the yellow fever outbreak. He remained confident in his abilities and approach to both the fever and medicine in general, while his meticulous writings ended up influencing generations of American physicians. As one scholar stated, Rush would "have a significant impact on how disease—not merely yellow fever, but disease in general—was treated in America."[10]

Indeed, he was hailed by the great Oliver Wendell Holmes who, while addressing the Massachusetts Medical Society in 1860, said of one of the founders of American medicine, "If I wish [students] to understand the tendencies of the American medical mind . . . I would make him read the life and writings of Benjamin Rush." Holmes goes on to say, "He taught thousands of American students, he gave a direction to the medical mind of the country more than any other one man; perhaps he typifies it better than any other."[11]

Rush not only saw an impressive number of patients in all stages of the fever, but bravely and repeatedly risked his life for his patients. He was also relentless in documenting every facet of the affliction. The scholar Paul Kopperman, writing in the *Bulletin of the History of Medicine*, concluded, "It was from the epidemic of 1793 that his coherent philosophy of pathology and therapeutics would spring."[12] Through his detailed notes, relationships with other physicians, and his collection of books, he developed a detailed understanding of pathology for the time. As Rush recorded in his journals, "Many painful hours have I spent in contemplating this subject. At length light broke in upon my mind. The phenomena of fever suddenly appeared to me in a new order: I instantly combined them into a new theory." He proudly boasted that "the conquest of this formidable disease, was not the effect of accident, nor of the application of a single remedy; but, it was the triumph of a principle in medicine!"[13]

Rush was well educated and, without question, a brilliant and courageous physician. He was vigilant in reading the texts from antiquity and putting to practice noted medical thinkers and practitioners. But he also borrowed from some physicians before him whose ideas had become discredited or were embroiled in controversy. Similarly, for a man of medicine and science, Rush was also a zealot, believing "there does not exist a disease for which the goodness of Providence has not a remedy," believing that God would guide his hand. Rush was therefore often unquestioning of his subsequent methods, irrespective of the results and facts before him.[14]

At the time, most physicians avoided weighing in on matters of politics as well as pontificating on topics of which they were uncertain. This never stopped Rush. He was blatantly political, allowed his political views to shape his approach to medicine, and was often thin-skinned to the point of being vindictive. Rush, it has been said, "seldom held back, even when he had little or no hard evidence to serve as his base." In his eyes, he did not need the evidence—he was supremely confident and his faith, as much as science, guided him.[15]

Rush's former student, Dr. Charles Caldwell, ended up disagreeing with his former mentor. Caldwell lived well into the nineteenth century and later wrote, "Dr. Rush had not an *original* mind," adding "for it is not known to me that he ever made a discovery in science."[16]

The criticism of Rush grew during the outbreak, with the publisher William Cobbett decrying "remorseless bleeding." Rush sued the paper and others for libel. "Blood, blood! Still they cry more blood," Cobbett continued, suggesting Rush's patients would "bleed to death." Another publisher Rush sued suggested Rush's "thirst for popularity" guided his public works. Another Rush critic, William Patterson, scoffed, "A physician, who is constantly busied, *sees* to much, and does not *think* enough." Another physician was so distraught over Rush's obviously dangerous methods that he challenged the famous surgeon to a duel! Indeed, Rush's contributions had nothing to do with his effectiveness during the yellow fever outbreak, but rather came from his charisma, political connections, and penchant for self-promotion. The scholar Bob Arnebeck concluded that Rush did little to stop the spread of the disease or save lives—and likely cost far more lives through his aggressive treatments and overconfidence.[17]

Rush looked back on his efforts through rose-colored glasses, still believing he was correct on every issue. Even after the disease passed, he wrote, "This victory . . . has not been a cheap one. It has been purchased at the expense of much labour and obloquy. The number of patients who died under my care, has been much exaggerated, and the most affecting stories have been circulated of their dying under the immediate use of my remedies."[18]

Despite his many difficult qualities and mixed record during the pandemic, Rush's writings remain a treasure trove for both physicians and historians. He was as meticulous and dedicated as he was vain and dogmatic. Aware that the eyes of history would be cast on the 1793 outbreak and his leadership during it, Rush hoped that his books would "throw additional light upon the disorder," while also offering an important "lesson" for future generations facing health crises. Rush hoped his example would inspire those "placed in similar circumstances, to commit their lives without fear, to the protection of that BEING who is able to save to the uttermost, not only from future, but from present evil."[19]

His legacy remains considerable, though despite the praise that continues to surround him, it was undeniably complicated. At the same time, Rush's legacy will forever be inextricably tied to the first great pandemic in American history. The scholar Paul Kopperman offered an interesting assessment that, in a way, Rush needed yellow fever not only to develop his theories of pathology, but to feed his considerable ego.[20] The celebrated doctor lived until April 19, 1813, passing at sixty-eight years old in Philadelphia during a typhus outbreak. He was buried at Christ Church not far from the grave of Benjamin Franklin. The American Medical Association erected a statue of him in Philadelphia in 1904.

As for the College of Physicians, one of the oldest professional medical organizations in the country, it also survived the yellow fever pandemic and is still a hallowed institution in Philadelphia. The nonprofit continues to keep alive the history of medicine with a museum on medical history as well as promoting public health.[21]

Philadelphians

Fortunately, several other leaders, physicians, and residents in Philadelphia wrote their accounts of the yellow fever ordeal, providing an array of perspectives. One of them was the Rev. Justus Henry Christian Helmuth, the Lutheran pastor from Germany, who penned *A Short Account of the Yellow Fever in Philadelphia* in 1794. Philadelphia had one of the largest German populations in the young nation and Helmuth's congregation was one of the largest in the city. One can almost forgive Helmuth for casting the wrath of God on much of the city, as fully 641 German Lutherans perished from the fever.[22]

Helmuth survived the outbreak and remained as the pastor at Philadelphia's St. Michael's and Zion Parish, the largest Lutheran congregation in the United States. He also served as a professor of German language and went on to be a trustee at the University of Philadelphia. He also founded the first Lutheran church newspaper in the United States, *Evangelisches Magasin*, in 1812. Helmuth lived until the ripe age of eighty, passing in 1825.

The diarist Elizabeth Drinker also lived a long life, passing at the then-advanced age of seventy-three on December 1, 1807. Fortunately, as a young woman she developed a "fondness for literature" which prompted her to keep a detailed diary; her writing survived and a few of her accounts are included throughout this book. The diary was organized and published many years after her death by one of her descendants under the title *Extracts from the Journal of Elizabeth Drinker*.

Besides the books by Rush, another medical account of the yellow fever titled *A Description of the Malignant, Infectious Fever Prevailing at Present in Philadelphia* was published in the midst of the pandemic by Dr. William Currie, who was a prolific writer of scores of medical essays and books. Currie also survived the disease, living until 1828.

The leaders of the Free African Society, Richard Allen and Absalom Jones, also survived the fever and wrote their account of the heroic work done by the Black community. Under the title *A Narrative of the Proceedings of the Black People*, it was meant to set the record straight and rebut the criticisms from Mathew Carey. It would become the first book published in the new nation by an African American. Today, streets and schools in the area are named for Allen and Jones. Happily, the two men remained lifelong friends, enjoyed long lives, and went on to numerous other worthy accomplishments. Jones was the first African American to become an ordained priest, which he accomplished in 1802 with the Diocese of Pennsylvania. He also founded a day school for Black children—the Female Benevolent Society—and other educational and social organizations. In 1800, Rev. Jones called upon Congress and President John Adams to abolish the slave trade. He did not live to see that happen; the man affectionately known as "The Black Bishop" passed in 1818.[23]

Allen's first wife died in 1801. He married his second wife, Sarah Bass, a freed slave from Virginia. She became his partner in the establishment of the African Methodist Episcopal Church in Philadelphia and other AME congregations around the country, earning her the name "Founding Mother" of the AME Church. The couple had six children who, like Jones, were angered to observe that schools and White churches would not provide equal educational opportunities to Black children, even in Philadelphia. As such, they promoted equal education for Black children, offered literacy classes at their church, and helped to organize the first "Negro Convention," held in Philadelphia in 1830, which was attended by church leaders. They later opened their Spruce Street home as a "station" on the Underground Railroad, helping escaped slaves until the reverend's death on March 26, 1831. Allen was buried in the cemetery of the church he founded.[24]

Mayor Matthew Clarkson served in office until 1796. He remained popular and was widely recognized for his enlightened leadership during the yellow fever outbreak. He passed in the city he loved on October 5, 1800, at the age of sixty-seven. He is buried at Christ Church Cemetery, the church used by many of the founding fathers during their time in Philadelphia.

Mathew Carey, the publisher from Ireland, also survived yellow fever. He went on to write multiple accounts of the fever, including his controversial and critical book of the city's Black workers and the leaders of the Free African Society. The rebuttal of his book prompted him to offer a more charitable telling in the subsequent edition. He continued publishing and enjoyed further success, most especially of his map of Washington, DC, released in 1802 and considered the best map of the new capital. Because of that book Carey is credited with being the originator of the name "The Mall" for the area in front of the Capitol Building. Other successful books and publications followed. Carey retired in 1825, passing his publishing company to his son and son-in-law. The company went on to publish the *Encyclopedia Americana* and books by such noted authors as Sir Walter Scott and James Fenimore Cooper. He lived a long life—especially for the time—passing on September 16, 1839, at age seventy-nine.

Stephen Girard, the director of Bush Hill, lived through the fever outbreak. As was mentioned earlier, the wealthy, self-made financier purchased most of the shares of the First Bank of the United States after its charter expired in 1811, largely because of opposition by Republicans. He reestablished the bank, hired his own managers, and permitted trustees of the former Bank of the United States to use its offices. Girard extended credit to many people and organizations and helped to fund the War of 1812. He was also long-lived, passing in Philadelphia at the age of eighty-one the day after Christmas in 1831. He was still in vigorous health the year before but was struck by a horse-drawn wagon on December 22, 1830, while crossing the road near Market Street. The wagon wheel ran over his head, and Girard never fully recovered. He was perhaps the wealthiest man in the country at the time of his death, leaving the lion's share of his fortune to charities. Today, streets and parks in the city are named in his honor.[25]

Jean Devèze survived the ordeal of treating many patients at Bush Hill. He also penned a short account of the disease, *An Enquiry into, and Observations Upon the Causes and Effects of the Epidemic Disease*. In it, he credits the leadership and volunteers at the fever hospital for their selfless and tireless work, which he called "the most meritorious acts of benevolence and charity."[26] Though never attaining a fraction of the acclaim of Rush, Devèze, by today's standards, "treated his patients with the greater humanity and knowledge" and was also willing to adapt his treatments to his experiences and observations. It has been said of Devèze that he has been "overlooked by almost all subsequent medical writers . . . and even today is not fully appreciated." The scholars Bob Arnebeck and John Lane, both of whom have written on the yellow fever outbreak, noted that "Benjamin Rush has been given credit where it did not belong to him" rather, "Credit belongs to Devèze." His noble service is all the more impressive when one considers that he had lost everything when forced to flee his home in Saint-Domingue. Devèze lived until 1826.[27]

These many heroic figures from the yellow fever pandemic were fortunate to have survived the outbreak. Thousands of their fellow citizens were not as lucky. A long, descriptive, and helpful letter about the disease, written at the height of the outbreak in the city, was penned by a young law clerk named Isaac Heston. Not much is known about Heston, except that he was born in October of 1770 in Philadelphia and was a Quaker. The letter, written from his home on 72 North Front Street on September 19, was to his brother Abraham. As was excerpted throughout this book, the letter contains touching accounts of the struggles faced by those living in the city. Heston died the day after mailing the letter, just days shy of his twenty-third birthday.[28]

At Last, a Cure

The 1793 scourge was not the end of yellow fever in the United States, or even in Philadelphia. There were additional outbreaks each summer from 1794 to 1799 in Philadelphia and elsewhere, along with a few episodes in the early 1800s. More people died in outbreaks of the yellow fever in New Orleans in 1853 and in Memphis in 1878. The 1793 pandemic, in the words of one scholar, "retains almost mythical status" in the history of American diseases. The nation was new and struggling and the 1793 outbreak would end up having a profound impact on the country and public health as a whole.[29]

Other cities, from Baltimore to Boston and Norfolk to New Haven all had minor outbreaks in subsequent years. However, in these and other future incidents, the common belief was that the fever was not contagious, so there was less use of quarantines and less panic from the public. However, the debates over Rush's treatments continued, as did quarrels among politicians and concerns about trade and immigration by the public. Those living in coastal or low-lying communities, with the means to do so, typically moved out of cities in the "sickly season" of late summer, a practice that continued until the dawn of the twentieth century.[30] From 1793 to 1905, it is estimated that roughly 100,000 Americans died from yellow fever. In 1905, the last serious outbreak occurred in New Orleans.[31]

The quest to understand and then develop a cure for yellow fever was a long, complicated, and deadly ordeal. The theory that the disease was caused by the lowly mosquito was not popularized until 1881, courtesy of a Cuban physician named Carlos Finlay.

Yellow fever had been recorded in Cuba since 1649, and outbreaks there claimed thousands, the worst of which killed an estimated one-third of Havana's population. Interestingly, Dr. Finlay claimed that it was none other than Dr. Rush's account of the 1793 outbreak that gave him the idea that mosquitoes were to blame. Rush, without realizing it, recorded that "mosquitoes (the usual attendants of a sickly autumn) were uncommonly numerous" at the time and he also recorded red marks on his patients that resembled mosquito bites. Sadly, Finley's work was initially dismissed by both the public and medical community.[32]

Finlay's mosquito was the perfect transmitter. Essentially an airborne syringe, the insect's long, hollow proboscis is designed to cut into skin, find a capillary, and drink blood. Mosquitoes consume nectar from flowers and fruits, but the females will supplement their diet with blood, which enhances the development of their eggs. Although the insects prefer animal blood, they will use human hosts. There are 2,500 varieties of mosquitoes and all of them are nearly invisible, voracious hunters, spreading such illnesses as dengue fever, encephalitis, malaria, West Nile virus, and yellow fever. As a result, these tiny insects have likely killed more humans than sharks, snakes, lions, or any other animal.

A breakthrough in the science of yellow fever came during the Spanish-American War of 1898, when American, Cuban, and Spanish soldiers all contracted the deadly scourge. In the relatively short, successful conflict, the United States lost just over four hundred soldiers in combat, but many times that amount were either sick or succumbed to yellow fever, malaria, or one of the other tropical diseases found on the island. As was the case with the slave uprising in Saint-Domingue against their French colonial masters, the disease helped to defeat the Spanish. It is estimated that of the 230,000 Spanish troops stationed in Cuba, only about 55,000 were able to fight. The rest were sick or dying. At the same time, yellow fever and malaria were slaughtering French engineers and Panamanian workers attempting to build a canal across the isthmus in 1899. The leader of the endeavor, Count Ferdinand de Lesseps, ignored warnings about the tropical diseases until it was too late. At least thirty thousand workers died during the failed attempt.

In 1900 and 1901, while studying the illnesses among the army in the same part of the world, American pathologist Dr. Walter Reed read Finlay's work. Major Reed wrote that some kind of "alien parasite" was the source of infection. His discovery came while organizing a sanitary hospital in Cuba in an effort to address the diseases that were running rampant. Reed and three other physicians tested their theory in experiments by allowing themselves and volunteers to be bitten by infected mosquitoes![33] He then confirmed Dr. Finlay's theory—yellow fever was transmitted by a particular mosquito species.[34]

It is, we now know, transmitted by females of the mosquito species *Aedes aegypti*, who pass on the disease by biting the next victim. The yellow fever virus was successfully isolated in 1927 and a vaccine developed one decade later by Dr. Max Theiler, a South African–born American virologist.[35] Today, the vaccine is safe, widely available, and a single dose provides protection for life for most people. Yellow fever can be diagnosed in simple laboratory tests as well as through observable symptoms. Tragically, the vaccine and testing are less accessible in sub-Saharan Africa, the place where people are most at risk of infection.

The first scientist to identify *Aedes aegypti* was the Danish naturalist Johann Christian Fabricius, who made the discovery around 1800. A colleague of Dr. Fabricius brought two samples of the insect back to Denmark from the Dutch island of St. Croix. It turned out that Fabricius was a student of the great Linnaeus and was working on a classification system for the insect kingdom. He observed that *Aedes aegypti* was slightly smaller than other mosquitoes and had unique black and silver stripes on its back. In another interesting twist, Fabricius studied in Edinburgh, Scotland, with a young Benjamin Rush.[36]

It is also known that the disease can be rather effectively prevented by wearing long-sleeve shirts and long pants, avoiding times when mosquitoes are most active, and through common insect repellents. Likewise, public health officials encourage people to not let stagnant water collect during warm months in places like birdbaths, planters, buckets, discarded tires, and potholes. Such places can function as nurseries for mosquitoes. Yet even today, globally there are some 200,000 yellow fever infections per year, and the disease still kills 30,000 people annually, the lion's share in Africa.

APPENDIX A

Time Line of Events

1741
Yellow fever strikes Virginia

1762
Yellow fever strikes Philadelphia

1776
Declaration of Independence signed in Philadelphia

1787
Convention in Philadelphia produces the US Constitution

1790
June 20: A deal struck between Alexander Hamilton and Thomas Jefferson/James Madison arranges for an interim capital for a decade, during which time the future seat of government will be built by the Potomac River

December 6: The federal government relocates from its temporary home in New York City to Philadelphia

1791
A slave uprising starts in Saint-Domingue

1792
French government sends troops to Saint-Domingue to put down the uprising

April 13: William Clarkson begins first term as mayor of Philadelphia

November: The ship *Hankey* flees the West African island of Bolama, carrying yellow fever

February 13: Congress counts the Electoral College votes and George Washington is unanimously elected to a second term

March 4: George Washington's second inauguration

Spring: White French colonial refugees begin fleeing Saint-Domingue

July: Refugees from Saint-Domingue arrive in the United States, including about one thousand in Philadelphia, bringing yellow fever; one of the ships is the *Hankey*, whose passengers are ill with yellow fever

July 22: French Privateer *Sans Culottes* docks at Philadelphia with the *Flora*, a ship she captured; both ships may be carrying yellow fever

July 24: Ship *Amelia* docked at Philadelphia with her captain and crew sick with yellow fever; crew unloads rotted coffee at the docks

August 4: Mr. Moore dies at Denny's Lodging House on Water Street

August 6 or 7: Dr. Hodge's child dies in Philadelphia

August 7: Mrs. Parkinson died at Denny's Lodging House; the *Mary*, a ship with refugees from Saint-Domingue, arrives in Philadelphia

August 7–18: Dr. Rush visits sick patients near the waterfront

August 19: Peter Aston's death prompts Dr. Rush to diagnose and identify the contagion

August 20: Mrs. Lemaigre dies; Dr. Rush sees Mayor Clarkson and Governor Mifflin to inform them of the epidemic

August 22: Mayor Clarkson issues first public "notice" about the disease

August 23: Newspapers begin to publish advice on dealing with the disease

August 24: Dr. Rush notifies Dr. Hutchinson of the disease

August 25: On Mayor Clarkson's request, the College of Physicians meets to make recommendations about the disease

August 26–31: The exodus out of Philadelphia begins

August 27: Governor Mifflin orders Dr. Hutchinson to inspect the docks for the disease

August 29: Governor Mifflin addresses the state legislature about the disease; the Guardians of the Poor meet with city leaders about the need for a hospital

August 31: Letter from the College of Physicians containing guidelines about the disease is published in city newspapers; Guardians of the Poor establish Bush Hill as a fever hospital

September: Reverends Allen and Jones organize the Black community to help with relief; Pennsylvania Assembly was scheduled to meet the first week in September in Philadelphia; annual meeting of the Society of Friends was scheduled to meet in Philadelphia

September 2: Believing those of African descent are immune, Dr. Rush publishes an appeal in the newspaper asking for assistance from the city's Black community

September 6: Treasury Secretary Hamilton, ill with disease, is unable to attend an emergency Cabinet meeting

September 7: Dr. Hutchinson dies of the disease

September 8: Forty-two people die in Philadelphia

September 10: Dr. Rush releases his guide for treating epidemic in Philadelphia; President Washington departs the city on a previously scheduled vacation back to Virginia; mayor announces that the Guardians and Bush Hill need assistance

September 11: Hamilton begins publishing newspaper essays with his concerns about the medical treatment; Hamilton contacts the College of Physicians about his concerns

September 12: Mayor issues another announcement for assistance in dealing with the disease and forms a committee to take over the Guardians' work and supervise response to the disease; Governor Clinton of New York issues proclamation against Philadelphians traveling to his state; governor of Maryland does the same; within days, cities and states across the country issue similar quarantines and prohibitions

September 13: Mayor's Committee issued their report about deplorable conditions at Bush Hill

September 14: Committee borrows money from Bank of North America to fund Bush Hill and relief efforts

September 15: Frenchman Stephen Girard steps forward to assume control of Bush Hill; Peter Helm agrees to assist Girard; parishioners flock to Reverend Helmuth's Lutheran church in fear and defiance

September 16: Girard and Helm issue their own report on conditions at Bush Hill and the need for relief

September 17: Girard and Helm hire physicians and nurses, as well as Dr. Devèze, who had practiced medicine in Saint-Domingue

September 18: President Washington lays cornerstone for a Capitol in the new federal city; Secretary of State Jefferson returns to Virginia; State Department had only one clerk remaining in Philadelphia

September 19: Secretary of War Knox departs Philadelphia, eventually going to New England; Hamilton departs for New York after his bout with the fever; Comptroller Oliver Wolcott Jr. departed with Knox; committee procures housing for all the orphans in the city

October 1: Beginning in October, over 100 people per day die in the city; roughly 130 of Reverend Helmuth's parishioners die in first week of October

October 3: With death toll rising, the Mayor's Committee obtains a library for the growing population of orphans

October 15: Bank of Pennsylvania begins offering leniency for customers struggling with pandemic

October 16: Weather cools a bit

October 17: Articles start to appear in New York City newspapers suggesting Philadelphia is unsafe and Congress can come back to New York to meet

October 25: Some former residents return to Philadelphia; some stores open

October 27: Weather turns cold for a day

October 31: White flag raised above Bush Hill signaling there were no new sick patients for the first time

November 1793: Congress scheduled to being next session in Philadelphia

November 1: On advice from Hamilton, President Washington convenes his cabinet in Germantown on outskirts of Philadelphia

November 11: President Washington visits Philadelphia

November 14: Mayor's committee issues report on how to purify houses

1794
Dr. Rush, Dr. Devèze, Allen/Jones, Mathew Carey, and others all publish accounts of the pandemic

1802
French troops temporarily regain control of Saint-Domingue

1803
Uprising in Saint-Domingue defeats French troops

1900
Dr. Water Reed establishes sanitary hospital in Cuba where yellow fever was decimating the population

1927
Yellow fever virus finally isolated and identified by scientists

APPENDIX B
Map of Philadelphia

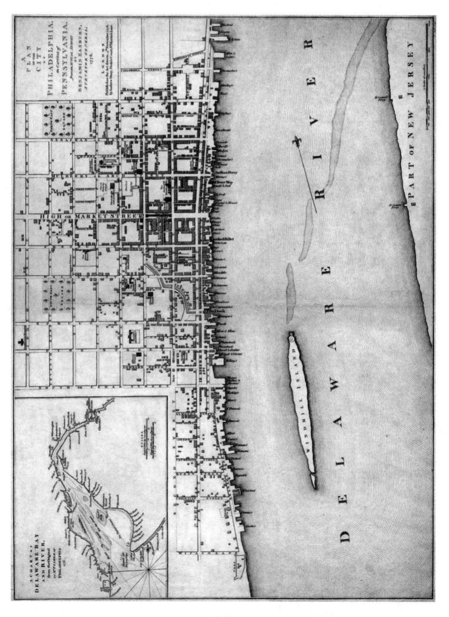

ABBREVIATIONS

ADA	*American Daily Advertiser*
CoP	College of Physicians
FG	*Federal Gazette*
FO	*Founders Online*
GUS	*Gazette of the United States*
GA	*General Advertiser*
IC	*Independent Chronicle*
IG	*Independent Gazetteer*
LoR	Letters of Rush
NG	*National Gazette*
NIH	National Institutes of Health
PG	*Philadelphia Gazette*
PoJ	Papers of Jefferson
WM	*Weekly Museum*
WHO	World Health Organization

NOTES

Prologue

1. A variation of the British rhyme reads: "Beware, beware, the bight of Benin; one comes out where fifty went in."

2. Billy G. Smith, *Ship of Death: A Voyage That Changed the Atlantic* (New Haven, CT: Yale University Press, 2013), 1–2.

3. Smith, *Ship of Death*, 1.

4. Smith, *Ship of Death*, 2.

5. Wilberforce lived from 1759 to 1833.

6. Carol Bolton, "The Bolama Colony and Abolitionary Reform in Captain Beaver's African Memoranda, 1805," *Romance, Revolution and Reform: The Journal of the Southampton Centre for Nineteenth Century Research* 3 (January 2021): 106.

7. Thomas Lewis, "Transatlantic Slave Trade," Encyclopedia Britannica, accessed February 1, 2022, http://www.britannica.com/topic/transatlantic-slave-trade; Steven Mintz, "Historical Context: Facts About the Slave Trade and Slavery," The Gilder-Lehrman Institute of American History, http://www.gilder-lehrman.org/history-resources/teacher-resources/historical-context-facts-about-slave-trade-and-slavery.

8. The Middle Passage is the name for the route across the Atlantic Ocean used for the forcible transportation of enslaved Africans.

9. The courts initially ruled in favor of Collingwood and that the insurers had to pay, but on appeal the decision was overturned.

10. Trevor Burnard, "A New Look at the Zong Case of 1783," *Revue de la Société d'Etudes Anglo-Américains* 76 (2019), www.journals.openedition.org/1718/1808.

11. The 1807 statute did not eliminate the legal status of individuals enslaved before its enactment. The United States would end the slave trade the next year, but not the practice of slavery, which would have to wait until 1865.

12. "William Wilberforce: Leader of the British Abolition Campaign," https://21wilberforce.org/william-wilberforce-leader-of-the-british-abolition -campaign/?utm_source=rss&utm_medium=rss&utm_campaign=william-wilber force-leader-of-the-british-abolition-campaign.

13. Lewis, "Transatlantic Slave Trade"; Mintz, "Historic Context."

14. Captain Beaver lived from 1766 to 1813.

15. Beaver, *African Memoranda*, 3.

16. Beaver, *African Memoranda*, 4.

17. Smith, *Ship of Death*, 2.

18. Quoted in Robin Law, Suzanne Schwarz, and Silke Strickrodt, *Commercial Agriculture, the Slave Trade and Slavery in Atlantic Africa* (Woodbridge, England: Boydell & Brewer, 2013), 2.

19. Smith, *Ship of Death*, 2.

20. Bolton, "Bolama Colony," 106.

21. Deidre Coleman, "Bulama and Sierra Leone: Utopian Islands and Visionary Interiors," in *Islands in History and Representations*, eds. Rod Edmond and Venessa Smith (London: Routledge, 2003), 63–81; Schwarz, "Commerce," 270.

22. The historic record gives different spellings for Bolama.

23. Sometimes referred to as the Bijagós Islands.

24. Smith, *Ship of Death*, 75.

25. See UNESCO's World Heritage List at www.whc.unesco.org/en/list/.

26. Smith, *Ship of Death*, 3.

27. Beaver, *African Memoranda*, 14.

28. In 1788, the British started sending convicts to Australia. After the Revolutionary War, they could no longer send them to America.

29. Smith, *Ship of Death*, 3.

30. Beaver, *African Memoranda*, 426; Smith, *Ship of Death*, 8.

31. Smith, *Ship of Death*, 12.

32. Smith, *Ship of Death*, 49–50.

33. "An Act for the Gradual Abolition of Slavery—March 1, 1780," Pennsylvania Historical & Museum Commission, www.phmc.state.pa.us/portal/com munities/documents/1776-1865/abolition-slavery.html.

34. Beaver, *African Memoranda*, 431.

35. Beaver, *African Memoranda*, 427–28.

36. Smith, *Ship of Death*, 49.

37. Smith, *Ship of Death*, 7.

38. Smith, *Ship of Death*, 36.

39. Smith, *Ship of Death*, 11.
40. Smith, *Ship of Death*, 36–37.
41. Marcus Rediker, *Between the Devil and the Deep Blue Sea: Merchant Seamen, Pirates, and the Anglo-American Maritime World, 1700–1750* (Cambridge: Cambridge University Press, 1989), 47.
42. Smith, *Ship of Death*, 4.
43. Smith, *Ship of Death*, 5, 9–10.
44. James Boswell, *The Life of Samuel Johnson*, vol. I (Boston: Carter, Hendee, 1832), 151.
45. Smith, *Ship of Death*, 10–11.
46. Smith, *Ship of Death*, 65.
47. Smith, *Ship of Death*, 26–27.
48. Some people in the region spoke Portuguese, but not many on the remote archipelago.
49. Smith, *Ship of Death*, 68.
50. Smith, *Ship of Death*, 70.

Chapter One

1. When an organism lives in symbiosis with another or other living things.
2. "How Pandemics Change Society," *HUB: Johns Hopkins Magazine*, April 9, 2020, www.hub.jhu.edu/2020/04/09/alexandre-white-how-pandemics-shape-society/.
3. Justinian lived from 527 to 565.
4. John Horgan, "Justinian's Plague," *World History Encyclopedia*, December 26, 2014, www.worldhistory.org/article/782/justinians-plague-541-542.ce/.
5. See "Thucydides on the Plague," accessed March 2, 2022, Livius, www.livius.org/sources/content/thucydides-historian/the-plague/ and Joshua J. Mark, "Thucydides on the Plague of Athens: Text & Commentary," World History Encyclopedia, accessed March 2, 2022, www.worldhistory.org/article/1535/thucydides-on-the-plague-of-athens-text-commentary/.
6. Yersin lived from 1863 to1943.
7. Barbara J. Hawgood, "Alexander Yersin: Discoverer of the Plague Bacillus, Explorer, and Agronomist," *PubMed: National Library of Medicine* 16, no. 3 (August 2008): 167–69.
8. Ker Than, "Two of History's Deadliest Plagues Were Linked: With Implications for Another Outbreak," *National Geographic* (January 11, 2014), www.nationalgeographic.com/animals/article/140129-justinian-plague-black-death-bacteria-bubonic-pandemic.

9. "Black Death," History (July 6, 2020), www.history.com/topics/middle-ages/black-death; C. J. Duncan and S. Scott, "What Caused the Black Death?" *Postgraduate Medical Journal* 81, no. 955 (2005): 315–20.

10. "The Determinants of Mortality," *Bulletin on Aging & Health*, no. 2 (June 2006): https://www.nber.org/bah/spring06/determinants-mortality; Lambert, "A History of Life Expectancy in the UK," *Local Histories*, accessed March 3, 2022, https://localhistories.org/a-history-of-life-expectancy-in-the-uk/.

11. John Seven, "The Black Death: A Timeline of the Gruesome Pandemic," *History* (April 16, 2020), www.history.com/news/black-death-timeline.

12. Than, "Two of History's."

13. The papal bull "*De sepolturis*" was issued in 1299.

14. Sanjib Kumar Ghosh, "Human Cadaveric Dissection: A Historical Account from Ancient Greece to the Modern Era," *Anatomy & Cell Biology* 48, no. 3 (September 2015): 154.

15. Frans Van Liere, "The Pope and the Plague," *Historical Horizons* (March 27, 2020), www.historicalhorizons.org/2020/03/27/the-pope-and-the-plague.

16. Perhaps on account of Jews being forced to live separately, keeping kosher, and practicing hygiene.

17. Dan Freedman, "Why Were Jews Blamed for the Black Death?" *Moment Magazine* (March 31, 2021), www.momentmag.com/why-were-jews-blamed-for-the-black-death/; Samuel K. Cohn Jr., "The Black Death and the Burning of Jews," *Past & Present* 196, no. 1 (August 2007): 3–36.

18. K. Park, *Secrets of Women: Gender, Generation and the Origins of Human Dissection* (Brooklyn, NY: Zone Books, 2006), 9–20 and A. R. Brown, "Authority, the Family, and the Dead in Late Medieval France," *French Historical Studies* 16, no. 4 (1990): 803–32.

19. Hippocrates lived from 460 to 377 BCE.

20. See Christos F. Kleisiaris and Ioanna V. Papathanasiou, "Health Care Practices in Ancient Greece: The Hippocratic Ideal," *Journal of Medical Ethics and History of Medicine* 7 (2014): 1–5.

21. Sara Toth Stub, "Venice's Black Death and the Dawn of Quarantine," *Sapiens: Anthropology Magazine* (April 24, 2020), www.sapiens.org/archaeology/venice-guarantine-history.

22. Siang Yong and Yvonne Tatsumura, "Alexander Fleming: Discoverer of Penicillin," *Singapore Medical Journal* 56, no. 7 (2015): 366–67.

23. Davod Cook, "Sickness, Starvation, and Death in Early Hispaniola," *Journal of Interdisciplinary History* 32, no. 3 (Winter 2002): 349–86.

24. Present-day Mexico City.

25. "Aztec Capital Falls to Cortés," *History* (February 9, 2010), www.history.com/this-day-in-history/aztec-capital-falls-to-cortes.

26. Arno Karlen, *Man and Microbes: Disease and Plague in History and Modern Times* (New York: G. P. Putnam's Sons, 1995), 16.

27. Thayer Watkins, "The Expedition of Hernando de Soto to Southeastern North America, 1538–1543," San Jose State University, accessed March 5, 2022, www.sjsu.edu/faculty/watkins/desoto.htm.

28. Cotton Mather lived from 1663 to 1728 in Massachusetts.

29. Robert Tindol, "Getting the Pox Off All Their Houses: Cotton Mather and the Rhetoric of Puritan Science," *Early American Literature* 46, no. 1 (2011): 1–29.

30. "Jeffrey Amherst and Smallpox Blankets," collection of Lord Amherst's letters discussing germ warfare against American Indians (University of Massachusetts: www.umass.edu/legal/derrico/amherst/lord_jeff.html).

31. John Harvey, *Bring Out Your Dead: The Great Plague of Yellow Fever in Philadelphia in 1793* (Philadelphia: University of Pennsylvania Press, 1949). Reprint: Mansfield Center, CT: Martino Publishing, 2016, 13.

Chapter Two

1. Billy G. Smith, *Ship of Death: A Voyage That Changed the Atlantic World* (New Haven, CT: Yale University Press, 2013), 71.

2. Smith, *Ship of Death*, 85.

3. Smith, *Ship of Death*, 108.

4. Smith, *Ship of Death*, 98.

5. J. K. Laughton and Andrew Lambert, "Beaver, Philip," *Oxford Dictionary of National Biography*, accessed December 2, 2021, http://www.oxforddnb.com.

6. Smith, *Ship of Death*, 109.

7. Smith, *Ship of Death*, 69 and 124.

8. Carol Bolton, "Bolama Colony and Abolitionary Reform in Captain Beaver's African Memoranda, 1805," *Romance, Revolution and Reform: The Journal of the Southampton Centre for Nineteenth Century Research* 3 (January 2021)," 121.

9. Philip Beaver, *African Memoranda: Relative to an Attempt to Establish a British Settlement on the Island of Bulama, on the Western Coast of Africa, in the Year 1792...* (London: C and R Baldwin, 1805), 82–83.

10. The ship was named for the *Charon* which, interestingly, was lost during the pivotal Battle of Yorktown in 1781 when General George Washington and his French allies defeated a large British army under Lord Cornwallis and a naval squadron sent to rescue them.

11. Peter Hicks, "The British Navy, 1793–1802," history website of the Foundation Napoleon, https://www.napoleon.org/en/history-of-the-two-empires /articles/the-british-navy-1792-1802/.

12. One of several British warships to carry that name over history.

13. Smith, *Ship of Death*, 162.

14. Smith, *Ship of Death*, 157.

15. Chisholm, *An Essay on the Malignant Pestilential Fever Introduced into the West Indian Islands from Boulam, on the Coast of Guinea, as It Appeared in 1793 and 1794* (London: J Mawman, 1795; Philadelphia: Dobson, 1799) [Evans Early American Collection, University of Michigan Libraries: www.quod.lib.umich .edu/e/evans/N26554.0001.001?view=toc].

16. Chisholm, "Essay," 89.

17. Smith, *Ship of Death*, 176.

18. Roger N., Buckley, ed., *The Haitian Journal of Lieutenant Howard, York Hussars, 1796–1798* (Knoxville: University of Tennessee Press, 1985), 42–50.

19. Buckley, *Haitian Journal*, 49–50.

20. Chishom, *Essay*, 111 and 123.

21. John B. Blake, "Yellow Fever in Eighteenth Century America," *Bulletin of the New York Academy of Medicine* 44 (1968): 676.

22. Smith, *Ship of Death*, 169.

23. Also known as "Le Cap" and called "Cap-Haitian" today.

24. Laurent Dubois, *Avengers of the New World: The Story of the Haitian Revolution* (Cambridge, MA: Belknap, 2004), 215–16.

25. Francis Alexander Stanislaus, *A Voyage to Saint-Domingue, in the Years 1788, 1789, and 1790* (London: T. Cadell and W. Davies, 1791), 228.

26. Present-day Haiti. In 1804, the island was renamed Haiti, a name derived from the indigenous Arawak people.

27. "Cap-Français" in *Slavery and Remembrance, Colonial Williamsburg*, accessed November 10, 2021, www.slaveryandremembrance.org.

28. Dubois, *Avengers*, 21–24.

29. "Haiti" Saint-Domingue," *Slavery and Remembrance*, Colonial Williamsburg, accessed November 10, 2021, www.slaveryandremembrance.org.

30. Franklin W. Knight, "The Haitian Revolution," *American Historical Review* 105, no. 1 (February 2000): 103–15.

31. Dubois, *Avengers*, 273; J. R. McNeill, *Mosquito Empires: Ecology and War in the Greater Caribbean* (Cambridge: Cambridge University Press, 2010), 253.

Chapter Three

1. "The United States and the Haitian Revolution, 1791–1804," Office of the Historian, U.S. Department of State, https://history.state.gov/milestones /1784-1800/haitian-rev.

2. John B. Blake, "Yellow Fever in Eighteenth Century America," *Bulletin of the New York Academy of Medicine*, vol. 44 (1968), 673.

3. Blake, "Yellow Fever," 637.

4. Blake, "Yellow Fever," 637–38.

5. Ibid.

6. "History of Yellow Fever in the U.S.," American Society for Microbiology (May 17, 2021): www.asm.org/articles/2021/may/history-of-yellow-fever-in -the-u-s.; Rickard Christophers, *Aëdes Aegypti: The Yellow Fever Mosquito: Its Life History, Bionomics and Structure* (Cambridge: Cambridge University Press, 2009).

6. "History of the Yellow Fever in the US."

7. The black color comes from it containing a lot of blood.

8. "Yellow Fever," National Institutes of Health, accessed November 10, 2021, www.nihlibrary.nih.gov/resources/subject-guides/infectious-diseases/ yellow-fever.

9. "Yellow Fever Breaks Out in Philadelphia," Accessed November 10, 2021, history.com: www.history.com/this-day-in-history/yellow-fever-breaks-out-in -philadelphia.

10. Currie, *A Description of the Malignant Infectious Fever Prevailing at Present in Philadelphia; with an Account of the Means to Prevent Infection, and the Remedies and Method of Treatment, which Have Been Found Most Successful* (Philadelphia: Thomas Dobson, 1793), 4.

11. Currie, *Description*, 4–5.

12. "Yellow Fever," World Health Organization, accessed November 10, 2021, www.who.int/news-room/fact-sheets/detail/yellow-fever; "The History of Vaccines: Yellow Fever," The College of Physicians of Philadelphia, accessed November 11, 2021, www.historyofvaccines.org/timeline/yellow-fever.

13. Noah Webster, *A Brief History of Epidemic and Pestilential Diseases; with the Principal Phenomena of the Physical World, which Precede and Accompany Them, and Observations Deduced from the Facts Stated*. [Evans Early American Collection, University of Michigan Libraries: www.quod.lib.umich.edu/e/evans/N2753 1.0001.001/1:11?rgn=div1;view=fulltext].

14. N. M. Crouse, *The French Struggle for the West Indies, 1665–1713* (New York: Columbia University Press, 1943), 182–88; Noah Webster, *A Brief History of Epidemic and Pestilential Diseases; with the Principal Phenomena of the Physical World, which Precede and Accompany Them, and Observations Deduced from the Facts Stated*.

[Evans Early American Collection, University of Michigan Libraries: www.quod
.lib.umich.edu/e/evans/N27531.0001.001/1:11?rgn=div1;view=fulltext].

15. Saul Jarcho, "John Mitchell, Benjamin Rush, and Yellow Fever," *Bulletin
of the History of Medicine* 31, no 2 (1957): 132–36.

16. R. La Roche, *Yellow Fever, Considered in Its Historical, Pathological, Etiological and Therapeutical Relations*, vol. I (Philadelphia: Blanchard 1855), 40–65;
Chisholm *An Essay on the Malignant Pestilential Fever Introduced into the West
Indian Islands from Boulam, on the Coast of Guinea, as It Appeared in 1793 and
1794* (London: J. Mawman, 1795; Philadelphia: Dobson, 1799) [Evans Early
American Collection, University of Michigan Libraries, www.quod.lib.umich
.edu/e/evans/N26554.0001.001?view=toc], 281–95.

17. William Currie, *A Sketch of the Rise and Progress of the Yellow Fever* (Philadelphia: Budd, Bartram, 1800), 57–58.

18. Blake, "Yellow Fever," 675–76.

19. John Harvey Powell, *Bring Out Your Dead: The Great Plague of Yellow Fever
in Philadelphia in 1793* (Philadelphia: University of Pennsylvania Press, 1949).
Reprint: Mansfield Center, CT: Martino Publishing, 2016, vi.

20. Powell, *Bring Out*, vi; *The Broadside Mortality*, 1793. Reprinted in Xroads,
University of Virginia, accessed November 15, 2021, www.xroads.virginia.edu/
-ma96/forrest/ww/feverl.html.

21. Bob Arnebeck, *Destroying Angel: Benjamin Rush, Yellow Fever and the
Birth of Modern Medicine*, 1999. Online book. Bobarnebeck.com/fever1793.html,
chapter 1.

22. Billy G. Smith, *Ship of Death: A Voyage That Changed the Atlantic World*
(New Haven, CT: Yale University Press, 2013), 166.

23. Blake, "Yellow Fever," 677.

24. Blake, "Yellow Fever," 678.

25. Smith, *Ship of Death*, 170.

Chapter Four

1. "The Quaker Province: 1681–1776," *Pennsylvania History*. Pennsylvania
Historical & Museum Commission, accessed November 10, 2021, www.phmc
.state.pa.us/portal/communities/pa-history/1681-1776.html.

2. They met at Carpenters' Hall in September and October of 1774.

3. Franklin was born in Boston in 1706 but ran away at seventeen and moved
to Philadelphia.

4. "The Diseased City," *The Broadside Mortality* (1793) [University of Virginia: www.xroads.virginia.edu/-ma96/forrest/ww/feverl.html].

5. Robert P. Watson, *George Washington's Final Battle: The Epic Struggle to Build a Capital City and Nation* (Washington, DC: Georgetown University Press, 2021), 76–77, 106–7.

6. Paul Sivitz and Billy G. Smith, "Philadelphia and Its People in Maps: The 1790s." *The Encyclopedia of Greater Philadelphia*, accessed December 1, 2021, www.philadelphiaencyclopedia.org/archive/philadelphia-and-its-people -in-maps-the-1790s/.

7. Sivitz and Smith, "Philadelphia"; "Philadelphia" in *Africans*. PBS Series, www.pbx.org/wgbbh/aia/part3/3narr1.html.; "1681-1776: The Quaker Province," in *The Founding of Pennsylvania*, Pennsylvania Historical & Museum Commission, accessed December 1, 2021, www.phmc.state.pa.us/portal/com munities/pa-history/1681-1776.html.

8. Sivitz and Smith, "Philadelphia."

9. "Diseased City."

10. See Watson, *George Washington's*, 116–20.

11. Letter, "Thomas Jefferson to James Monroe," June 20, 1790, in Julian P. Boyd, *PoJ*, 16: 536–38.

12. Letter, "George Washington to James McHenry," July 31, 1788, in John C. Fitzpatrick, ed., *The Diaries of George Washington* (New York: Houghton Mifflin, 1925), 30: 29.

13. Watson, *George Washington's*, 121–34.

14. Ron Chernow, *Washington: A Life* (New York: Penguin, 2010), 630.

15. The vote was 13 to 11.

16. Watson, *George Washington's*, 135–46.

17. Infrastructure, by today's parlance.

18. Letter, "Thomas Jefferson to George Washington," September 9, 1792, *FO*.

19. Watson, *George Washington's*, 136 and 155–63.

20. Watson, *George Washington's*, 164–77.

21. Bruce G. Peabody, "George Washington, Presidential Term Limits, and the Problem of Reluctant Political Leadership," *Presidential Studies Quarterly* 31, no. 3 (September 2001): 441–42.

22. "George Washington's Second Presidential Term," *George Washington: Biography, History, and Facts*, accessed December 10, 2021. www.georgewashing ton.org/second-presidential-term.jsp.

23. L'Enfant Americanized his name to Peter while living in the states and also claimed that he resigned as opposed to being removed.

24. Watson, *George Washington's*, 206–17.

25. Letter, "George Washington to William Moultrie," August 28, 1793, *FO*.

26. Henry D. Biddle, ed., *Elizabeth Drinker, Extracts from the Journal of Elizabeth Drinker, from 1759 to 1807* (Philadelphia: J. B. Lippincott Co., 1889). 186, January 21, 1793.

27. John Harvey Powell, *Bring Out Your Dead: The Great Plague of Yellow Fever in Philadelphia in 1793* (Philadelphia: University of Pennsylvania Press, 1949). Reprint: Mansfield Center, Conn.: Martino Publishing, 2016, 64.

28. Powell, *Bring Out*, 1.

29. Mathew Carey, *A Short Account of the Malignant Fever, Lately Prevalent in Philadelphia: With a Statement of the Proceedings That Took Place on the Subject in Different Parts of the United States* (Philadelphia: Self-published, 1793) [National Library of Medicine: www.collections.nlm.nih.gov], 12–13.

30. Biddle, *Extracts*, 188, July 25, 1793.

31. Powell, *Bring Out*, 2.

Chapter Five

1. See *Independent Gazetteer*, June 2, 1784.

2. The next month, the *Sans-Culotte* would be converted by the French navy into a warship. It was then lost at sea the next year and was one of a few French ships to carry that name.

3. John Harvey Powell, *Bring Out Your Dead: The Great Plague of Yellow Fever in Philadelphia in 1793* (Philadelphia: University of Pennsylvania Press, 1949). Reprint: Mansfield Center, CT: Martino Publishing, 2016, 5.

4. Powell, *Bring Out*, 4.

5. Billy G. Smith, *Ship of Death: A Voyage That Changed the Atlantic World* (New Haven, CT: Yale University Press, 2013), 187–90.

6. Mathew Carey, *Short Account of the Malignant Fever, Lately Prevalent in Philadelphia: With a Statement of the Proceedings That Took Place on the Subject in Different Parts of the United States* (Philadelphia: Self-published, 1793) [National Library of Medicine: www.collections.nlm.nih.gov], 13.

7. Today known as Penn's Landing.

8. William Currie, *Historical Account of the Climate and Disease of the United States* (Philadelphia: Thomas Dobson, 1792), 29–30.

9. Isaac Weld, *Travels through the States of North America and the Provinces of Upper and Lower Canada During the Years 1795, 1796 and 1797*, 4th ed. (London: John Stockdale, 1807), 3–4.

10. It is sometimes spelled "Dennies" in the historical record.

11. Henry D. Biddle, Elizabeth Drinker, *Extracts from the Journal of Elizabeth Drinker, from 1759 to 1807* (Philadelphia: J. B. Lippincott Co., 1889), 188, August 4, 1793.

12. Jim Green, "Pandemic Reading: Yellow Fever in Philadelphia," The Library Company of Philadelphia, https://librarycompany.org/2020/04/27/pandemic-reading-yellow-fever/.

13. Rev. Justus Henry Christian Helmuth, *Short Account of the Yellow Fever in Philadelphia for the Reflecting Christian* (Philadelphia: Jones, Hoff & Derrick, 1794) [Harvard University's Library Open Collections Program on contagions; Sabin Americana Print Editions], 8.

14. Powell, *Bring Out*, 7.

15. It also spread dengue fever, Zika, and other diseases.

16. Paul E. Kopperman, "Venerate the Lancet": Benjamin Rush's Yellow Fever Therapy in Context," *Bulletin of the History of Medicine*, 78 (3) (Fall 2004), 539–74.

17. Powell, *Bring Out*, 12.

18. Customarily spelled "culottes."

19. Carey, *Short Account*, 16.

20. John B. Blake, "Yellow Fever in Eighteenth Century America," *Bulletin of the New York Academy of Medicine* 44 (1968): 677–79; "History of the Yellow Fever in the US," American Society for Microbiology (May 17, 2021), www.asm.org/articles/2021/may/history-of-yellow-fever-in-the-u-s.

21. Also known as the "Guardians of the Poor."

22. "Guardians of the Poor," Philadelphia Information Locater Service, Department of Records, City of Philadelphia: www.phila.gov/phils/docs/inventor/graphics/agencies/a035.htm#:~:text+by%20an%20act%20of%20januar.proceeds%20among%20the%20city's%20indigent.

23. Physick, whose first name is sometimes written "Philip" with one "l," lived until 1837, passing in Philadelphia.

24. "Dr. Phillip Syng Physick," Penn Medicine, www.uphs.upenn.edu/paharc/timeline/1751/tline8.html.

25. Cathrall lived until 1819.

26. See Isaac Cathrall, *A Medical Sketch of the Synochus Maligna, or Malignant Contagious Fever; as It Lately Appeared in the City of Philadelphia: to Which Is Added, Some Account of the Morbid Appearances Observed after Death, on Dissection* (Philadelphia: T. Dobson, 1794).

27. Bob Arnebeck, *Destroying Angel: Benjamin Rush, Yellow Fever and the Birth of Modern Medicine*, 1999, chapter 1. Online book. Bobarnebeck.com/fever1793.html; Powell, *Bring Out*, 16.

28. Powell, *Bring Out*, 14.

29. "Samuel Powel," Washington Library, Mount Vernon, accessed December 10, 2021, www.mountvernon.org/library/digitalhistory/digital-encyclopedia/articl/samuel-powel/.

30. Powell, *Bring Out*, 16.
31. Sydenham lived from 1624 to 1689.
32. Including *Observations Medicae* (1676) and *An Account of Gout* (1683).
33. Powell, *Bring Out*, ix; Arnebeck, *Destroying Angel.*
34. Powel, *Bring Out*, ix.
35. Powell, *Bring Out*, ix and 8; Arnebeck, *Destroying Angel.*
36. "Epidemic in Philadelphia: The Great Fever," *American Experience*, PBS: www
.pbs.org/wgbh/americanexperience/features/fever-epidemic-philadelphia-1793/.
37. Currie, *Historical Account*, 112.
38. Rush, *Account*, 9–11.
39. Rush, *Account*, 9–12; Arnebeck, *Destroying Angel.*
40. Helmuth, *Short Account*, 4.
41. Biddle, *Excerpts*, 3–4.
42. Biddle, *Excerpts*, 188, August 10 and 16, 1793.
43. Helmuth, *Short Account*, 2.

Chapter Six

1. John Harvey Powell, *Bring Out Your Dead: The Great Plague of Yellow Fever in Philadelphia in 1793* (Philadelphia: University of Pennsylvania Press, 1949). Reprint: Mansfield Center, CT: Martino Publishing, 2016, 9.
2. Henry D. Biddle, ed., Elizabeth Drinker, *Extracts from the Journal of Elizabeth Drinker, from 1759 to 1807* (Philadelphia: J. B. Lippincott Co., 1889), 188, August 18, 1793.
3. Powell, *Bring Out*, 10
4. At the time, a rather common treatment for a number of afflictions, though often used with tea.
5. Benjamin Rush, *An Account of the Bilious Remitting Yellow Fever as It Appeared in Philadelphia, in the Year 1793* (Philadelphia: Thomas Dobson, 1794), 6.
6. Powell, *Bring Out*, 10.
7. Mathew Carey, *A Short Account of the Malignant Fever, Lately Prevalent in Philadelphia: With a Statement of the Proceedings That Took Place on the Subject in Different Parts of the United States* (Philadelphia: Self-published, 1793) [National Library of Medicine: www.collections.nlm.nih.gov], 20.
8. He was also a member of the influential American Antiquarian Society, living until 1839. He is buried at St. Mary's Catholic Church in Philadelphia.
9. Biddle, *Extracts*, 188–89, August 21, 1793.
10. Carey, *Short Account*, 21.
11. Biddle, *Extracts*, 188–89, August 21, 1793.
12. Rush, *Account*, 13.

13. Arnebeck, "Descriptions of Historic Yellow Fever Cases, Especially in Philadelphia and New York in the 1790s," *Yellow Fever Casebook* (October 26 2014): www.fevercasebook.blogspot.com."; Paul E. Kopperman, "'Venerate the Lancet': Benjamin Rush's Yellow Fever Therapy in Context," *Bulletin of the History of Medicine* 78 (2004): 539–74.

14. Rush, *Account*, 1794, 17.

15. Arnebeck, "Descriptions."

16. Bob Arnebeck, *Destroying Angel: Benjamin Rush, Yellow Fever and the Birth of Modern Medicine*, 1999. Online book. Bobarnebeck.com/fever1793.html, ch. 1.

17. Rush, *Account*; see also Powell, *Bring Out*, 12.

18. Arnebeck, "Descriptions."

19. Rush, *Account*, 13–15.

20. Hippocrates lived from 460 to 370 BCE.

21. Rush, *Account*, 127; John Mitchell, "Mitchell's Account of the Yellow Fever in Virginia in 1741-42," *Philadelphia Medical Museum Records* 1, no. 1 (1805): 5–10; John Mitchell, "Account of the Yellow Fever which Prevailed in Virginia in the Years 1737, 1741, and 1742." *American Medical and Philosophical Register* 4 (1814): 181–83.

22. Benjamin Rush, "Observations Upon the Origin of the Malignant Bilious, or Yellow Fever in Philadelphia, and Upon the Means of Preventing It: Addressed to the Citizens of Philadelphia," 1793 [Evans Early American Imprint Collection, www.quod.lib.umich.edu/e/evans/], 27.

23. Rush, *Account*, 193.

24. Rush, *Observations*, 27.

25. Biddle, *Extracts*, 189, August 23, 1793.

26. Rush, *Account*, 13–15.

27. Letter, "Benjamin Rush to wife," August 29, 1793., Butterfield, *LoR.*

28. Rush, Letter, "Benjamin Rush to wife."

29. Rush, Letter, "Benjamin Rush to wife."

30. Letter, "Benjamin Rush to Julia Rush," August 1793, Butterfield, *LoR.*

31. Arneback, "Descriptions."

32. Bob Arnebeck, "Ebola Africa 2014 and Yellow Fever Philadelphia 1793," *Yellow Fever Casebook* (October 26, 2014), www.fevercasebook.blogspot.com.

33. Rush, *Account*, 345; Arnebeck, "Ebola Africa."

34. Rush, *Account*, 352–53.

35. Rush, *Account*, 345–47.

36. Rush, *Account*, 347–48.

37. Rush, *Account*, 341–43, 355.

38. Rush, *Account*, 342–44, 352–53; Arnebeck, "Ebola Africa."

39. Rush, Account, 344; Arnebeck, "Ebola Africa."

40. Rush, *Account*, 362.

41. Rev. Justus Henry Christian Helmuth, *A Short Account of the Yellow Fever in Philadelphia for the Reflecting Christian* (Philadelphia: Jones, Hoff & Derrick, 1794) [Harvard University's Library Open Collections Program on contagions; Sabin Americana Print Editions], 10.

Chapter Seven

1. Matthew A. Carey, *A Short Account of the Malignant Fever, Lately Prevalent in Philadelphia: With a Statement of the Proceedings That Took Place on the Subject in Different Parts of the United States* (Philadelphia: Self-published, 1793) [National Library of Medicine: www.collections.nlm.nih.gov], 16.

2. Henry D. Biddle, ed., Elizabeth Drinker, *Extracts from the Journal of Elizabeth Drinker, from 1759 to 1807* (Philadelphia: J. B. Lippincott Co., 1889), 191–92, August 31, 1793.

3. Carey, *Short Account*, see August 22, 23, 24, 1793.

4. Rev. Justus Henry Christian Helmuth, *A Short Account of the Yellow Fever in Philadelphia for the Reflecting Christian* (Philadelphia: Jones, Hoff & Derrick, 1794) [Harvard University's Library Open Collections Program on contagions; Sabin Americana Print Editions], 4–5.

5. Helmuth, *Short Account*, 4–5.

6. Helmuth, *Short Account*, 4–6; Bob Arnebeck, "Descriptions of Historic Yellow Fever Cases, Especially in Philadelphia and New York in the 1790s," *Yellow Fever Casebook* (October 26 2014), www.fevercasebook.blogspot.com.

7. Biddle, *Extracts*, 89, August 25, 1793; Paul E. Kopperman, "'Venerate the Lancet': Benjamin Rush's Yellow Fever Therapy in Context," *Bulletin of the History of Medicine*, 78 (2004): 539–74.

8. Biddle, *Extracts*, 190, August 26, 1793.

9. Carey, *Short Account*, 22.

10. Edwin B. Bronner and J. Philip Goldberg, "Letter from a Yellow Fever Victim; Philadelphia, 1793," *Pennsylvania Magazine of History and Biography*, 1962, 205.

11. John Harvey Powell, *Bring Out Your Dead: The Great Plague of Yellow Fever in Philadelphia in 1793* (Philadelphia: University of Pennsylvania Press, 1949). Reprint: Mansfield Center, Conn.: Martino Publishing, 2016, 29–30.

12. Powell, *Bring Out*, 30.

13. Whitfield J. Bell, *The Colonial Physician & Other Essays* (New York: Science History Publications, 1975), 103.

14. Benjamin Rush, *An Account of the Bilious Remitting Yellow Fever as It Appeared in Philadelphia, in the Year 1793* (Philadelphia: Thomas Dobson, 1794), 127.

15. Laudanum is an alcohol solution containing morphine and/or opium as a painkiller.

16. Rush, *Account*, 128.

17. Rush, *Account*, 129.

18. John Purdon, "Reflections Caused by the Yellow Fever in the Year 1793," in *A Leisure Hour, or, a Series of Poetical Letters Mostly Written During the Prevalence of the Yellow Fever* (Philadelphia: 1804).

19. Rush's son Richard was thirteen at the time.

20. Lyman Henry Butterfield, ed., *Letters of Benjamin Rush*, vol. 2: 1793–1813 (Princeton: Princeton University Press, 1951), letter, "Benjamin Rush to Julia Rush," August 26, 1793 and September 1, 1793.

21. Helmuth, *Short Account*, 5–6.

22. Helmuth, *Short Account*, 40.

23. Bronner and Goldberg, "Letter," 206.

24. Letter, "Thomas Jefferson to James Madison," September 1, 1793, *FO*.

25. Letter, "Thomas Jefferson to James Madison," September 1, 1793, *FO*.

26. Paul Preston, "Some Incidents of the Yellow Fever Epidemic of 1793," *Pennsylvania Magazine of History and Biography* 38 (1914): 236–37.

27. Biddle, *Extracts*, 192–93, September 3, 1793.

28. Carey, *Short Account*, 34.

29. Carey, *Short Account*, 34.

30. Helmuth, *Short Account*, 34.

31. Biddle, *Extracts*, 194–95, September 4, 1793.

32. Carey, *Short Account*, 32.

33. Carey, *Short Account*, 34.

34. Carey, *Short Account*, 29–30.

35. Carey, *Short Account*, 29.

36. Carey, *Short Account*, 29.

37. Helmuth, *Short Account*, 26–27.

38. Helmuth, *Short Account*, 22.

39. Helmuth, *Short Account*, 30.

40. Biddle, *Extracts*, 194, September 6, 1793.

41. Biddle, *Extracts*, 194, September 6, 1793.

42. Jim Murphy, *An American Plague: The True and Terrifying Story of Yellow Fever in Philadelphia in 1793* (New York: Clarion Books, 2003), 80; Helmuth, *Short Account*, 29–31.

43. Carey, *Short Account*, 83–84.

44. Carey, *Short Account*, 83.

45. Carey, *Short Account*, 30–31.

46. Helmuth, *Short Account*, 10.

47. Helmuth, *Short Account*, 16 and 20.
48. Helmuth, *Short Account*, 16 and 18; Preston, "Some Incidents," 236–37.
49. Helmuth, *Short Account*, 14.
50. Helmuth, *Short Account*, 12–13.
51. Helmuth, *Short Account*, 14–15.
52. Helmuth, *Short Account*, 14–16.
53. Preston, "Some Incidents," 236–37.
54. Helmuth, *Short Account*, 11.
55. Helmuth, *Short Account*, 15 and 47.

Chapter Eight

1. Mathew Carey, *A Short Account of the Malignant Fever, Lately Prevalent in Philadelphia: With a Statement of the Proceedings That Took Place on the Subject in Different Parts of the United States* (Philadelphia: Self-published, 1793) [National Library of Medicine: www.collections.nlm.nih.gov], 20.
2. Carey, *Short Account*, 21.
3. *ADA*, August 28, 1793.
4. John Harvey Powell, *Bring Out Your Dead: The Great Plague of Yellow Fever in Philadelphia in 1793* (Philadelphia: University of Pennsylvania Press, 1949). Reprint: Mansfield Center, Conn.: Martino Publishing, 2016, 21.
5. It must be remembered that the federal government at the time contained only five departments: State, Treasury, War, Justice, and the Postal Service, and a few dozen employees.
6. Carey, *Short Account*, 71 and 82.
7. Also known as the "Society of Friends."
8. "Yearly Meeting Epistle 1793," Swarthmore College Library Quaker Collection and the letter, "Margaret Morris to her daughter," August 31, 1793, in the Haverford College library manuscript collection.
9. "Dolley Todd House," Independence National Historic Park, U.S. National Park Service: https://www.nps.gov/places/000/dolley-todd-house.htm.
10. Bob Arnebeck, "Ebola Africa 2014 and Yellow Fever Philadelphia 1793," *Yellow Fever Casebook* (October 26, 2014), www.fevercasebook.blogspot.com.
11. Carey, *Short Account*, 59.
12. Powell, *Bring Out*, 18.
13. Carey, *Short Account*, 21.
14. Carl Linnaeus, 1707–1778, was the Swedish botanist and physician noted for creating the taxonomy by which organisms are named.
15. Powell, *Bring Out*, 31; Carey, *Short Account*, 21.
16. Powell, *Bring Out*, 33.

17. Carey, *Short Account*, 22–23.

18. *FG*, August 31, 1793.

19. Henry D. Biddle, ed., Elizabeth Drinker, *Extracts from the Journal of Elizabeth Drinker, from 1759 to 1807* (Philadelphia: J. B. Lippincott Co., 1889), 190, August 28, 1793; Carey, *Short Account*, 23;Rev. Justus Henry Christian, *A Short Account of the Yellow Fever in Philadelphia for the Reflecting Christian* (Philadelphia: Jones, Hoff & Derrick, 1794) [Harvard University's Library Open Collections Program on contagions; Sabin Americana Print Editions], 7.

20. Paul E. Kopperman, "'Venerate the Lancet': Benjamin Rush's Yellow Fever Therapy in Context," *Bulletin of the History of Medicine*, 78 (2004).

21. Locals referred to the island as "State Island" or, disparagingly as "Mud Island."

22. Arnebeck, "Ebola Africa 2014;" Bob Arenebeck, "Descriptions of Historic Yellow Fever Cases, Especially in Philadelphia and New York in the 1790s," *Yellow Fever Casebook* (October 26 2014), www.fevercasebook.blogspot.com.

23. Camphor is a powder ground from the bark of the camphor tree.

24. Barbara J. Becker, "Plagues & People: Infectious and Epidemic Disease in History," University of California, Irvine: http://faculty.humanities.uci.edu /bjbecker/plaguesandpeople/week7ca.html.

25. Murphy, *An American Plague*, 11–19.

26. Carey, *Short Account*, 64–65.

27. US National Library of Medicine at www.collections.nlm.nih.gov.

28. Carey, *Short Account*, 22.

29. Martin Pernick, "Politics, Parties, and Pestilence: Epidemic yellow Fever in Philadelphia and the Rise of the First Party System," *The William and Mary Quarterly* 29, no. 4 (October 1972), 560.

Chapter Nine

1. Sometimes known as the "Visitors of the Poor."

2. Mathew Carey, *A Short Account of the Malignant Fever, Lately Prevalent in Philadelphia: With a Statement of the Proceedings That Took Place on the Subject in Different Parts of the United States* (Philadelphia: Self-published, 1793) [National Library of Medicine: www.collections.nlm.nih.gov], 56.

3. Carey, *Short Account*, 24–25.

4. Letter, "Abigail Adams to Elizabeth Smith."

5. Hamilton lived from 1676 to1741.

6. Regrettably, the home, whose property was later owned by Oliver Hazard Perry, was torn down in 1875.

7. Carey, *Short Account*, 19–20; John Harvey Powell, *Bring Out Your Dead: The Great Plague of Yellow Fever in Philadelphia in 1793* (Philadelphia: University of Pennsylvania Press, 1949). Reprint: Mansfield Center, CT: Martino Publishing, 2016, 58–62; Dennis B. Cornfield, "The Hospital at Bush Hill: Philadelphia's Response to the 1793 Yellow Fever Epidemic," *MD Advisor* (Summer 2020): MD Advantage: www.mdadvantageonline.com/feature-articles/the-hospital-at-bush-hill-philadelphias-respose-to-the-1793-yellow-fever-epidemic/.

8. Jim Murphy, *An American Plague: The True and Terrifying Story of Yellow Fever in Philadelphia in 1793* (New York: Clarion Books, 2003), 40.

9. Carey, *Short Account*, 25.

10. *FG*, September 10, 1793.

11. Carey, *Short Account*, 32 and 56; Philadelphia Common Council, "Minutes of the Proceedings of the Committee Appointed on the Date of 14 September to Alleviate the Suffering of the Afflicted" (1794), accessed December 12, 2021, http://pds.lib.harvard.edu/pds/view/6395244?n=30&printthumbnails=no.

12. Cornfield, "Hospital."

12. Richard Allen and Absalom Jones, *A Narrative of the Proceedings of the Black People, During the Late Awful Calamity in Philadelphia in the Year 1793: and a Refutation of Some Censures, Thrown Upon them in Some Late Publications* (Philadelphia: William W. Woodward, 1794), 9.

13. Carey, *Short Account*, 61–62.

14. John E. Lane, "Jean Devèze: Notes on the Yellow Fever Epidemic at Philadelphia in 1793," *Annals of Medical History* 8, no. 3 (1936), 203, www.ncbi.nlm.nih.gov/pmc/articles/pmc7939912/pdf/annmedhist147404-0024.pdf.

15. Amira Rose Schroeder, "Girard Stephen," Civil Rights in a Northern City: Philadelphia. Temple University Libraries, accessed December 10, 2021, www.northerncity.library.temple.edu/exhibits/show/civil-rights-in-a-northern-cit/people-and-places/girard—stephen.

16. Lane, "Jean Devèze," 203.

17. Lane, "Jean Devèze," 203.

18. Devèze would survive yellow fever outbreaks in both the islands and Philadelphia, and it is believed he lived until 1826.

19. Lane, "Jean Devèze," 202.

20. Lane, "Jean Devèze," 203.

21. Jean Devèze, *An Enquiry Into, and Observations Upon the Causes and Effects of the Epidemic Disease, which Raged in Philadelphia from the Month of August Till Towards the Middle of December, 1793* (Philadelphia: Parent, 1794) [Harvard Open Library, http://pds.lib.harvard.edu/pds/view/7374528?n=84&imagesize=1200&jp2Res=.25&printThumbnails=no], 1.

22. Devèze, *Enquiry*, 1; Powell, *Bring out*, 32–34.

23. Devèze, *Enquiry*, 4.
24. Powell, *Bring Out*, 32; Cornfield, "Hospital."
25. Devèze, *Enquiry*, 26–28.
26. Devèze, *Enquiry*, 26–28.
27. Devèze, *Enquiry*, 30.
28. Lane, "Jean Devèze," 204.
29. Carey, *Short Account*, 59–60.
30. Murphy, *American Plague*, 75; Cornfield, "Hospital."
31. Gregory J. Dehler, "Neutrality Proclamation," Washington Library, George Washington's Mount Vernon, accessed October 2, 2021. www.mount vernon.org/library/digitalhistory/digital-encyclopedia/article/neutrality-procla mation/.
32. Devèze, *Enquiry*, ii–iv.
33. Devèze, *Enquiry*, 30–32; Cornfield, "Hospital."
34. Devèze, *Enquiry*, 34 and 36.
35. Quinine is a treatment for malaria made from the bark of the cinchona tree.
36. Devèze, *Enquiry*, 28.
37. Devèze, *Enquiry*, ii & 46.
38. Benjamin Rush, *An Account of the Bilious Remitting Yellow Fever as It Appeared in Philadelphia, in the Year 1793* (Philadelphia: Thomas Dobson, 1794), 320.
39. Carey, *Short Account*, 63.
40. Devèze, *Enquiry*, ii–iv and 48.
41. Devèze, *Enquiry*, 8.
42. Devèze, *Enquiry*, 50.

Chapter Ten

1. Martin Pernick, "Politics, Parties, and Pestilence: Epidemic yellow Fever in Philadelphia and the Rise of the First Party System." *The William and Mary Quarterly* 29, no. 4 (October 1972), 560.
2. Pernick, "Politics," 560.
3. John Harvey Powell, *Bring Out Your Dead: The Great Plague of Yellow Fever in Philadelphia in 1793* (Philadelphia: University of Pennsylvania Press, 1949). Reprint: Mansfield Center, CT: Martino Publishing, 2016, 24.
4. Powell, *Bring Out*, 24.
5. Mark A. Smith, "Andrew Brown's "Earnest Endeavor": *The Federal Gazette's* Role in Philadelphia's Yellow Fever Epidemic of 1793," *Pennsylvania*

Magazine of History and Biography 120, no. 4 (October 1996), 331; Dunlap's newspaper, August 26 to September 14, 1793.

6. *FG*, August 23 and 24, 1793.

7. *FG*, August 26, 1793.

8. Thomas Collins, "Choice and Rare Experiments in Physick and Chirurgery," in *Old English Books*, http://quod.lib.umich.edu/e/eebo/A34011.0 001/1:7?rgn=div1;view=fulltext.

9. "Animalcule," "Recollections relative to Egypt," *PG*, August 4, 1802.

10. *ADA*, August 29, 1793.

11. Henry D. Biddle, ed., Elizabeth Drinker, *Extracts from the Journal of Elizabeth Drinker, from 1759 to 1807* (Philadelphia: J. B. Lippincott Co., 1889, 190, August 28, 1793.

12. Helmuth, *Short Account*, 6–8.

13. Helmuth, *Short Account*, 7–8.

14. Biddle, *Excerpts*, 189, August 23, 1793.

15. Rev. Justus Henry Christian Helmuth, *A Short Account of the Yellow Fever in Philadelphia for the Reflecting Christian* (Philadelphia: Jones, Hoff & Derrick, 1794) [Harvard University's Library Open Collections Program on contagions; Sabin Americana Print Editions], 9–10.

16. Bob Arnebeck, "Descriptions of Historic Yellow Fever Cases, Especially in Philadelphia and New York in the 1790s," *Yellow Fever Casebook* (October 26, 2014): www.fevercasebook.blogspot.com.

17. Ragusa is in Sicily and Martinico is another name for Martinique.

18. Mathew Carey, *A Short Account of the Malignant Fever, Lately Prevalent in Philadelphia: With a Statement of the Proceedings That Took Place on the Subject in Different Parts of the United States* (Philadelphia: Self-published, 1793) [National Library of Medicine: www.collections.nlm.nih.gov], 18–20.

19. A privateer is an armed ship crewed privately yet having a government commission for war or to capture enemy ships.

20. Carey, *Short Account*, 19.

21. Carey, *Short Account*, 16.

22. Carey, *Short Account*, 17.

23. Helmuth, *Short Account*, 6–8.

24. Bob Arnebeck, *Destroying Angel: Benjamin Rush, Yellow Fever and the Birth of Modern Medicine*, 1999. Online book. Bobarnebeck.com/fever1793.html.

25. Benjamin Rush, *An Account of the Bilious Remitting Yellow Fever as It Appeared in Philadelphia, in the Year 1793* (Philadelphia: Thomas Dobson, 1794), 339.

26. Lyman Henry Butterfield, ed., *Letters of Benjamin Rush*, vol. 2: 1793–1813 (Princeton: Princeton University Press, 1951), "Benjamin Rush to Julia Rush," September 3 and 5, 1793.

27. Rush, *Account*, 339.
28. Rush, *Account*, 340.
29. Rush, *Account*, 349.
30. Ruch, *Account*, 349–51.
31. Rush, *Account*, 211.
32. Mark A Smith, "Andrew Brown's "Earnest Endeavor": *The Federal Gazette's* Role in Philadelphia's Yellow Fever Epidemic of 1793," *Pennsylvania Magazine of History and Biography*, vol. 120, no. 4 (October 1996), 332.
33. Letters, "Adam Kuhn to Benjamin Rush," "Putrid Fever," September 7, 1793, and "Adam Kuhn and Edward Stevens to Matthew Clarkson," September 13, 1793, *FG.*
34. With the new nation deeply in debt, President Washington tasked Hamilton with solving the problem. After an explosive political debate, Hamilton's plan passed over the objections of the Jefferson faction and Southerners. It must be said that Hamilton's plan worked—it addressed the debt, gave the nation credit, stabilized the value of the currency, and allowed the fledgling government to govern.
35. Sarah Pruitt, "When the Yellow Fever Outbreak of 1793 Sent the Wealthy Fleeing Philadelphia," History Channel (June 11, 2020): www.history.com.
36. Boyd, *PoJ*, vol. 20, 718–53; "Jefferson, Freneau, and the Founding of the *National Gazette*," *FO.*
37. Rush, *Account*, 325–33.
38. Smith, "Andrew Brown's Earnest," 323.
39. Pruitt, "Yellow Fever Outbreak"; Jane Hampton Cook, "In the 1st U.S. Epidemic, Alexander Hamilton Leveraged Newspapers to Save Lives," *Genealogy Bank* (March 18, 2020), www.blog.genealogybank.com.
40. Letter, "Alexander Hamilton to College of Physicians," September 11, 1793]
41. Smith, "Andrew Brown's Earnest," 331; letters, "Benjamin Rush to Julia Rush," September 5 and 15, 1793; letter, "John Fenno to Alexander Hamilton," November 9, 1793, *FO.*
42. Alexander Hamilton, *WM* August 31, 1793, p. 3; Cook, "In the 1st Epidemic."
43. Alexander Hamilton, *ADA*, September 16, 1793, p. 2.
44. Alexander Hamilton, *IC*, September 23, 1793, p. 1.
45. Alexander Hamilton, *ADA*, September 16, 1793, p. 2
46. William Currie, *A Description of the Malignant Infectious Fever Prevailing at Present in Philadelphia; with an Account of the Means to Prevent Infection, and the Remedies and Method of Treatment, which Have Been Found Most Successful* (Philadelphia: Thomas Dobson, 1793), 7–8.

NOTES

47. Currie, *Description*, 6–7.
48. Currie, *Description*, 8–9.
49. Currie, *Description*, 8.
50. Currie, *Description*, 10.
51. Marion E. Brown, "Adam Kuhn: Eighteenth Century Physician and Teacher," *Journal of the History of Medicine and Allied Sciences* 5, no. 2 (Spring 1950), 163–77.
52. Currie, *Description*, 18–20.
53. Currie, *Description*, 3.
54. Currie, *Description*, 7.
55. Jean Devèze, *An Enquiry Into, and Observations Upon the Causes and Effects of the Epidemic Disease, which Raged in Philadelphia from the Month of August Till Towards the Middle of December, 1793* (Philadelphia: Parent, 1794) [Harvard Open Library, http://pds.lib.harvard.edu/pds/view/7374528?n=84&imagesize =1200&jp2Res=.25&printThumbnails=no], 50.
56. Devèze, *Enquiry*, 14.
57. See Edward Stevens, *GA*, September 11, 1793.
58. Currie, *Description*, 10.
59. Devèze, *Enquiry*, iv, 6, 50.
60. Butterfield, *Letters*, 1213–18.

Chapter Eleven

1. Mathew Carey, *A Short Account of the Malignant Fever, Lately Prevalent in Philadelphia: With a Statement of the Proceedings That Took Place on the Subject in Different Parts of the United States* (Philadelphia: Self-published, 1793) [National Library of Medicine: www.collections.nlm.nih.gov], 77–78; Everett Mendelsohn, "John Lining and his Contribution to Early American Science," *Isis: History of Science Society* 51, no. 3 (September 1960), 278–92.
2. *ADA*, September 2, 1793; Richard Allen and Absalom Jones *A Narrative of the Proceedings of the Black People, During the Late Awful Calamity in Philadelphia in the Year 1793: and a Refutation of Some Censures, Thrown Upon them in Some Late Publications* (Philadelphia: William W. Woodward, 1794); Mendelsohn, "John Lining," 278–92.
3. Benjamin Rush, *An Account of the Bilious Remitting Yellow Fever as It Appeared in Philadelphia, in the Year 1793* (Philadelphia: Thomas Dobson, 1794), 316.
4. Rush had published an antislavery pamphlet in 1773 titled *An Address to the Inhabitants of the British Settlements in America, Upon Slave-keeping.*
5. "Rush on Abolition and Race," Benjamin Rush Portal, University of Pennsylvania Libraries: www.guides.library.upenn.edu/benjaminrush/abolitionist.

238

6. "Black Founders: The Free Black Community in the Early Republic," Library Company of Philadelphia: www.librarycompany.org/blackfounders/ section4.htm; James Wolfinger, "African American Migration," *The Encyclopedia of Greater Philadelphia*: https://philadelphiaencyclopedia.org/archive/african -american-migration/.

7. Rush Letters, "Benjamin Rush to Julia Rush," September 6, 1793; Henry D. Biddle ed., Elizabeth Drinker, *Extracts from the Journal of Elizabeth Drinker, from 1759 to 1807* (Philadelphia: J. B. Lippincott Co., 1889), September 8, 1793, 194.

8. "Africans in America," part 3, PBS: https://www.pbs.org/wgbh/aia /part3/3p97.html.

9. "Absalom Jones (1746–1818)," BlackPast: https://blackpast.org/african -american-history/jones/absalom-1746-1818/ and "Absalom Jones—One of America's Founding Fathers," The Constitutional: https://www.theconstitu tional.com/blog/2020/10/08/absalom-jones-one-americas-founding-fathers.

10. This site remains the oldest continually Black-owned piece of real estate in the United States.

11. "Africans in America," part 3, PBS: https://www.pbs.org/wgbh/aia /part3/3p97.html; Allen and Jones, *Narrative*, 2–3.

12. Allen and Jones, *Narrative*, 3.

13. Allen and Jones, *Narrative*, 4.

14. Allen and Jones, *Narrative*, 5.

15. Allen and Jones, *Narrative*, 17–18.

16. Allen and Jones, *Narrative*, 18.

17. Allen and Jones, *Narrative*, 19.

18. Rev. Justus Henry Christian Helmuth, *A Short Account of the Yellow Fever in Philadelphia for the Reflecting Christian* (Philadelphia: Jones, Hoff & Derrick, 1794) [Harvard University's Library Open Collections Program on contagions; Sabin Americana Print Editions].

19. Allen and Jones, *Narrative*, 16–18.

20. Allen and Jones, *Narrative*, 17–18.

21. Allen and Jones, *Narrative*, 5, 20.

Chapter Twelve

1. Gregory J. Dehler, "Neutrality Proclamation," Washington Library, George Washington's Mount Vernon, accessed December 5, 2021, www.mountvernon.org/library/digitalhistory/digital-encyclopedia/article/neu trality-proclamation/.

NOTES

2. Henry D. Biddle, ed., Elizabeth Drinker, *Extracts from the Journal of Elizabeth Drinker, from 1759 to 1807* (Philadelphia: J. B. Lippincott Co., 1889), 187, April 23, 1793.

3. "Cabinet Opinion of Foreign Vessels and Consulting the Supreme Court," July 21, 1793. *Founders Online*: www.founders.archives.gov.

4. "Citizen Genêt Affair, 1793–1794," Archive, U.S. Department of State: www.state.gov/r/pa/ho/time/nr/88110.htm.

5. Mark A. Smith, "Andrew Brown's "Earnest Endeavor": *The Federal Gazette's* Role in Philadelphia's Yellow Fever Epidemic of 1793," *Pennsylvania Magazine of History and Biography* 120, no. 4 (October 1996), 324.

6. Letter, "John Adams to Thomas Jefferson," June 30, 1813, *FO*

7. Bob Arnebeck, "George Washington and Yellow Fever," *Yellow Fever Casebook* (January 20, 2012), www.fevercasebook.blogspot.com.

8. Letter, "George Washington to Alexander Hamilton, September 6, 1793, *FO*.

9. Letter, "George Washington to Henry Knox," September 9, 1793, *FO*.

10. Letter, "Thomas Jefferson to James Madison," September 8, 1793, *FO*.

11. Letter, "Thomas Jefferson to James Madison," September 8, 1793, *FO*.

12. Letter, "Thomas Jefferson to James Madison," September 8 & 12, 1793, *FO*.

13. Letter, "Thomas Jefferson to James Madison," September 12, 1793, *FO*.

14. Letter, "George Washington to Tobias Lear," September 25, 1793, *FO*; Robert P. Watson, *George Washington's Final Battle: The Epic Struggle to Build a Capital City and Nation* (Washington, D.C.: Georgetown University Press, 2021), 36 and 55.

15. Letter, "George Washington to Tobias Lear," September 25, 1793, *FO*.

16. Mathew Carey, *A Short Account of the Malignant Fever, Lately Prevalent in Philadelphia: With a Statement of the Proceedings That Took Place on the Subject in Different Parts of the United States* (Philadelphia: Self-published, 1793) [National Library of Medicine: www.collections.nlm.nih.gov], 58.

17. Letter, "Tobias Lear to George Washington," October 10, 1793, *FO*.

18. Letter, "George Washington Thomas Sim Lee."

19. Arnebeck, "George Washington and Yellow Fever."

20. Letter, "George Washington to Henry Lee," October 13, 1793, *FO*.

21. Dupont was the French minister; Joseph Wright was a London-trained artist who painted Washington in 1784 and was working at the U.S. Mint.

22. Letter, "Thomas Jefferson to George Washington," September 15, 1793, *FO*.

23. The Schuylkill River runs through Philadelphia.

24. Letter, "James Madison to Thomas Jefferson," September 16, 1793, *FO*.

25. Congress was not due back in session until November and the recommendation was for it to also reconvene in Germantown.

26. Dr. Washington was the grandson was the president's cousin. He died of the fever shortly after this letter was written. Pickering was the postmaster at the time and would later succeed Knox and Jefferson in running their cabinet departments.

27. Letter, "Henry Knox to George Washington," September 15, 1793, *FO*.

28. Letter, "Henry Knox to George Washington," September 15, 1793, *FO*.

29. Letter, "Henry Knox to George Washington," September 15 and 18, 1793, *FO*.

30. Letter, "Henry Knox to George Washington," September 18, 1793, *FO*.

31. Letter, "Thomas Jefferson to George Washington," September 15, 1793, *FO*.

32. Letter, "Henry Knox to George Washington," September 18, 1793, *FO*.

33. Letter, "Henry Knox to George Washington," September 24, 1793, *FO*.

34. 34. Rev. Justus Henry Christian Helmuth, *A Short Account of the Yellow Fever in Philadelphia for the Reflecting Christian* (Philadelphia: Jones, Hoff & Derrick, 1794) [Harvard University's Library Open Collections Program on contagions; Sabin Americana Print Editions], 32.

35. Letter, "Henry Knox to George Washington," September 24, 1793, *FO*; Benjamin Rush, *An Account of the Bilious Remitting Yellow Fever as It Appeared in Philadelphia, in the Year 1793* (Philadelphia: Thomas Dobson, 1794), 330.

36. Letter, "Henry Knox to George Washington," September 18, 1793, *FO*.

Chapter Thirteen

1. Samuel A. Gum, "Philadelphia Under Siege: The Yellow Fever of 1793," Pennsylvania Center for the Book, accessed November 10, 2021, www.pabook .libraries.psu.edu.

2. Rev. Justus Henry Christian Helmuth, *A Short Account of the Yellow Fever in Philadelphia for the Reflecting Christian* (Philadelphia: Jones, Hoff & Derrick, 1794) [Harvard University's Library Open Collections Program on contagions; Sabin Americana Print Editions], 31.

3. Edwin B. Bronner and J. Philip Goldberg, "Letter from a yellow fever victim; Philadelphia, 1793," *Pennsylvania Magazine of History and Biography*, 1962, 206: www.journals.psu.edu/pmhb/article/view/41767/41498.

4. Mathew Carey, *A Short Account of the Malignant Fever, Lately Prevalent in Philadelphia: With a Statement of the Proceedings That Took Place on the Subject in Different Parts of the United States* (Philadelphia: Self-published, 1793) [National Library of Medicine: www.collections.nlm.nih.gov], 38.

5. Carey, *Short Account*, 45–46.

6. Carey, *Short Account*, 40.

7. Carey, *Short Account*, 48–50.

8. Bob Arnebeck, "Descriptions of Historic Yellow Fever Cases, Especially in Philadelphia and New York in the 1790s," *Yellow Fever Casebook* (October 26 2014): www.fevercasebook.blogspot.com; Carey, *Short Account*, 38.

9. Jim Murphy, *An American Plague: The True and Terrifying Story of Yellow Fever in Philadelphia in 1793* (New York: Clarion Books, 2003), 77.

10. Sarah Pruitt, "When the Yellow Fever Outbreak of 1793 Sent the Wealthy Fleeing Philadelphia," History Channel (June 11, 2020): www.history.com.

11. This is a somewhat common epitaph that dates back centuries, with various derivations, that can be found across the country and throughout Europe.

12. Letter, "Thomas Jefferson to James Madison," September 15, 1793, *FO*; Murphy, *American Plague*, 29.

13. Mickey Herr, "A Woman Rediscovered: A False-Bottomed Trunk and a Love of Citron Cake," Philadelphia Society for the Preservation of Landmarks (June 14, 2017), www.philalandmarks.org.

14. Arnebeck, "Samuel Powel."

15. Letter, "Samuel Powel to Benjamin Rush," undated, Rush Papers, vol. 36.

16. Bob Arnebeck, "Samuel Powel," *Yellow Fever Casebook* (April 18, 2011), www.fevercasebook.blogspot.com.; Herr, "A Woman Discovered."

17. Letter, "Elizabeth Willing Powel to George Washington," September 9, 1793, *FO*.

18. Rush, *Account*, 329.

19. New York City functioned as the interim capital for one year from 1789 to 1790 before it relocated to Philadelphia. See Robert P. Watson, *George Washington's Final Battle: The Epic Struggle to Build a Capital City and Nation* (Washington, D.C.: Georgetown University Press, 2021), 116–20.

20. Helmuth, *Short Account*, 31.

21. Benjamin Rush, *An Account of the Bilious Remitting Yellow Fever as It Appeared in Philadelphia, in the Year 1793* (Philadelphia: Thomas Dobson, 1794), 330.

22. Lillian Rhoades, *The Story of Philadelphia* (Philadelphia: American Book Company, 1900).

23. Helmuth, *Short Account*, 30.

24. The inviter was sometimes called the "aanspreecker," a term from the Dutch settlement of New Amsterdam.

25. Helmuth, *Short Account*, 29.

26. Carey, *Short Account*, 50–53.

27. Rush, *Account*, X, 330–32.

28. Henry D. Biddle, ed., Elizabeth Drinker, *Extracts from the Journal of Elizabeth Drinker, from 1759 to 1807* (Philadelphia: J. B. Lippincott Co., 1889).

Chapter Fourteen

1. The 1790 Residence Act.

2. Robert P. Watson, *George Washington's Final Battle: The Epic Struggle to Build a Capital City and Nation* (Washington, D.C.: Georgetown University Press, 2021), 155–63.

3. Watson, *George Washington's*, 218–26.

4. Germantown sat just a few miles north of Philadelphia.

5. Letter, "George Washington to Alexander Hamilton," September 25, 1793, *FO*.

6. Letter, "George Washington to Henry Knox," September 25, 1793, *FO*.

7. Letter, "George Washington to Thomas Jefferson," October 11, 1793, *FO*.

8. Trumbull was still serving in the House and would soon serve in the US Senate and as governor.

9. Letter, "George Washington to Thomas Jefferson," October 11, 1793, *FO*.

10. Letter, "George Washington to Alexander Hamilton," October 14, 1793, *FO*.

11. Letter, "George Washington to Alexander Hamilton," October 14, 1793, *FO*.

12. Letter, "George Washington to Henry Knox," October 15, 1793, *FO*.

13. Letter, "Thomas Jefferson to George Washington," October 17, 1793, *FO*.

14. Letter, "Alexander Hamilton to George Washington," October 24, 1793, *FO*.

15. Letter, "Alexander Hamilton to George Washington," October 24, 1793, *FO*.

16. Bob Arnebeck, "Descriptions of Historic Yellow Fever Cases, Especially in Philadelphia and New York in the 1790s," Yellow Fever Casebook: http://fevercasebook.blogspot.com/2012/01/george-washington-and-yellow-fever.html.

17. *FG*, October 16, 1793.

18. Henry D. Biddle, ed., Elizabeth Drinker, *Extracts from the Journal of Elizabeth Drinker, from 1759 to 1807* (Philadelphia: J. B. Lippincott Co., 1889). October 21, 1793, 209.

19. Biddle, *Extracts*, October 24, 1793, 210.

20. *FG*, October 25, 1793

21. Mathew Carey, *A Short Account of the Malignant Fever, Lately Prevalent in Philadelphia: With a Statement of the Proceedings That Took Place on the Subject in Different Parts of the United States* (Philadelphia: Self-published, 1793) [National

Library of Medicine: www.collections.nlm.nih.gov], 72; Mark A. Smith, "Andrew Brown's "Earnest Endeavor": *The Federal Gazette's* Role in Philadelphia's Yellow Fever Epidemic of 1793," *Pennsylvania Magazine of History and Biography*, vol. 120, no. 4 (October 1996), November 1, 1793.

22. Letter, "George Washington to Thomas Jefferson," October 7, 1793, *FO*.

23. Letter, "Thomas Jefferson to James Madison," November 2, 1793, *FO*.

24. Circular letters were meant to be widely circulated, often passed around among leaders and reprinted in newspapers.

25. Letter, "Alexander Hamilton to George Washington," November 3, 1793.

26. Letter, "George Washington to Tobias Lear," September 25, 1793; "Henry Knox to George Washington," September 18, 1793.

27. Letter, "Thomas Jefferson to James Madison," November 9, 1793.

28. Carey, *Short Account*, 67–69.

29. Biddle, *Extracts*, November 13 and 16, 1793, 214.

Chapter Fifteen

1. Mathew Carey, *A Short Account of the Malignant Fever, Lately Prevalent in Philadelphia: With a Statement of the Proceedings That Took Place on the Subject in Different Parts of the United States* (Philadelphia: Self-published, 1793) [National Library of Medicine: www.collections.nlm.nih.gov], 7.

2. The disease had African origins but was brought to the city by mosquitoes aboard slave and trade vessels, including the *Hankey*, all owned and captained by White people.

3. Carey, *Short Account*, 63.

4. Carey, *Short Account*, 77.

5. Carey, *Short Account*, 76–77.

6. Carey, *Short Account*, 75 and 79.

7. Sarah Pruitt, "When the Yellow Fever Outbreak of 1793 Sent the Wealthy Fleeing Philadelphia," History Channel (June 11, 2020), www.history.com.

8. Richard Allen and Absalom Jones, *A Narrative of the Proceedings of the Black People, During the Late Awful Calamity in Philadelphia in the Year 1793: and a Refutation of Some Censures, Thrown Upon them in Some Late Publications* (Philadelphia: William W. Woodward, 1794), 3.

9. Allen and Jones, *Narrative*, 7.

10. Allen and Jones, *Narrative*, 10–11.

11. Allen and Jones, *Narrative*, 11–12.

12. Allen and Jones, *Narrative*, 8.

13. Allen and Jones, *Narrative*, 4.

14. Allen and Jones, *Narrative*, 9–11.

15. Allen and Jones, *Narrative*, 8.

16. Allen and Jones, *Narrative*, 5–7.

17. Edwin Bronner and J. Philip Goldberg, "Letter from a Yellow Fever Victim; Philadelphia, 1793," *Pennsylvania Magazine of History and Biography*, 1962, 205, www.journals.psu.edu/pmhb/article/view/41767/41498.

18. Carey, *Short Account*, 106.

19. Allen and Jones, *Narrative*, 5.

20. From 1789 to 1791, the Federalist and anti-Federalist factions formed as political parties.

21. Letter, "James Madison to Thomas Jefferson," September 2, 1793

22. Mark A. Smith, "Andrew Brown's "Earnest Endeavor": *The Federal Gazette's* Role in Philadelphia's Yellow Fever Epidemic of 1793," *Pennsylvania Magazine of History and Biography*, vol. 120, no. 4 (October 1996), 322.

23. Martin Pernick, "Politics, Parties, and Pestilence: Epidemic yellow Fever in Philadelphia and the Rise of the First Party System." *The William and Mary Quarterly* 29, no. 4 (October 1972), 574.

24. Pernick, "Politics, Parties, and Pestilience," 565; Lyman Henry Butterfield, ed., *Letters of Benjamin Rush*, vol. 2: 1793–1813 (Princeton: Princeton University Press, 1951), 681; John Harvey Powell, *Bring Out Your Dead: The Great Plague of Yellow Fever in Philadelphia in 1793* (Philadelphia: University of Pennsylvania Press, 1949). Reprint: Mansfield Center, CT: Martino Publishing, 2016, 43.

25. Butterfield, *Letters*, "Benjamin Rush to Elias Boudinot,"692.

26. Butterfield, *Letters*, "Benjamin Rush to Horatio Gates," December 26, 1795, 793; Butterfield, *Letters*, "Benjamin Rush to Julia Rush," October 3, 1793.

27. Butterfield, *Letters*, "Thomas Jefferson to James Madison," September 8, 1793.

28. Benjamin Rush, *An Account of the Bilious Remitting Yellow Fever as It Appeared in Philadelphia, in the Year 1793* (Philadelphia: Thomas Dobson, 1794).

29. Powell, *Bring Out*, 52–53.

30. Edwin B. Bronner and J. Philip Goldberg, "Letter," 206.

31. *NG*, October 26, 1793.

32. See Fred Lewis Pattee, ed., *Poems of Philip Freneau*, Vol. III, The Project Gutenberg, https://www.gutenberg.org/files/39909/39909-h/39909-h.htm.

33. Smith, "Andrew Brown's Earnest," 329–30; *NG*, October 26, 1793.

34. Donald H. Stewart, *The Opposition Press of the Federalist Period* (Albany: State University of New York Press, 1969).

35. *NG*, September 23, 1793.

36. *GA*, November 30, 1793; Butterfield, *Letters*, 729–30, October 28, 1793.

37. Records of CoP, vol. I, 175, November 19, 1793; Pernick, "Politics, Parties, and Pestilence," 564; Rush, *Account*, 146; *IG*, January 22.

38. Benjamin Rush, "Observations Upon the Origin of the Malignant Bilious, or Yellow Fever in Philadelphia, and Upon the Means of Preventing It: Addressed to the Citizens of Philadelphia," 1793 [Evans Early American Imprint Collection, www.quod.lib.umich.edu/e/evans/].

39. *GUS*, December 19, 1793; *GA*, January 6, 1794; *NG*, October 16, 1793]

40. Butterfield, *Letters*, "Benjamin Rush to Mathew Carey," 807; *NG*, October 9 and 16, 1793; Carey, *Short Account*, 10.

41. *GUS*, December 14, 1793.

42. Pernick, "Politics, Parties, and Pestilence," 562, 568–69; John B. Blake, "Yellow Fever in Eighteenth Century America," *Bulletin of the New York Academy of Medicine*, vol. 44 (1968), 68.

43. Minutes of the Mayor's Committee, 120; Bob Arnebeck, "Ebola Africa 2014 and Yellow Fever Philadelphia 1793," *Yellow Fever Casebook* (October 26, 2014): www.fevercasebook.blogspot.com.

44. Jean Devèze, *An Enquiry Into, and Observations Upon the Causes and Effects of the Epidemic Disease, which Raged in Philadelphia from the Month of August Till Towards the Middle of December, 1793* (Philadelphia: Parent, 1794) [Harvard Open Library, http://pds.lib.harvard.edu/pds/view/7374528?n=84&imagesize=1 200&jp2Res=.25&printThumbnails=no], 136–38.

45. Devèze, *Enquiry*, 140 and 142.

Epilogue

1. Mathew Carey, *A Short Account of the Malignant Fever, Lately Prevalent in Philadelphia: With a Statement of the Proceedings That Took Place on the Subject in Different Parts of the United States* (Philadelphia: Self-published, 1793) [National Library of Medicine: www.collections.nlm.nih.gov], 73–75.

2. Bob Arnebeck, "A Short History of Yellow Fever in the U.S.," in *Benjamin Rush, Yellow Fever and the Birth of Modern Medicine* (2008); Carey, *Short Account*, 94 and 96; Martin Pernick, "Politics, Parties, and Pestilence: Epidemic yellow Fever in Philadelphia and the Rise of the First Party System." *The William and Mary Quarterly* 29, no. 4 (October 1972), 559; John Harvey Powell, *Bring Out Your Dead: The Great Plague of Yellow Fever in Philadelphia in 1793* (Philadelphia: University of Pennsylvania Press, 1949). Reprint: Mansfield Center, CT: Martino Publishing, 2016.

3. "Epidemic in Philadelphia: The Great Fever," *American Experience*, PBS: www.pbs.org/wgbh/americanexperience/features/fever-epidemic-philadel phia-1793/.

4. Carey, *Short Account*, 72–73.

5. Report of the Mayor's Committee, "Committee to Attend to and Alleviate the Sufferings of the Afflicted with the Malignant Fever" [University of Pennsylvania Library, call No. CAASAMF, 1793], 51.

6. Billy G. Smith, *Ship of Death: A Voyage That Changed the Atlantic World* (New Haven: Yale University Press, 2013).

7. "The First Yellow Fever Pandemic: Slavery and its Consequences," New York American Center for History (October 15, 2018): www.nyamcenterforhistory.org/2018/10/15/yellow-fever-pandemic/; Nancy Szokan, In 1792 They Set Off to Undo Slavery but Ended up Sending Yellow Fever Across the Atlantic," *Washington Post* (November 11, 2013); Ann Marie Ackerman, "The Hankey, Yellow Fever, and Nautical Signal Flags," https://www.annmarieackermann.com.

8. "The First Yellow Fever"; Szokan, "In 1792"; Smith, *Ship of Death*.

9. Powell, *Bring Out*, v; Ackerman, "The Hankey."

10. Paul E. Kopperman, "'Venerate the Lancet': Benjamin Rush's Yellow Fever Therapy in Context," *Bulletin of the History of Medicine* 78 (2004), 540; Rush, *Medical Inquiries and Observations, Containing an Account of the Bilious Remitting and Intermitting Yellow Fever* (Philadelphia: Thomas Dobson, 1794), 246.

11. Oliver Wendell Holmes, *Currents, and Counter-Currents in Medical Science; with Other Addresses and Essays* (Boston: Ticknor and Fields, 1861), 25–27.

12. Kopperman, "Venerate," 549–50.

13. Rush, *Account*, 204 (1793 edition) and 122 (1794 edition).

14. Rush, *Account*, 196.

15. Kopperman, "Venerate," 551.

16. Harriot W. Warner, ed.,*The Autobiography of Charles Caldwell, M.D.* (Philadelphia. Lippincott, Grambo, 1855), 316–17.

17. Arnebeck, "Ebola Africa," chapter 12; *PG*, September 12 and 15, 1797; William Patterson, *Remarks on Some of the Opinions of Dr. Rush Respecting the Yellow Fever which Prevailed in the City of Philadelphia in the Year 1793* (Londonderry: Douglas, 1795), 8.

18. Rush, *Account*, 117.

19. Rush, *Account*, 339.

20. Kopperman, "Venerate," 549–50.

21. See their website at www.collegeofphysicians.org/about-us.

22. Rev. Justice Henry Christian Helmuth, *A Short Account of the Yellow Fever in Philadelphia for the Reflecting Christian* (Philadelphia: Jones, Hoff & Derrick, 1794) [Harvard University's Library Open Collections Program on contagions; Sabin Americana Print Editions], ii.

23. Carol V. R. George, *Segregated Sabbaths: Richard Allen and the Emergence of Independent Black Churches, 1760–1840* (New York: Oxford University Press, 1973).

24. James Henretta, "Richard Allen and African-American Identity," *Early America Review* (Spring 1997).

25. Businessmen, eager to cash in on the good name, opened a bank named Girard Trust Company. It was later known as Girard Bank, which merged with Mellon Bank in 1983.

26. Jean Devèze, *An Enquiry Into, and Observations Upon the Causes and Effects of the Epidemic Disease, which Raged in Philadelphia from the Month of August Till Towards the Middle of December, 1793* (Philadelphia: Parent, 1794) [Harvard Open Library, http://pds.lib.harvard.edu/pds/view/7374528?n=84&im agesize=1200&jp2Res=.25&printThumnails=no], vi.

27. Arnebeck ; John E. Lane, "Jean Devèze: Notes on the Yellow Fever Epidemic at Philadelphia in 1793," *Annals of Medical History* 8, no. 3 (1936), 202.

28. One account suggests Heston died on September 28. He was buried at the Quaker Cemetery on Third and Arch Streets.

29. Kopperman, "Venerate," 539.

30. John B. Blake, "Yellow Fever in Eighteenth Century America," *Bulletin of the New York Academy of Medicine*, vol. 44 (1968), 679.

31. According to the National Museum of Health and Medicine, Washington, DC.

32. Rush, *Account*, 108; "History of Yellow Fever in the US."

33. Reed's work occurred at Camp Lazear in Cuba, a base named by the physician for his friend Jesse Lazear, a fellow physician who died from the fever after allowing himself to be bitten in order to test their theory.

34. See US Centers for Disease Control and Prevention, "Yellow Fever": cdc .gov/yellowfever/index.html.

35. Theiler won the Nobel Prize in Medicine for his vaccine. Perhaps appropriately, he was from Africa, the source of the disease.

36. Bob Arnebeck, "Dr Jean Devèze during the 1793 Epidemic," *Destroying Angel: Benjamin Rush, Yellow Fever and the Birth of Modern Medicine*: www.bob arnebeck.com/deveze.html., Prologue.

BIBLIOGRAPHY

Period Newspapers

American Daily Advertiser
Federal Gazette
Gazette of the United States
General Advertiser
Independent Gazetteer
National Gazette

Historic Sources

Allen, Richard, and Absalom Jones. *A Narrative of the Proceedings of the Black People, During the Late Awful Calamity in Philadelphia in the Year 1793: and a Refutation of Some Censures, Thrown Upon them in Some Late Publications.* Philadelphia: William W. Woodward, 1794.

Banneker, Benjamin. *Banneker's Almanac, for the Year 1793; Being the Third After Leap Year: Containing (Besides Every Thing Necessary in an Almanac) an Account of the Yellow Fever, Lately prevalent in Philadelphia.* Philadelphia: William Young, Bookseller, 1794.

Beaver, Philip. *African Memoranda: Relative to an Attempt to Establish a British Settlement on the Island of Bulama, on the Western Coast of Africa, in the Year 1792.* London: C and R Baldwin, 1805.

Biddle, Henry D., ed. Elizabeth Drinker, *Extracts from the Journal of Elizabeth Drinker, from 1759 to 1807*. Philadelphia: J. B. Lippincott Co., 1889.

Bronner, Edwin B., and J. Philip Goldberg. "Letter from a Yellow Fever Victim; Philadelphia, 1793," *Pennsylvania Magazine of History and Biography* (1962), 204–9, https://journals.psu.edu/pmhb/article/view/41767.

Boswell, James. *The Life of Samuel Johnson*, vol. I. Boston: Carter, Hendee, 1832.

Boyd, Julian P., et al., eds., *The Papers of Thomas Jefferson*. Princeton, NJ: Princeton University Press, 1950–1965, 1982.

Buckley, Roger N., ed. *The Haitian Journal of Lieutenant Howard, York Hussars, 1796–1798*. Knoxville: University of Tennessee Press, 1985.

Butterfield, Lyman Henry, ed. *Letters of Benjamin Rush*, vol. 2: 1793–1813. Princeton: Princeton University Press, 1951.

"Cabinet Opinion of Foreign Vessels and Consulting the Supreme Court," July 21, 1793, *Founders Online*: www.founders.archives.gov.

"Cabinet Opinion on French Privateers," June 1, 1793, *Founders Online*: www .founders.archives.gov.

Carey, Matthew, *A Short Account of the Malignant Fever, Lately Prevalent in Philadelphia: With a Statement of the Proceedings That Took Place on the Subject in Different Parts of the United States*. Philadelphia: Self-published, 1793; National Library of Medicine: www.collections.nlm.nih.gov.

Cathrall, Isaac. *A Medical Sketch of the Synochus Maligna, or Malignant Contagious Fever; as It Lately Appeared in the City of Philadelphia: to Which Is Added, Some Account of the Morbid Appearances Observed after Death, on Dissection*. Philadelphia: T. Dobson, 1794.

Chisholm, Colin. *An Essay on the Malignant Pestilential Fever Introduced into the West Indian Islands from Boulam, on the Coast of Guinea, as It Appeared in 1793 and 1794*. London: J Mawman, 1795; Philadelphia: Dobson, 1799, Evans Early American Collection, University of Michigan Libraries, www.quod.lib.umich .edu/e/evans/N26554.0001.001?view=toc.

"Citizen Genêt Affair, 1793-1794." Archive, U.S. Department of State: www .state.gov/r/pa/ho/time/nr/88110.htm.

"Committee for Relieving the Sick and Distressed, Appointed by a Meeting of the Citizens of Philadelphia, Summoned by Advertisement in the Public Papers,

September 13, 1793," U.S. National Library of Medicine: www.collections.nlm .nih.gov.

Currie, William. *A Description of the Malignant Infectious Fever Prevailing at Present in Philadelphia; with an Account of the Means to Prevent Infection, and the Remedies and Method of Treatment, which Have Been Found Most Successful.* Philadelphia: Thomas Dobson, 1793.

———. *An Historical Account of the Climate and Disease of the United States.* Philadelphia: Thomas Dobson, 1792.

———. *A Sketch of the Rise and Progress of the Yellow Fever.* Philadelphia: Budd, Bartram, 1800.

Devèze, Jean. *An Enquiry Into, and Observations Upon the Causes and Effects of the Epidemic Disease, which Raged in Philadelphia from the Month of August Till Towards the Middle of December, 1793.* Philadelphia: Parent, 1794, Harvard Open Library, http://pds.lib.harvard.edu/pds/view/7374528?n=84&imagesize=1200 &jp2Res=.25&printThumnails=no.

"The Diseased City." *The Broadside Mortality* (1793), University of Virginia: www.xroads.virginia.edu/-ma96/forrest/ww/feverl.html.

Fitzpatrick, John. C., ed. *The Diaries of George Washington.* New York: Houghton Mifflin, 1925.

Founders Online. National Archives: https://founders.archives.gov.

Helmuth, Rev. Justus Henry Christian. *A Short Account of the Yellow Fever in Philadelphia for the Reflecting Christian.* Philadelphia: Jones, Hoff & Derrick, 1794, Harvard University's Library Open Collections Program on contagions; Sabin Americana Print Editions.

Holmes, Oliver Wendell. *Currents, and Counter-Currents in Medical Science; with Other Addresses and Essays.* Boston: Ticknor and Fields, 1861.

Hoth, David R., ed. *The Papers of George Washington: Presidential Series*, vol. 14, September 1–December 31, 1793. Charlottesville: University Press of Virginia, 2008.

"Jeffrey Amherst and Smallpox Blankets." Collection of Lord Amherst's letters discussing germ warfare against American Indians, University of Massachusetts, www.umass.edu/legal/derrico/amherst/lord_jeff.html.

La Roche, R. *Yellow Fever, Considered in Its Historical, Pathological, Etiological and Therapeutical Relations*, vol. I. Philadelphia: Blanchard, 1855.

BIBLIOGRAPHY

Mason, John Mitchell. "Sermon Preached September 20th, 1793; a day set apart, in the city of New York, for public fasting, humiliation and prayer, on account of a malignant and mortal fever prevailing in the city of Philadelphia." New York: Samuel Loudon & Son, 1793, https://archive.org/details/sermonpreachedse00maso.

Mitchell, John. "Account of the Yellow Fever which Prevailed in Virginia in the Years 1737, 1741, and 1742." *American Medical and Philosophical Register* 4 (1814): 181–215.

————. "Mitchell's Account of the Yellow Fever in Virginia in 1741-42." *Philadelphia Medical Museum Records* 1, no. 1 (1805): 1–20.

The Papers of Thomas Jefferson, vol. 26: May to August 1793. Princeton: Princeton University Press, 1995.

The Papers of Thomas Jefferson, vol. 27: September to December 1793. Princeton: Princeton University Press, 1997.

Patrick, Christine S., ed. *The Papers of George Washington: Presidential Series*, vol. 13: June 1–August 31, 1793. Charlottesville: University Press of Virginia, 2007.

Patterson, William. *Remarks on Some of the Opinions of Dr. Rush Respecting the Yellow Rever which Prevailed in the City of Philadelphia in the Year 1793*. Londonderry: Douglas, 1795.

Philadelphia Common Council. "Minutes of the Proceedings of the Committee Appointed on the Date of 14 September to Alleviate the Suffering of the Afflicted" (1794), http://pds.lib.harvard.edu/pds/view/6395244?n=30&printthumb nails=no.

Preston, Paul. "Some Incidents of the Yellow Fever Epidemic of 1793." *Pennsylvania Magazine of History and Biography* 38 (1914): 236–37.

Purdon, John. "Reflections Caused by the Yellow Fever in the Year 1793." In *A Leisure Hour, or, a Series of Poetical Letters Mostly Written During the Prevalence of the Yellow Fever*, Philadelphia: P. Stewart,1804.

Report of the Mayor's Committee. "Committee to Attend to and Alleviate the Sufferings of the Afflicted with the Malignant Fever." University of Pennsylvania Library, call No. CAASAMF, 1793.

Rush, Benjamin, *An Account of the Bilious Remitting Yellow Fever as It Appeared in Philadelphia, in the Year 1793*. Philadelphia: Thomas Dobson, 1794.

————. *Medical Inquiries and Observations, Containing an Account of the Bilious Remitting and Intermitting Yellow Fever* Philadelphia: Thomas Dobson, 1794.

————. "Observations Upon the Origin of the Malignant Bilious, or Yellow Fever in Philadelphia, and Upon the Means of Preventing It: Addressed to the Citizens of Philadelphia," 1793, Evans Early American Imprint Collection, www.quod.lib.umich.edu/e/evans/.

Stanislaus, Francis Alexander. *A Voyage to Saint-Domingue, in the Years 1788, 1789, and 1790.* London: T. Cadell and W. Davies, 1791.

Syrett, Harold C., ed. *The Papers of Alexander Hamilton, Digital Edition*, vol. 15, June 1, 1793–January 31, 1794. Charlottesville: University Press of Virginia, 2011–2021.

Webster, Noah. *A Brief History of Epidemic and Pestilential Diseases; with the Principal Phenomena of the Physical World, which Precede and Accompany Them, and Observations Deduced from the Facts Stated.* Evans Early American Collection, University of Michigan Libraries, www.quod.lib.umich.edu/e/evans/N27531.00 01.001/1:11?rgn=div1;view=fulltext].

Weld, Isaac. *Travels through the States of North America and the Provinces of Upper and Lower Canada During the Years 1795, 1796 and 1797*, 4th ed. London: John Stockdale, 1807.

"Yearly Meeting Epistle 1793," Swarthmore College Library Quaker Collection and the letter, "Margaret Morris to her daughter," August 31, 1793, in the Haverford College library manuscript collection.

"The Yellow Fever Epidemic in Philadelphia, 1793." Harvard University Library Open Collections, http://ocp.hul.harvard.edu/contagion/yellowfever.html.

Books

Apel, Thomas A. *Feverish Bodies, Enlightened Minds: Science and the Yellow Fever Controversy in the Early American Republic.* (Palo Alto, CA: Stanford University Press, 2016.

Arnebeck, Bob. *Destroying Angel: Benjamin Rush, Yellow Fever and the Birth of Modern Medicine*, 1999. Online book. Bobarnebeck.com/fever1793.html.

Bell, Whitfield, J. *The Colonial Physician & Other Essays.* New York: Science History Publications, 1975.

Buckley, Roger N., ed. *The Haitian Journal of Lieutenant Howard, York Hussars, 1796–1798.* Knoxville: University of Tennessee Press, 1985.

BIBLIOGRAPHY

Chernow, Ron. *Washington: A Life.* New York: Penguin, 2010.

Childs, Frances S. *French Refugee Life in the United States, 1790–1800: An American Chapter of the French Revolution.* Baltimore: Johns Hopkins University Press, 1940.

Christophers, Rickard. *"Aëdes Aegypti": The Yellow Fever Mosquito: Its Life History, Bionomics and Structure.* Cambridge: Cambridge University Press, 2009.

Crouse, N. M. *The French Struggle for the West Indies, 1665–1713.* New York: Columbia University Press, 1943.

Dubois, Laurent. *Avengers of the New World: The Story of the Haitian Revolution.* Cambridge, Mass: Belknap, 2004.

Estes, J. Worth, and Billy G Smith, eds. *Melancholy Scenes of Devastation: The Public Response to the 1793 Philadelphia Yellow Fever Epidemic.* Canton, MA: Science History Publications, 1997.

Fried, Stephen. *Rush: Revolution, Madness & The Visionary Doctor Who Became a Founding Father.* New York: Broadway Books, 2018.

George, Carol V. R. *Segregated Sabbaths: Richard Allen and the Emergence of Independent Black Churches, 1760–1840.* New York: Oxford University Press, 1973.

Hofstadter, Richard. *The Idea of a Party System: The Rise of Legitimate Opposition in the United States, 1780–1840.* Berkeley: University of California Press, 1969.

Karlen, Arno. *Man and Microbes: Disease and Plague in History and Modern Times.* New York: G. P. Putnam's Sons, 1995.

Law, Robin, Suzanne Schwarz, and Silke Strickrodt, eds. *Commercial Agriculture, the Slave Trade and Slavery in Atlantic Africa.* Woodbridge: Boydell and Brewer, 2013.

McNeill, J. R. *Mosquito Empires: Ecology and War in the Greater Caribbean.* Cambridge: Cambridge University Press, 2010.

Murphy, Jim. *An American Plague: The True and Terrifying Story of Yellow Fever in Philadelphia in 1793.* New York: Clarion Books, 2003.

Park, K. *Secrets of Women: Gender, Generation and the Origins of Human Dissection.* (New York: Zone Books, 2006.

Powell, John Harvey. *Bring Out Your Dead: The Great Plague of Yellow Fever in Philadelphia in 1793.* Philadelphia: University of Pennsylvania Press, 1949. Reprint: Mansfield Center, CT: Martino Publishing, 2016.

Rediker, Marcus. *Between the Devil and the Deep Blue Sea: Merchant Seamen, Pirates, and the Anglo-American Maritime World, 1700–1750.* Cambridge: Cambridge University Press, 1989.

Rhoades, Lillian. *The Story of Philadelphia.* Philadelphia: American Book Company, 1900.

Smith, Billy G. *Ship of Death: A Voyage That Changed the Atlantic World.* New Haven: Yale University Press, 2013.

Stewart, Donald H. *The Opposition Press of the Federalist Period.* Albany: State University of New York Press, 1969.

Warner, Harriot W., ed. *The Autobiography of Charles Caldwell, M.D.* Philadelphia. Lippincott, Grambo, 1855.

Watson, Robert P. *George Washington's Final Battle: The Epic Struggle to Build a Capital City and Nation.* Washington, DC: Georgetown University Press, 2021.

Articles and Online Sources

"1681–1776: The Quaker Province," in *The Founding of Pennsylvania.* Pennsylvania Historical & Museum Commission, www.phmc.state.pa.us/portal/communities/pa-history/1681-1776.html.

"Absalom Jones," *Black History Now* (June 6, 2014), www.blackhistorynow.com.

Ackermann, Ann Marie, "The Hankey, Yellow Fever, and Nautical Signal Flags," https://www.annmarieackermann.com.

Arnebeck, Bob, "A Short History of Yellow Fever in the U.S.," in *Benjamin Rush, Yellow Fever and the Birth of Modern Medicine* (2008).

———. "Descriptions of Historic Yellow Fever Cases, Especially in Philadelphia and New York in the 1790s," *Yellow Fever Casebook* (October 26 2014), www.fevercasebook.blogspot.com.

———. "Dr Jean Devèze during the 1793 Epidemic," *Destroying Angel: Benjamin Rush, Yellow Fever and the Birth of Modern Medicine,* www.bobarnebeck.com/deveze.html.

———. "Ebola Africa 2014 and Yellow Fever Philadelphia 1793," *Yellow Fever Casebook* (October 26, 2014), www.fevercasebook.blogspot.com.

———. "George Washington and Yellow Fever," *Yellow Fever Casebook* (January 20, 2012), www.fevercasebook.blogspot.com.

———. "Samuel Powel," *Yellow Fever Casebook* (April 18, 2011), www.fevercase book.blogspot.com.

"Aztec Capital Falls to Cortés," *History* (February 9, 2010), www.history.com /this-day-in-history/aztec-capital-falls-to-cortes.

"Black Death," *History* (July 6, 2020), www.history.com/topics/middle-ages /black-death.

"Black Founders: The Free Black Community in the Early Republic," Library Company of Philadelphia, www.librarycompany.org/blackfounders/section4.htm.

Blake, John B. "Yellow Fever in Eighteenth Century America," *Bulletin of the New York Academy of Medicine* 44 (1968): 680.

Bolton, Carol. "The Bolama Colony and Abolitionary Reform in Captain Beaver's African Memoranda, 1805," *Romance, Revolution and Reform: The Journal of the Southampton Centre for Nineteenth Century Research*, issue 3 (January 2021): 105–27.

Brown, Elizabeth A. R. "Authority, the Family, and the Dead in Late Medieval France," *French Historical Studies* 16, no. 4 (1990): 803–32.

Brown, Marion E. "Adam Kuhn: Eighteenth Century Physician and Teacher," *Journal of the History of Medicine and Allied Sciences* 5, no. 2 (Spring 1950), 163–77.

Burnard, Trevor. "A New Look at the Zong Case of 1783," *Revue de la Société d'Etudes Anglo-Américains*, vol. 76 (2019), www.journals.openedition .org/1718/1808.

"Cap-Français." *Slavery and Remembrance, Colonial Williamsburg*: www.slavery andremembrance.org.

Cohen, Amy. "Bravery and Bad Deeds During the Yellow Fever Outbreak of 1793," *Hidden City* (May 11, 2020), www.hiddencityphila.org.

Cohn, Samuel K. Jr., "The Black Death and the Burning of Jews," *Past & Present* 196, issue 1 (August 2007): 3–36.

Coleman, Deirdre. "Bulama and Sierra Leone: Utopian Islands and Visionary Interiors." In *Islands in History and Representations*, Rod Edmond and Venessa Smith, eds., 63–81. London: Routledge, 2003.

College of Physicians of Philadelphia, www.collegeofphysicians.org.

Cook, Jane Hampton. "In the 1st U.S. Epidemic, Alexander Hamilton Leveraged Newspapers to Save Lives," *Genealogy Bank* (March 18, 2020), www.blog.genealogybank.com.

Cook, Noble David. "Sickness, Starvation, and Death in Early Hispaniola." *Journal of Interdisciplinary History* 32, no. 3 (Winter 2002): 349–86.

Cornfield, Dennis B. "The Hospital at Bush Hill: Philadelphia's Response to the 1793 Yellow Fever Epidemic," *MD Advisor* (Summer 2020): MD Advantage, www.mdadvantageonline.com/feature-articles/the-hospital-at-bush-hill-philadelphias-respose-to-the-1793-yellow-fever-epidemic/.

Dehler, Gregory J. "Neutrality Proclamation," Washington Library, George Washington's Mount Vernon, www.mountvernon.org/library/digitalhistory/digital-encyclopedia/article/neutrality-proclamation/.

"The Determinants of Mortality." *Bulletin on Aging & Health*, no 2 (June 2006), https://www.nber.org/bah/spring06/determinants-mortality.

"The Diseased City." *The Broadside Mortality*, 1793. Reprinted in Xroads, University of Virginia, www.xroads.virginia.edu/-ma96/forrest/ww/feverl.html.

"Dr. Phillip Syng Physick." Penn Medicine, www.uphs.upenn.edu/paharc/time line/1751/tline8.html.

Duncan, C. J., and S. Scott. "What Caused the Black Death?" *Postgraduate Medical Journal* 81, no. 955 (2005): 315–20.

"Epidemic in Philadelphia: The Great Fever." *American Experience*, PBS, www.pbs.org/wgbh/americanexperience/features/fever-epidemic-philadelphia-1793/.

"The First Yellow Fever Pandemic: Slavery and its Consequences." New York American Center for History (October 15, 2018), www.nyamcenterforhistory.org/2018/10/15/yellow-fever-pandemic/.

Freedman, Dan. "Why Were Jews Blamed for the Black Death?" *Moment Magazine* (March 31, 2021), www.momentmag.com/why-were-jews-blamed-for-the-black-death/.

Frerichs, Ralph R. "Competing Theories of Cholera." University of California, Los Angeles, www.ph.ucla.edu/epi/snowcholeratheories.html.

"George Washington's Second Presidential Term." *George Washington: Biography, History, and Facts*, www.georgewashington.org/second-presidential-term.jsp.

BIBLIOGRAPHY

Ghosh, Sanjib Kumar. "Human Cadaveric Dissection: A Historical Account from Ancient Greece to the Modern Era" *Anatomy & Cell Biology* 48, no. 3 (September 2015): 153–69.

"Great Fever. The" *American Experience*, PBS, www.pbs.org/wgbh/americanex perience/films/fever/.

"Guardians of the Poor." Philadelphia Information Locater Service, Department of Records, City of Philadelphia, www.phila.gov/phils/docs/inventor/graph ics/agencies/a035.htm#:~:text+by%20an%20act%20of%20Januar.proceeds%20 among%20the%20city's%20indigent.

Gum, Samuel A. "Philadelphia Under Siege: The Yellow Fever of 1793," Pennsylvania Center for the Book, www.pabook.libraries.psu.edu.

"Haiti (Saint-Domingue). " *Slavery and Remembrance*, Colonial Williamsburg, www.slaveryandremembrance.org.

Hawgood, Barbara J. "Alexandre Yersin: Discoverer of the Plague Bacillus, Explorer, and Agronomist," *PubMed: National Library of Medicine* 16, no. 3 (August 2008): 167–72.

Henretta, James. "Richard Allen and African-American Identity," *Early America Review* (Spring 1997).

Herr, Mickey. "A Woman Rediscovered: A False-Bottomed Trunk and a Love of Citron Cake," Philadelphia Society for the Preservation of Landmarks (June 14, 2017), www.philalandmarks.org.

"The History of Vaccines: Yellow Fever." The College of Physicians of Philadelphia, www.historyofvaccines.org/timeline/yellow-fever.

"History of Yellow Fever in the U.S." American Society for Microbiology (May 17, 2021), www.asm.org/articles/2021/may/history-of-yellow-fever-in-the-u-s.

Horgan, John. "Justinian's Plague," *World History Encyclopedia* (December 26, 2014), www.worldhistory.org/article/782/justinians-plague-541-542.ce/.

"How Pandemics Change Society." *HUB: Johns Hopkins Magazine* (April 9, 2020), www.hub.jhu.edu/2020/04/09/alexandre-white-how-pandemics-shape -society/.

Jaracho, Saul. "John Mitchell, Benjamin Rush, and Yellow Fever," *Bulletin of the History of Medicine* 31, no 2 (1957): 132–36.

Kannadan, Ajesh. "History of the Miasma Theory of Disease," *ESSAI* 16, article 18 (Spring 2018), www.dc.cod.edu/essai/vol16/iss1/18.

Kleisiaris, Christos F., Chrisanthos Sfakianakis, and Ioanna V. Papathanasiou. "Health Care Practices in Ancient Greece: The Hippocratic Ideal," *Journal of Medical Ethics and History of Medicine* 7 (2014): 6.

Knight, Franklin W. "The Haitian Revolution," *American Historical Review* 105, no. 1 (February 2000): 103–15.

Kopperman, Paul E. "'Venerate the Lancet': Benjamin Rush's Yellow Fever Therapy in Context," *Bulletin of the History of Medicine* 78 (2004): 539–74.

Lambert, Tim. "A History of Life Expectancy in the UK," *Local Histories*, https://localhistories.org/a-history-of-life-expectancy-in-the-uk/.

Lane, John E. "Jean Devèze: Notes on the Yellow Fever Epidemic at Philadelphia in 1793," *Annals of Medical History* 8, no. 3 (1936): 202–25, www.ncbi.nlm.nih.gov/pmc/articles/pmc7939912/pdf/annmedhist147404-0024.pdf.

Laughton, J. K., and Andrew Lambert. "Beaver, Philip," *Oxford Dictionary of National Biography*.

Lewis, Thomas. "Transatlantic Slave Trade," *Encyclopedia Britannica*, www.britannica.com/topic/transatlantic-slave-trade.

Mark, Joshua J. "Thucydides on the Plague of Athens: Text & Commentary," *World History Encyclopedia*, www.worldhistory.org/article/1535/thucydides-on-the-plague-of-athens-text-commentary/.

Mendelsohn, Everett. "John Lining and his Contribution to Early American Science," *Isis: History of Science Society* 51, no. 3 (September 1960): 278–92.

Meredith, Mark. "Bush Hill." *House Histree* (May 21, 2020), www.househistree.com/houses/bush-hill.

Mintz, Steven. "Historical Context: Facts About the Slave Trade and Slavery," The Gilder-Lehrman Institute of American History, www.gilder-lehrman.org/history-resources/teacher-resources/historical-context-facts-about-slave-trade-and-slavery.

"Neutrality Proclamation." Washington Library, Mount Vernon, www.mountvernon.org/library/digitalhistory/digital-encyclopedia/article/neutrality-proclamation/.

Peabody, Bruce G. "George Washington, Presidential Term Limits, and the Problem of Reluctant Political Leadership," *Presidential Studies Quarterly* 31, no. 3 (September 2001): 439–53.

BIBLIOGRAPHY

Pernick, Martin. "Politics, Parties, and Pestilence: Epidemic yellow Fever in Philadelphia and the Rise of the First Party System," *The William and Mary Quarterly* 29, no. 4 (October 1972): 559–86.

"Philadelphia." *Africans*. PBS Series, www.pbx.org/wgbbh/aia/part3/3narr1.html.

Preston, Paul. "Some Incidents of the Yellow Fever Epidemic of 1793," *Pennsylvania Magazine of History and Biography* (Vol 38, 1914): 236–37.

Pruitt, Sarah. "When the Yellow Fever Outbreak of 1793 Sent the Wealthy Fleeing Philadelphia," History Channel (June 11, 2020), www.history.com.

"The Quaker Province: 1681–1776." *Pennsylvania History*. Pennsylvania Historical & Museum Commission, www.phmc.state.pa.us/portal/communities /pa-history/1681-1776.html.

Ruane, Michael E. "Yellow Fever Led Half of Philadelphians to Flee the City, Ten Percent of the Residents Still Died," *Washington Post* (April 4, 2020).

"Rush on Abolition and Race." Benjamin Rush Portal, University of Pennsylvania Libraries, www.guides.library.upenn.edu/benjaminrush/abolitionist.

"Samuel Powel." Washington Library, Mount Vernon, www.mountvernon.org /library/digitalhistory/digital-encyclopedia/articl/samuel-powel/.

Schroeder, Amira Rose. "Girard Stephen," Civil Rights in a Northern City: Philadelphia. Temple University Libraries, www.northerncity.library.temple.edu/ exhibits/show/civil-rights-in-a-northern-cit/people-and-places/girard--stephen.

Schwarz, Suzanne. "Commerce, Civilization and Christianity: The Development of the Sierra Leone Company." In *Liverpool and Transatlantic Slavery*, edited by David Richardson, Suzanne Schwarz, and Anthony Tibbles, 252–70. Liverpool: Liverpool University Press, 2007.

Seven, John. "The Black Death: A Timeline of the Gruesome Pandemic," *History* (April 16, 2020), www.history.com/news/black-death-timeline.

Sivitz, Paul, and Billy G. Smith. "Philadelphia and Its People in Maps: The 1790s." *The Encyclopedia of Greater Philadelphia*, www.philadelphiaencyclopedia. org/archive/philadelphia-and-its-people-in-maps-the-1790s/.

Smith, Mark A. "Andrew Brown's "Earnest Endeavor": *The Federal Gazette's* Role in Philadelphia's Yellow Fever Epidemic of 1793." *Pennsylvania Magazine of History and Biography* 120, no. 4 (October 1996): 321–42.

Stub, Sara Toth. "Venice's Black Death and the Dawn of Quarantine." *Sapiens: Anthropology Magazine* (April 24, 2020), www.sapiens.org/archaeology/venice -guarantine-history.

Szokan, Nancy. "In 1792 They Set Off to Undo Slavery but Ended up Sending Yellow Fever Across the Atlantic." *Washington Post* (November 11, 2013).

Tan, Siang Yong, and Yvonne Tatsumura. "Alexander Fleming: Discoverer of Penicillin." *Singapore Medical Journal* 56, no. 7 (2015): 366–67.

Than, Ker. "Two of History's Deadliest Plagues Were Linked: With Implications for Another Outbreak." *National Geographic* (January 11, 2014), www.nation algeographic.com/animals/article/140129-justinian-plague-black-death-bacteria -bubonic-pandemic.

"Thucydides on the Plague." Livius: www.livius.org/sources/content/thucydides -historian/the-plague/.

Tindol, Robert. "Getting the Pox Off All Their Houses: Cotton Mather and the Rhetoric of Puritan Science." *Early American Literature*. 46, no. 1 (2011): 1–23.

Van Liere, Frans. "The Pope and the Plague." *Historical Horizons* (March 27, 2020), www.historicalhorizons.org/2020/03/27/the-pope-and-the-plague.

Watkins, Thayer. "The Expedition of Hernando de Soto to Southeastern North America, 1538–1543." San Jose State University, www.sjsu.edu/faculty/watkins /desoto.htm.

"William Wilberforce: The Politician." *The Abolition Project*, www.abolition .e2bn.org/people_24.html.

Wolfinger, James. "African American Migration." *The Encyclopedia of Greater Philadelphia*: https://philadelphiaencyclopedia.org/archive/african-american-mi gration/.

"Yellow Fever." Centers for Disease Control and Prevention, www.cdc.gov/yel lowfever/index.html.

"Yellow Fever." National Institutes of Health, www.nihlibrary.nih.gov/resources /subject-guides/infectious-diseases/yellow-fever.

"Yellow Fever." World Health Organization, www.who.int/news-room/fact -sheets/detail/yellow-fever.

"Yellow Fever Breaks Out in Philadelphia." history.com: www.history.com/this -day-in-history/yellow-fever-breaks-out-in-philadelphia.

INDEX

Photo plate images between pages 116 and 117 are indicated by *p1*, *p2*, *p3*, etc.

"A.B." (*Federal Gazette* contributor), 118–19
abolitionists, xviii, xxi, 136, 161, 195
Absalom Jones (Peale), *p7*
Academy and College of Philadelphia. *See* University of Pennsylvania
Adams, Abigail, 105
Adams, Henry, 36
Adams, John, 42, 104–5, 147
Aedes aegypti (mosquito), 27–29, 52, 205
Africa, yellow fever in, 27–28, 136
African chiefs, slavers aided by, xx
African Methodist Episcopal Church (AME Church), 201
Africans, immunity and, 135–38
Allen, Flora, 140
Allen, Richard, 140–43, 181–82, 201, *p8*; Bush Hill described by, 107; Free African Society defended by,

179–80, 200; slavery experienced by, 138–39
almshouses, 38, 94, 104
AME Church. *See* African Methodist Episcopal Church
Amelia (ship), 48, 53
America. *See specific topics*
American Daily Advertiser (newspaper), 118–19
American Philosophical Society, in Philadelphia, 95, 118
American Revolution, xxiv, 36–37
Amherst, Jeffrey, 11
Amos III, verse 6, 87
Annan, William, 109, 113
"Anthony Benezet" (pseudonym), 136. *See also* Rush, Benjamin
anti-Federalists, 39, 40, 126, 186, 245n20
Anti-Slavery Society, xviii

Arch Street Ferry, Philadelphia (Birch), *p2*
Arch Street Meeting House, 93
Arnebeck, Bob, 32, 198, 202
Articles of Confederation, 35, 95
Aston, Peter, 63–64, 65
Athens, Plague of, 4
Aztecs, smallpox killing, 10

Bache, Benjamin Franklin, 187
Bank of North America, 107
Bank of Pennsylvania, 95
Barbados (British colony), 17–18
"bargain of 1790," 40–41
Bass, Sarah, 180, 201
Battle of Yorktown, 221n10
Beakly, Ann, 109
Beaver, Philip, xxi, xxiv–xxv, xxx, 15
Beggar's Benison (ship), xxv, xxix, xxx, 33
Bell, C. M., *p8*
Benge, Samuel, 100–101
Bethel African Methodist Episcopal Church. *See* African Methodist Episcopal Church
Biafada (tribe), Bolama owned by, 14
Bickham, Sally, 108
Biddle, Charles, 80
Birch, W., *p2*
Bissau, xxii, xxx, 16
Black community, of Philadelphia, 37–38, 136–37, 200; Bush Hill staffed by, 107; Carey on, 178–79, 182; Clarkson helped by, 179; dedication of, 180. *See also* Free African Society
Black Death, Europe decimated by, 4–7
Blake, John, 27, 31

bleeding and purging (treatment), 81; of McNair, 64; potion for purging during, 123; Republican supporting, 184; Rush using, 58, 70–71, 75, 123–26, 142–43
Blount, William, 43
bodies, Free African Society collecting, 141, 181
Bodinot, Elias, 184
Bolama (island), xxii, 13; Biafada owning, 14; colonists on, xxx–xxxi; initial plan to settle, xxiii–xxiv; map of, *p1*; women traveling to, xxv; yellow fever on, 15–16. *See also* Bulama Association
Bolama experiment, xviii, xxi, xxi–xxv, 33
"Bolama Fever." *See* yellow fever
Bolívar, Simón, 23
Bonaparte, Napoleon, 22–23, 26
Boniface VIII (pope), 6–7
Book of Common Prayer, on plague, 157
Boyles, Thomas, 105
Bradford, Polly, 58
Bradford, Thomas, 58
Breck, Samuel, 66
Britain: France warring with, 145–47; slave trade ended in, xx; Spain in relations with, xxix. *See also* England; West Indies
British Foreign Ministry, xxi
Brown, Andrew, 79, 147, 183
Brown, Edward, 127
bubonic plague, 4–6
Bulama, Island of, *p1*
Bulama Association: American Revolution inspiring, xxiv; charter by, xxiv; funding of, xxiii; working class of, xxii
burials, 100–101, 142

Burke, Edmund, xx
Bush Hill, 104, 111, 136–37, 178, *p4*;
Black community staffing, 107;
Carey assessing, 106–7; death at,
115; Free African Society staffing,
142; Girard supervising, 108–9,
111–12; Guardians of the Poor
commandeering, 105; Hamilton,
A., reclaiming, 189–90; yellow fever
overrunning, 105–6

Caldwell, Charles, 105, 198
Callender, James Thomson, 183
Calypso (ship), xxv, xxviii, xxxi;
England left for by, 15; near Bissau,
xxx; smallpox on, xxix
camphor, in treatments, v, 96, 99,
118–19, 233n23
Camp Lazear, in Cuba, 249n33
Canabacs (tribe), xxxi, 13–14, 15
Canaries (islands), xxix
Cape Verde (islands), xix, xxix– xxx, 16
Cap Français, Saint-Domingue: Cox
sailing for, 21–22; France priding,
20; *Hankey* at, 25–26; slaves
attacking, 22, 110
capital, of U.S., 172; disease
threatening, 168–69; Hamilton, A.,
suggesting, 173; New York City
as, 242n19; Philadelphia as, 39–42,
187; Washington, G., prioritizing,
43, 167–68
Capitol, cornerstone laid at, 167–68
Carey, Mathew, v, 65–66, 83–85,
100, *p6*; on Black community,
178–79, 182; Bush Hill assessed
by, 106–7; on coffee, 53; on federal
government, 151; Free African
Society criticized by, 178, 201; on
Helm, 112; *Narrative* questioning,

181–82; on origin, 121–22; on
Philadelphia, 44, 49; on Rush,
165; terror described by, 78, 93; on
weather, 176; Weed confusing, 87;
on yellow fever, 77, 177–78, 193
Cathrall, Isaac, 54–56, 58–59, 82, 109,
125–26
Charles II (king), 35
Charleston, South Carolina, 135
Charon (ship), 16, 221n10
Chernow, Ron, 40
Chestnut Street Theater, preachers
targeting, 188
Chew, Benjamin, 138
children, orphaned, 84–85
Chisholm, Colin, 17, 18
Christ Church, 142
Christians, flagellation by, 7
"The Citizen Genêt Affair," 146
Clarkson, Matthew, 69, 94, 106–7,
189, 201, *p6*; Black community
helping, 179; College of Physicians
met with by, 95; Committee
to Attend to and Alleviate the
Sufferings of the Afflicted with the
Malignant Fever established by, 99;
disease limited by, 98, 101; Free
African Society contacted by, 137;
Hutchinson counseling, 96
Clement VI (pope), 7
climate change, starvation influenced
by, 5
Cobbett, William, 198
coffee, rotted, 52–53, 69, 95, 113,
121–23
College of Physicians, 69, 199;
Clarkson meeting, 95; Hamilton,
A., writing to, 127; on origin, 187;
recommendations by, 96–98
Collingwood, Luke, xix

colonists, xxv, 16; on Bolama, xxx–xxxi; Canabacs killing, xxxi, 15; *Hankey* boarded by, 26; as refugees, 48; yellow fever killing, 14–15, 33

Columbus, Christopher, 9, 22

Committee for the Relief of the Sick, 84

Committee of Distribution (subcommittee), 100

Committee to Attend to and Alleviate the Sufferings of the Afflicted with the Malignant Fever, 99–101

Congress, U.S., 176; Executive power over, 170–72, 175; First and Second Continental, 35; Philadelphia met outside of, 168–72

Connelly, John, 100

conservatives, threatened by Philadelphia, 183

Constitution, U.S., 36, 42, 149, 168, 172, 175

Constitutional Convention, xxvi, 40, 69, 78, 172

Cooper, Fenimore, 201

Cortés, Hernán, 10

Courtney, Richard, 155–56

COVID-19 pandemic, xi–xii

Cox, John, xxviii, xxx, 16, 21–22, 25–26

Cranchal, Caesar, 180

Cuba, Camp Lazear in, 203–4

Currie, William, 29, 96, 125–26, 129–31, 200

Daily Advertiser (newspaper), 128

Dalrymple, Henry Hew, 15

Davidson, Lucretia Maria, 47

Dawson, Joshua, 92

death, 72–73, 81–82, 163; at Bush Hill, 115; in Committee to Attend to and Alleviate the Sufferings of the Afflicted with the Malignant Fever, 101; Drinker, E., recording, 51, 66; Hamilton, A., recording, 155; Helmuth on, 51, 78–79; of infants, 6, 58; of LeMaigre, C., 65; mortality rates, 93, 141; Rush impacted by, 74; from yellow fever, 55–56, 193–94

Declaration of Independence, 36

Deforest, Henry, 100

Delaware River, 89

Democratic Society, Pennsylvania, 147

Denmark, xix, 205

Denny, Richard, 49–50

Denny's Boardinghouse, 49–50, 54–55, 226n10

A Description of the Malignant, Infectious Fever Prevailing at Present in Philadelphia (Currie), 200

Deshler, David, 174

Dessalines, Jean-Jacques, 23, 26

Devèze, Jean, 129–32; Girard impressed by, 111, 113; Rush contrasted with, 114–15, 190, 202; yellow fever known to, 109–10

"dinner table bargain," 40–41

disease, 49, 128, 157, 163–64, 244n2; capital threatened by, 168–69; Clarkson limiting, 98, 101; combatting of, 8; contagiousness lacked by, 80, 113, 129–30; Drinker, E., chronicling, 59; etiology studying, 8; Europeans carrying, 9–11; factions impacted by, 182–83; fascination with, xi; *Federal Gazette* politicizing, 127; federal government threatened by, 92–93, 148; *Hankey* isolated by, 21–22; hemorrhagic, 28;

Hutchinson dismissing, 122; medical community debating, 54; microbes spreading, 3–4; during Peloponnesian War, 4; in port, 121; public influenced by, 99; on ships, xxviii; state government strained by, 91; Tartars spreading, 5; U.S. impacted by, 196; in West Indies, 9. *See also* immunity; pestilence; smallpox; yellow fever

Dispensary, physicians from, 54

dissection, of human body, 6–7

docks, in Philadelphia, 38, 51; Falconer inspecting, 92; *Hankey* at, 49–50; as origin, 131; refugees housed at, 50; yellow fever at, 52–56, 92. *See also* Water Street

Dodd (captain), 16–17

Drinker, Elizabeth, 83–84, 120–21, 138, 146, 176, 200; death recorded by, 51, 66; disease chronicled by, 59; fear expressed by, 165; on Hutchinson, 71; privateers noted by, 146; on Water Street, 86; weather recorded by, 44, 79; on yellow fever, 173–74

Drinker, Henry, 59

drought, Philadelphians impacted by, 44–45

"Dr. Rush's Directions for Curing and Treating Yellow Fever" (Rush), 123

Dundas, Henry, 18

economy, of Philadelphia, 44, 86

Encyclopedia Americana (Scott, W., and Cooper), 201

L'Enfant, Pierre Charles, 43, 225n23

England: *Calypso* leaving for, 15; economy impacted by, 44; Isle of Wight in, xxvi; London in, 118

An Enquiry into, and Observations Upon the Causes and Effects of the Epidemic Disease (Devèze), 202

essential services, for Philadelphia: collapse of, 86; Free African Society performing, 138, 182; of Guardians of the Poor, 106

etiology, disease studied by, 8

Europe, Black Death decimating, 4–7

Europeans: disease carried by, 9–11; lives of, 6; yellow fever contracted by, 30

evacuation, of Philadelphia, 79–80, 86, 98, 127–28; by federal government, 149; Philadelphia after, 157–58; Republicans disparaging, 186; Rush and, 72, 164; Washington, G., ordering, 150

"Evangeline" (Longfellow), 23

Evangelisches Magasin (newspaper), 200

Executive power, over Congress, 170–72, 175

Exodus 9:15, 3

Extracts from the Journal of Elizabeth Drinker (Drinker, E.), 200

Fabricius, Johann Christian, 205

factions, partisan, 41–42, 126–27, 182–83. *See also* anti-Federalists; Federalists; Republicans

Falconer, Nathaniel, 92

famine, fascination with, xi

The Federal Gazette and Philadelphia Daily Advertiser (newspaper), 79, 85, 118, 127, 147, 173; on Guardians of the Poor, 106

federal government, U.S., 41, 167–69; Carey on, 151; disease threatening,

92–93, 148; evacuation by, 149; in
Philadelphia, 35–36, 39–41
Federalists, 127, 184; anti-, 39,
40, 126, 186, 245n20; Freneau
attacking, 186; Jefferson criticizing,
185; Madison opposing, 183
Fenno, John, 127, 147, 183
Ferris, J. L. G., *p8*
fever. *See* yellow fever
fever hospital, Guardians of the Poor
developing, 103–4
Finlay, Carlos, 203
First Bank, of the United States, 108,
202
Fisher, Edward, 142
Fisher's Island, in Delaware River, 89
flagellation, by Christians, 7
Flaviviridae (virus family), 28
Fleming, Alexander, 9, 124–25
Flora (ship), 48, 121–22
Foulke, John, 64–65
France, 21; Britain warring with, 145–
47; Cap Français prided by, 20;
against Maroons, 22; refugees and,
147; yellow fever impacting, 23. *See
also* Saint-Domingue
Franklin, Benjamin, 36
Free African Society, 140, 143; Allen,
R., defending, 179–80, 200; bodies
collected by, 141, 181; Bush Hill
staffed by, 142; Carey criticizing,
178, 201; Clarkson contacting, 137;
essential services performed by, 138,
182; payment of, 178, 181–82
Freedom Journal (newspaper), 137
French Revolution, 22
Freneau, Philip, xv, 126, 147;
Federalists attacked by, 186;
partisans blamed by, 185;
Washington, G., disparaged by, 188

funerals, of Philadelphians, 165

Gardiner, Henry, xxxi
Garrettson, Freeborn, 139. *See also*
Allen, Richard
Gates, Horatio, 184
Gazette of the United States
(newspaper), 127, 147, 183
General Advertiser (newspaper), 187
Genêt, Edmond Charles, 146, 151
Genghis Khan, leading Tartars, 5
Germantown, Pennsylvania, 174
Gillenham, John, 59
Gilpin, Joseph, 18
Girard, Stephen, 107–9, 111–14,
201–2, *p7*
government, Philadelphia without,
151–52
Gradual Abolition Act (1780), in
Pennsylvania, xxiv
gravediggers, Philadelphia lacking, 86
Great Plague, of London, 118
Grenada (British colony), 17
Griffitts, Samuel, 96
Guardians of the Poor (organization),
38, 54, 109, 140; Bush Hill
commandeered by, 105; essential
services of, 106; fever hospital
developed by, 103–4
Guinea-Bissau, xxii
gunpowder, burning of, 97–98

Haiti. *See* Saint-Domingue
Hamilton, Alexander, 42, 92, 148,
152–53, 175; capital suggested by,
173; College of Physicians written
to by, 127; death recorded by, 155;
debt solved by, 40–41, 237n34;
Jefferson contrasted with, 145, 171–
72; Rush contrasted with, 125–27,

184–85; Stevens treating, 125–26, 128–29; Washington, G., writing, 169–70

Hamilton, Eliza, 126

Hamilton, William, 189–90

Hammond, George, 146

Hankey (ship), xxv, 13–14; at Cape Verde, xxix–xxx; at Cap Français, 25–26; colonists boarding, 26; crew of, xxvi; disease isolating, 21–22; at docks, 49–50; Grenada infected by, 17; mosquitoes carried by, 16, 32, 195, 244n2; as origin, 33; passengers not prioritized on, xxvii–xxviii; in Philadelphia, 47–48; West Indies sailed for by, xvii–xviii, 17; yellow fever spread by, 19, 45

Hell Town (neighborhood), in Philadelphia, 51, 67, 78, 121

Helm, Peter, 108–9, 112

Helmuth, Justus Henry Christian, 58, 85–87, 121, 158, 163, 199–200; burials noted by, 142; on death, 51, 78–79; origin questioned by, 120; Philadelphia described by, 82; wrath of God described by, 59, 87–89

Heston, Isaac, 79–80, 82–83, 158, 182, 185–86, 202–3

Hippocrates (physician), 8, 70, 130

Hispaniola (island), 9. *See also* Saint-Domingue

History of the Peloponnesian War (Thucydides), 4

Hodge, Hugh, 57, 64–65, 77

Holmes, Oliver Wendell, 197

homelessness, of Philadelphians, 189

hospitals, yellow fever overrunning, 103

Howard, Thomas, 18–19

Howe, William, 174

humoral theory, Rush accepting, 69–70

Hunter, John, 54

Hutchinson, James, 69, 148; Clarkson counseled by, 96; disease dismissed by, 122; Drinker, E., on, 71; Jefferson on, 186; Kuhn treating, 81; Rush disagreeing with, 80, 92

Ill Constante (ship), 121

immunity, to disease: Africans and, 135–38; indigenous people without, 9; Rush misunderstanding, 135–36; from yellow fever, 110

Independent Chronicle (newspaper), 128

indigenous people, without immunity, 9

Inskeep, Joseph, 178

Ipomoea purge (plant), 70

Ireland, 65

Isaiah 5 and 6, 89

Island of Bulama, colonial undertakings in, *p1*

Isle of Wight, England, xxvi

Israel, Israel, 100

jail, without yellow fever, 87

Jefferson, Thomas, 26, 39–41, 80–81, 148–49, 160–70, 174–75; Declaration of Independence produced by, 36; Federalists criticized by, 185; Hamilton, A., contrasted with, 145, 171–72; on Hutchison, 186; Neutrality Proclamation frustrating, 147; on yellow fever, 83, 152, 176

Jewish community, scapegoating of, 7

Johnson, Samuel, xxvii

Jones, Absalom, 107, 138–43, 179–81, 200, *p7*

Jones, Mary, 139
Jumelia (poet), 193
Justice Department, U.S., 93
Justinian, plague of, 4

King, John, xxiv
Knox, Henry, 43, 148, 154, 169–71; on Philadelphians, 155; on Rush, 156; Washington, G., relying on, 151, 153
Kopperman, Paul, 197, 199
Kuhn, Adam, 81, 96, 125–26, 129, 130

Lane, John, 202
Latrobe, Benjamin Henry, 190
Lazear, Jesse, 249n33
Lear, Tobias, 150, 151, 174
LeClerc, Charles, 23
Leib, Michael, 109
LeMaigre, Catherine, 64–65
LeMaigre, Peter, 64–65
de Lesseps, Ferdinand, 204
Letson, Meghan, 167
Lewis, Samuel, 51
Lining, John, 135
Linnaeus, Carl, 233n14
Loganian Library, as orphanage, 100
London, England, 118
Longfellow, Henry Wadsworth, 23
Louisiana (territory), 26
Louis XVI (king), 145
Lownes, Caleb, 99–100
Lum, Mary, 108

Madeira Islands (archipelago), xix
Madison, Dolley, 94
Madison, James, 40–42, 83, 148–49, 152, 183

Maroons (rebels), 22
Marshall, John, 54
Martinique (island), 30, 121, 236n18
Mary (ship), 121, 131–32, 147
Maryland, 159
Mason, Richard, 180
Mather, Cotton, 11, 29
Mayflower Compact, xxiv
McNair, bleeding and purging of, 64
medical community, of Philadelphia, xi–xii, 52; consensus lacked by, 122; disease debated by, 54; feuding in, 129; misunderstanding within, 8; Rush leading, 56–57, 196; yellow fever confusing, 117. *See also* College of Physicians; physicians
medicine, as unregulated, 96
"mephitic" (vapor), 52–53
mercury, in treatments, 70–71, 123–24
miasmas, yellow fever blamed on, 8, 52–53, 67, 69, 113, 121
Michell, John, 70
microbes, disease spread by, 3–4
Middle Passage (Atlantic Ocean), xix, 217n8
Mifflin, Thomas, 69, 91–92, 97–98, 174, 189
Mitchell, John, 30, 70
Montefiore, Joshua, xxxi
Moore (Englishman), 51, 53, 55
Morris, Robert, 40, 42
mosquitoes, 87, 119–20; *Aedes Aegypti*, 27–29, 52, 205; *Hankey* carrying, 16, 32, 195, 244n2; *petechiae* suggesting, 67; Reed studying, 204–5
Motolinia, Toribio, 10
Mount Vernon, 150, 175
mumps, in Philadelphia, 43–44

A Narrative of the Proceedings of the Black People (Allen, R., and Jones, A.), 179–82, 200
de Narváez, Pánfilo, 10
National Gazette (newspaper), 147, 186, 188
National Institutes of Health, U.S., 28
National Troupe of the Northern Province, 110
Native Americans, 43
Native people, smallpox killing, 11
Neutrality Proclamation, of Washington, G., 145, 147
"new Africa policy," slavery contrasted with, xxii
New Jersey, 94, 152, 154–55, 159–60
Newsam, Albert, *p7*
newspapers, 120; physicians contrasted with, 118–19; port disregarded by, 51; Rush dividing, 183–84. *See also specific newspapers*
Newton, John, xviii
New York (state), Philadelphians banned from, 154
New York City, New York: as capital, 242n19; quarantine required by, 154; yellow fever in, 158–59
Nobel Prize, in Medicine, 249n35
Numbers 16:46, 91

Old Slaughter's Coffee House, xviii
"On where to go from here" (Carey), 177
origin, of yellow fever outbreak, 27–28, 53, 95; Carey on, 121–22; College of Physicians on, 187; docks as, 131; *Hankey* as, 33; Helmuth questioning, 120; weather believed to be, 120–21; West Indies as, 11
orphanage, Loganian Library as, 100

orphans, yellow fever creating, 38, 78, 100, 141, 163
L'ouverture, Toussaint "Black Napoleon," 23, 26
Overseers of the Poor. *See* Guardians of the Poor

Parkinson (Mrs.), 51, 55
Parkinson, Richard, 54
parties, political, 39–40, 182–84, 196. *See also* factions, partisan; Federalists; Republicans
Pasteur, Louis, 5
Peale, Betsy, 160–61
Peale, Charles Willson, 160–61
Peloponnesian War, disease during, 4
penicillin (*penicillium notatum*), 9
Penington (Dr.), 125
Penn, William, 11, 35
Pennsylvania: Bank of, 95; Germantown in, 174; Gradual Abolition Act in, xxiv; slavery ended in, 137; University of, 36, 54, 200. *See also* Philadelphia, Pennsylvania
Pennsylvania Assembly, 91
Pennsylvania Democratic Society, 147
Pennsylvania Hospital, 103
Pennsylvania State House, 36
Pericles, 'father of democracy,' 4
Pernick, Martin, 117, 118, 183–84
pestilence: Exodus on, 3; Psalm 91 on, 145; rivers inviting, 31–32
Pestilence (Freneau), xv
petechiae (skin spots), 67
Philadelphia, Pennsylvania, xi–xiii, 27, 30–31, 103, 191, *p2*; abolitionists in, 136; American Philosophical Society in, 95, 118; as capital, 39–42; Carey on, 44, 49; cartoon depicting, *p4*; cleaning of, 189;

Congress meeting outside, 168–72; conservatives threatened by, 183; economy of, 86; epidemic in, 68; after evacuation, 157–58; federal government in, 35–36, 39–41; without government, 151–52; gravediggers lacked by, 86; *Hankey* in, 47–48; Hell Town in, 51, 67, 78, 121; Helmuth describing, 82; mumps in, 43–44; physicians in, 117–18; poem from, 77; population of, 37; Powel, E., remaining in, 161–62; refugees straining, 49, 147, 183; Sabbath broken in, 89; sewage in, 38–39; "sickly season" in, 19, 31, 69, 122, 158, 203; theater in, 88; Washington, G., returning to, 175–76; waterfront of, *p2*; water system constructed in, xiii, 190–91; yellow fever spread from, 156. *See also* Black community; docks; essential services; evacuation; medical community; port; residents; Water Street; weather

Philadelphia Gazette (newspaper), 119

Philadelphians: banning of, 154, 159; bells unnerving, 98; drought impacting, 44–45; funerals of, 165; homelessness of, 189; Knox on, 155; New York banning, 154; violence against, 160. *See also* residents

physicians, 194–95; from Dispensary, 54; newspapers contrasted with, 118–19; in Philadelphia, 117–18; preachers defying, 158; residents resisting, 96–97; Rush contrasted with, 113–14, 122–23, 125, 198; treatments debated by, 123; yellow fever treated by, 103. *See*

also College of Physicians; *specific physicians*

Physick, Phillip Syng, 54–56, 109, 112

Pickering, Timothy, 153

Piercy, Christian, 160

Pitt, William "the Younger," xviii, xx

Pizarro, Francisco, 10

plague. *See specific topics*

port, of Philadelphia, 32, 71; disease in, 121; Genêt threatening, 146; newspapers disregarded by, 51; yellow fever at, 52–53, 111. *See also* docks; Water Street

Portugal, slave trade dominated by, xviii, xxx

Potomac River, 39, 168, 191

Potter's Field (cemetery), 101, 107

Powel, Elizabeth Willing, 42, 55, 153, 161–63

Powel, Samuel, 91, 125, 150, 161–62

Powell, J. M., 196

Powell, John Harvey, 57, 95

preachers, 88, 118, 158, 188. *See also specific preachers*

privateers (ship type), 48, 121–22, 146, 151, 226n2, 236n19

Psalm 91, 145

purging. *See* bleeding and purging

Quakers, 37–38, 93, 139, 187

quarantine (*quaranta giorni*), xxix, 8–9, 89, 159; New York City requiring, 154; paranoia prompting, xii; of refugees, 98; Rush opposing, 185

Ragusa, Sicily, 121, 236n18

"Recollections relative to Egypt" (anonymous), 119

Redman, John, 96, 127

Reed, Walter, 204–5, 249n33

refugees, 71; colonists as, 48; docks housing, 50; France and, 147; Philadelphia strained by, 49, 147, 183; quarantine of, 98; residents blaming, 53; Saint-Domingue fled by, 48–49, 110–11

religious communities, wrath of God suggested by, 188

Republicans, 126; bleeding and purging supported by, 184; Brown promoting, 183; evacuation disparaged by, 186

Residence Act (1790), 41–42

residents, of Philadelphia, 88–89, 96–97; American Revolution influencing, 36–37; avoidance among, v, 85; panic influencing, 83–84; physicians resisted by, 96–97; refugees blamed by, 53; yellow fever documented by, 199–200. *See also specific residents*

Revolutionary War, xxiv, 35. *See also* American Revolution

Rey, Jacob, xxiv

Rhoades, Lillian, 164

Richard Allen (Bell), *p8*

Ricketts, John Bill, 104

Ricketts' Circus, 104

Rittenhouse, David, 45

rivers, pestilence invited by, 31–32

Roehampton (ship), 151

rumors, on yellow fever, 83–84, 131–32, 187

Rush, Benjamin, xi, 65, 82, 95–96, 163, *p5*; bleeding and purging used by, 58, 70–71, 75, 123–26, 142–43; Carey on, 165; Clarkson meeting with, 95; Currie disagreeing with, 129–30; death impacting, 74; Devèze contrasted with, 114–15,

202; evacuation and, 72, 164; Hamilton, A., contrasted with, 125–27, 184–85; humoral theory accepting, 69–70; Hutchinson disagreeing with, 80, 92; immunity misunderstood by, 135–36; Knox on, 156; legacy of, 199; medical community led by, 56–57, 196; miasmas blamed by, 52–53, 67; Mitchell studied by, 30, 70; newspapers divided on, 183–84; patients risked by, 197; physicians contrasted with, 113–14, 122–23, 125, 198; poem dedicated to, 63; Powel, S., with, 91, 162; quarantine opposed by, 185; Stevens criticizing, 132; Washington, G., served by, 56–57; at Water Street, 58, 64–65; yellow fever and, 66–68, 71–75

Sabbath, broken in Philadelphia, 89

Saint-Domingue (French colony), 19; independence of, 26; refugees fleeing, 48–49, 110–11; slaves in, 20–21, *p2*; starvation on, 26. *See also* Cap Français

St. Croix (Dutch colony), 205

St. George, Grenada, 18

St. George's Methodist Church, 139

St. Michael's and Zion Parish (church), 200

St. Peter's Episcopal (church), 142

St. Vincent (British colony), 17–18

Sandwith, William, 59

Sans-Culottes (privateer), 48, 121–22, 226n2

Sansom, William, 106

Saville, Mary, 109

Say, Benjamin, 63–64, 96

Schuylkill River, 190

Scorpion (ship), 17
Scott, Mary, 180
Scott, Walter, 201
Seagrove, James, 43
servants, indentured, xxiii
sewage, 6, 38–39
Sharwood, James, 100
Shewell, Mary, 63
Shipley, "Wm," 59
Shippen, Edward, 161
Shippen, William, 96
ships, xxvii; disease on, xxviii; smallpox on, xxvi; yellow fever carried by, 49–50. *See also specific ships*
Shōei (monk), sutra from, 117
A Short Account of the Malignant Fever (Carey), 178
A Short Account of the Yellow Fever in Philadelphia (Helmuth), 199
"sickly season," in Philadelphia, 19, 31, 69, 122, 158, 203
Sierra Leona, colonial undertakings in, *p1*
Silk Road, 5
slavers, African chiefs aiding, xx
slavery, xviii, xix, 195–96, 218n11; Allen, R., experiencing, 138–39; movement against, xx; "new Africa policy" contrasted with, xxii; Pennsylvania ending, 137
slaves: Cap Français attacked by, 22, 110; heroism by former, xii; in Saint-Domingue, 20–21, *p2*
slave trade, xxi, 31; Britain abolishing, xx; Portugal dominating, xviii, xxx; U.S. and, 195–96; Wilberforce against, xviii; yellow fever transported by, 27

smallpox: Aztecs killed by, 10; on *Calypso*, xxix; Native people killed by, 11; on ships, xxvi
Smith, Billy G., 19, 32, 195
Smith, Elizabeth, 105
Society for Effecting the Abolition of the Slave Trade. *See* Anti-Slavery Society
Society of Friends, 37, 93–94
de Soto, Hernando, 10–11
South Carolina, 135
Spain, Britain in relations with, xxix
Spanish-American War, yellow fever influencing, 204
Spanish flu (1918), xi
Stanislaus, Francis, 21
Stansbury, Joseph, 82
State Department, U.S., 93, 151
state government, disease straining, 91
"Stella Caeli Exstirpavit" (chant), 135
Stephen Girard (Newsam), *p7*
Stevens, Edward, 125–26, 128–29, 132, 187
Sturgis, Stokley, 138
sutra, from Shōei, 117
Swanwick, John, 100
Sydenham, Thomas, 56
syphilis, in Western Hemisphere, 9

Tartars (army), 5
Tenochtitlán (Aztec capital), 10
theater, yellow fever blamed on, 88, 188
Theiler, Max, 205, 249n35
Thucydides (historian), 4
Timkins, Jacob, 106
Todd, John, 94
"To Toussaint L 'Overture" (Wordsworth), 13

Town and Country Almanac, 119
Treasury Department, U.S., 92
treatments, for yellow fever: camphor in, v, 96, 99, 118–19, 233n23; Currie listing, 130–31; homemade, 120; implausible, 118; mercury in, 70–71, 123–24; Mitchell informing, 30, 70; physicians debating, 123; vinegar in, v, 8, 71, 73–74, 99, 118–19. *See also* bleeding and purging
Treaty of Rijswijk (1697), 20
Trumbull, Jonathan, 170, 243n8

United States (U.S.): Constitution, 36, 42, 149, 168, 172, 175; disease impacting, 196; First Bank of, 108, 202; Justice Department, 93; National Institutes of Health, 28; slave trade and, 195–96; State Department, 93, 151; Treasury Department, 92; yellow fever in, 203. *See also* capital; Congress; federal government; *specific places*
University of Pennsylvania, 36, 54, 200
U.S. *See* United States

vaccine, for yellow fever, 205, 249n35
vapor, "mephitic," 52–53
vinegar, in treatments, v, 8, 71, 73–74, 99, 118–19
Virginia, 30, 159
virus, yellow fever as, 28

Wadstrom, C. B., xxiii
Washington (Mrs.), 150
Washington, DC, 191
Washington, George, 37, 39, 162, 171–73; capital prioritized by, 43, 167–68; evacuation ordered by, 150; Freneau disparaging, 188;

Hamilton, A., written by, 169–70; Hammond meeting with, 146; inaugurations of, 42, *p8*; Knox relied on by, 151, 153; Neutrality Proclamation of, 145, 147; Philadelphia returned to by, 175–76; Rush serving, 56–57; yellow fever concerning, 148–49
Washington, Warner, 153, 241n26
Washington's 1793 Inaugural at Philadelphia (Ferris), *p8*
water, drinkable, 39
Water Street, Philadelphia, 64; Drinker, E., on, 86; Rush at, 58, 64–65; Weld describing, 50
water system, Philadelphia constructing, xiii, 190–91
Watson, James, xxiv, 33
weather, in Philadelphia, 156, 165, 174; Carey on, 176; Drinker, E., recording, 44, 79; origin believed to be, 120–21
Weed, Elijah, 87
Weekly Museum (newspaper), 127
Weld, Isaac, 50
West Africa, sailor's warning of, xvii
Western Hemisphere, syphilis in, 9
West Indies (British colonies), 11, 18–19; disease in, 9; *Hankey* sailing for, xvii–xviii, 17; as origin, 11; yellow fever in, 28, 120
Weyman, John, 63
"W.F." (editorialist), 119
Wheeler, Francis, 30
Wilberforce, William, xviii, xx
The William and Mary Quarterly (newspaper), 117, 183
Willing, Thomas, 161
Wilson, James, 106
Wistar, Caspar, 148

Wistar, Thomas, 99
Wolcott, Oliver, Jr., 154
women, traveling to Bolama, xxv
women's groups, Wadstrom writing
    to, xxiii
Woodhouse, James, 74
Wordsworth, William, 13
working class, in Bulama Association,
    xxii–xxiii
wrath of God, outbreak blamed on, 59,
    87–89, 188

Yearly Epistle (publication), 94
yellow fever, xi–xiii, 11, 17–18, 30,
    168, 195; *Aedes aegypti* causing, 52;
    in Africa, 27–28, 136; on Bolama,
    15–16; Bush Hill overrun with,
    105–6; Carey on, 77, 177–78,
    193; cartoons depicting, *p3*, *p4*; in
    Charleston, 135; climate impacting,
    28; colonists killed by, 14–15, 33; in
    Cuba, 203–4; Currie describing, 29;
    death from, 55–56, 193–94; Devèze
    knowing about, 109–10; discourse
    of blame on, 189; at docks, 52–56,
    92; Drinker, E., on, 173–74;
    Europeans contracting, 30; France
    impacted by, 23; *Hankey* spreading,
    19, 45; heroic figures surviving,
    202–3; history of, 27; hospitals
    overrun with, 103; immunity
    from, 110; interdependency

demonstrated by, 196; jail without,
    87; Jefferson on, 83, 152, 176;
    medical community confused by,
    117; miasmas blamed for, 8, 52–53,
    67, 69, 113, 121; *National Gazette*
    downplaying, 186; in New York
    City, 158–59; orphans created by,
    38, 78, 100, 141, 163; Peale, C.,
    contracting, 160–61; Philadelphia
    spreading, 156; physicians
    treating, 103; at port, 52–53,
    111; Quakers contracting, 93–94;
    reforms following, 189; residents
    documenting, 199–200; rumors
    on, 83–84, 131–32, 187; Rush
    and, 66–68, 71–75; ships carrying,
    49–50; slave trade transporting, 27;
    Spanish-American War influenced
    by, 204; theater blamed for, 88,
    188; in U.S., 203; vaccine for, 205,
    249n35; as virus, 28; Washington,
    G., concerned with, 148–49; in
    West Indies, 28, 120. *See also*
    origin; treatments
"Yellow Fever" (Jumelia), 193
"The Yellow Fever" (Davidson), 47
"Yellow fever 1793" (Letson), 167
yellow jack. *See* yellow fever
Yersin, Alexander, 5
Yersinia pestis (bactirium), 5, 6

Zong (ship), massacre on, xix

ABOUT THE AUTHOR

Robert P. Watson, PhD, historian, media commentator, and author, has published over forty books, several of which won awards and were featured on C-SPAN's *Book TV* and at prominent literary festivals. His recent works include: *America's First Crisis* (2014), *The Nazi Titanic* (2016), *The Ghost Ship of Brooklyn* (2017), *George Washington's Final Battle* (2021), and *When Washington Burned* (2023). *Affairs of State* (2012) and *Escape!* (2021) were published by Rowman & Littlefield. He lives in Boca Raton, Florida, where he holds the titles Distinguished Professor of American History and Avron Fogelman Research Professor at Lynn University.